Game Audio Programming 4

Welcome to the fourth volume of *Game Audio Programming: Principles and Practices* – the first series of its kind dedicated to the art, science, and craft of game audio programming. This volume contains 17 chapters from some of the top game audio programmers in the industry and dives into subjects that apply to diverse game genres and from low-level topics such as thread-safe command buffers and pitch detection to high-level topics such as object management, music systems, and audio tools.

With such a wide variety of topics, game audio programmers of all levels will find something for them in this book. The techniques presented in this book have all been used to ship games, including some large AAA titles, so they are all practical and many will find their way into your audio engines. There are chapters about timed ADSRs, data-driven music systems, background sounds, and more.

This book collects a wealth of advanced knowledge and wisdom about game audio programming. If you are new to game audio programming or a seasoned veteran, or even if you've just been assigned the task and are trying to figure out what it's all about, this book is for you!

Guy Somberg has been programming audio engines for his entire career. From humble beginnings writing a low-level audio mixer for slot machines, he quickly transitioned to writing game audio engines for all manner of games. He has written audio engines that shipped AAA games like *Hellgate: London*, *Bioshock 2*, *The Sims 4*, and *Torchlight 3*, as well as smaller titles like *Minion Master*, *Tales from the Borderlands*, and *Game of Thrones*. Guy has also given several talks at the Game Developer Conference, the Audio Developer Conference, and CppCon. When he's not programming or writing game audio programming books, he can be found at home reading, playing video games, and playing the flute.

Game Audio
Programming 4
Principles and Practices

Edited by
Guy Somberg

CRC Press
Taylor & Francis Group
Boca Raton London New York

CRC Press is an imprint of the
Taylor & Francis Group, an **informa** business

Designed cover image: Shutterstock

First edition published 2024
by CRC Press
2385 NW Executive Center Drive, Suite 320, Boca Raton, FL 33431

and by CRC Press
4 Park Square, Milton Park, Abingdon, Oxon, OX14 4RN

CRC Press is an imprint of Taylor & Francis Group, LLC

© 2024 selection and editorial matter, Guy Somberg; individual chapters, the contributors

ISBN: 978-1-032-36239-7 (hbk)
ISBN: 978-1-032-36107-9 (pbk)
ISBN: 978-1-003-33093-6 (ebk)

DOI: 10.1201/9781003330936

Typeset in Minion Pro
by KnowledgeWorks Global Ltd.

*To Mila, who will see the results
of hard work and enthusiasm.*

---

*And to Emily, who is always there
for me through everything.*

Contents

Acknowledgments

Every book in this series accumulates more and more people to whom I am indebted for its creation. This page in each volume is my opportunity to name them all again and again, which I do with relish.*

My contributors are the lifeblood of these books, and this volume is no exception. I always learn so much from all of you – thank you all!

Throughout my career, folks have taken me under their wing, taken chances on me, and allowed me to grow and flourish. Tyler Thompson, David Brevik, and Brian Fitzgerald I have mentioned in previous volumes, and I am still indebted to you all. New to this volume is Justin Miller, who has been a great boss.

It's entirely possible that Thomas Buckeyne will never see these books and will never know that he is acknowledged in every single one, but without him I would never have discovered my joy of audio programming.

David Steinwedel hasn't been a sound designer for a while, but he still gets acknowledgment here for working with me on my first big game, Hellgate: London.

I have learned so much from the sound designers I've worked closely with over the years: David Steinwedel, Jordan Stock, Andy Martin, Pam Aranoff, Michael Kamper, Michael Csurics, and Erika Escamez.

Another new name in this volume is Fiach O'Donnell, the first audio programmer I've ever had the opportunity to work alongside. Thanks for joining me, Fiach!

Thanks to Rick Adams from CRC Press, who got me started writing the first volume of this series, and thanks to Will Bateman, Simran Kaur, and the rest of the team at CRC Press, who are working on this volume.

I appreciate all of your hard work on my behalf in making this book a reality.

This book is dedicated to my wife, Emily, but she deserves an extra mention here for her support, and for taking care of me.

NOTE

* And mustard and catsup! (Finishing this book has made me loopy, I think.)

Foreword

INTRODUCTION

Welcome to the fourth volume of *Game Audio Programming: Principles and Practices*! Every one of these volumes opens with this phrase: a greeting to all who have opened this book, either its physical pages or selected this volume in their e-reader application. These words are in some ways ceremonial, but I also mean them with all of the warmth and enthusiasm that I can muster in black and white text. Game audio programming is a passion that I and the contributors to this book all share, and we are all excited to share our knowledge with you, the reader, in its pages. As always, everybody who contributed to this work has done a fantastic job of laying out their knowledge and skills.

When the first volume of this series was published, little to none of the combined wisdom of the game audio programming community was documented, or even written down. It was with great joy that I had to coordinate with several of the contributors to this volume in order to make sure that their chapters for this volume didn't overlap with similar topics from previous volumes. The fact that we have this much collective wisdom written down means that we can all stand on our colleagues' giant shoulders and see further for future games.

This Book

As with the previous volumes, there are two broad categories of chapters in this book. The first are high-level overviews of topics, the thinking behind them, and some techniques to approach certain aspects of them. The second are deep dives into code and specific approaches to solving problems.

Here are brief summaries of all of the chapters in this book:

- **Audio Object Management Techniques** by Christian Tronhjem –
  Creating and managing audio objects that we can play sounds on is a
  fundamental and foundational part of any audio engine. This chapter

covers techniques for handling these objects and optimizing them, including techniques for object pooling and spatial partitioning.

- **State-Based Dynamic Mixing** by Colin Walder – Cyberpunk 2077 is a complex game with a complex mix. This chapter describes the Director System that was developed for use in Cyberpunk, which can perform various mixing actions after selecting objects in the scene and making decisions about them. The system is state based, so the mix and the mixing decisions can change from moment to moment as the game transitions through states.

- **Timed ADSRs for One-Shot Sounds** by Guy Somberg – The ADSR curve is a great tool to implement effect changes over time with looped audio tracks, but it breaks down when applied to repeated one-shot sounds. This chapter introduces a new concept, the Timed ADSR, which adapts the ADSR curve to be applicable to one-shot sounds. Two solutions are presented: one which uses mostly built-in functionality in the audio middleware (but which requires complex setup) and the other which implements the feature in code.

- **Systemic Approaches to Random Sound Effects** by Michael Filion – In large open world games, adding randomization to environmental effects can help to increase realism and immersion. This chapter introduces a system to trigger randomized sound effects around the listener, along with discussions around the subtleties of triggering them and their location in 3D space.

- **The Jostle System: A Baked Solution to Environmental Interaction Sounds** by Alex Pappas – As players walk around a 3D game space, the characters implicitly interact with (jostle) the objects in their surroundings. This chapter introduces a system for triggering various kinds of jostle sounds, and also an offline mechanism to track changes in level layouts when assets are changing rapidly.

- **Background Sounds** by Guy Somberg – Creating the feeling of being in an environment requires splitting the sound into multiple layers, both looped and one-shot. This chapter shows a system that plays ambiences, handling the looped and one-shot sounds differently. Looped sounds are played at randomized intervals, fading in and out and to new volumes. One-shot sounds are triggered individually with randomized panning, but can optionally be placed into groups of repeated sounds. Implementations are presented both using built-in tools from the audio middleware and using C++.

- **Data-Driven Music Systems for Open Worlds** by Michelle Auyoung – Open world games have a challenge with music, where the music must always be present and reactive to the player's actions. This chapter describes how to implement a system that reacts to game parameters, using Time of Day and Threat Level as examples.

- **Finding the Intersection of a Box and a Circle** by Guy Somberg – When implementing volumetric sounds, you may find the need to intersect an axis-aligned box with a circle. This chapter dives deep into the details of the algorithm and code and runs through several optimizations to drastically reduce the number of boxes from the result.

- **Building a Pitch Tracker: Fundamentals** by David Su – Games where the player sings or hums into the microphone need to be able to track the pitch that the player is singing in order to feed that information to the game. This chapter explains the math of basic pitch tracking and shows how to set up a plugin to track the pitch of a playing sound.

- **Building a Pitch Tracker: Practical Techniques** by David Su – This chapter builds on the previous one, which has only provided a good starting point. It covers improving the accuracy of tracking, handling noise, and ways to improve the efficiency of the code so that the effect can be used in a real-time context.

- **Flexible Delay Lines** by Robert Bantin – A delay line is a buffer that delays audio data by a certain amount of time. This chapter shows the implementation of a flexible delay line, then shows how to apply it in several gameplay scenarios such as a car racing game and a procedural walking simulator.

- **Thread-Safe Command Buffer** by Guy Somberg – When sending commands to the mixer thread, we have hard real-time requirements. This chapter dives deep into a lock-free triple buffer implementation that solves the problem of sending messages to another thread that cannot take a mutex to read the commands.

- **Optimizing Audio Designer Workflows** by Matias Lizana – Working with sound designers means understanding what it is that they do and where they are spending their time. This chapter runs through questions that you can ask your sound designers and tools that you can build for them, along with effective techniques for designing audio engines to make them toolable.

- **An Introduction to "An Introduction to Audio Tools Development"** by Simon N Goodwin – Audio tools programming is a key specialism that demands unique knowledge. This analytical introduction to Jorge Garcia's chapter explains what's special about audio tools, and why a runtime audio specialist insists on working with experts like Jorge when AAA audio projects include a substantial tool-development component. This chapter discusses audio tool integration, cross-platform aspects, and how the audio tool programmer works with others on the game team, not just specialists in sound.

- **An Introduction to Audio Tools Development** by Jorge Garcia – This chapter provides an overview of the various tools, architectures, and techniques that go into making audio-specific tools. It discusses implementing fundamental features like undo/redo, architectures like model-view-controller, and tool programming patterns that come up frequently,

- **Audio Debugging Tools and Techniques** by Stéphane Beauchemin – Game developers in general – and sound designers and audio programmers in particular – spend much of their time debugging problems. This chapter describes why you should implement debugging tools early in development, then shows how to apply progressively more complex debugging techniques, starting with simple flags and console commands and moving up to using ImGui to implement audio tools in-game quickly and easily.

- **Automatic Manual Foley and Footsteps** by Pablo Schwilden Diaz – When faced with a massive manual process, sound designers need tools to make their lives better. This chapter shows the code of how to solve a problem of hooking footsteps and foley sounds up to many animations with a reasonable level of accuracy. The philosophy is to write code that does what an intern would do if faced with the same task.

Parting Thoughts

At a recent Game Developers Conference, I had several people come up to me and tell me how valuable this book series has been to them and their careers. These stories make me happy and really inspire me to continue doing the work and putting in the effort to make them. I always learn so much and get so much inspiration from my fellow game audio programmers; hopefully, you do as well!

Contributors

Michelle Auyoung is an experienced Audio Software Engineer with a focus on game audio programming who has worked on *Avowed* (Obsidian Entertainment), *Halo Infinite* (343 Industries), and *Dolby Atmos for Xbox* (Dolby Laboratories). She is passionate about building audio systems to help designers create immersive soundscapes to enhance gameplay as well as narrative experiences. Additionally, she has supported tools development like integrating audio-related plugins in game projects and improving audio design workflows. Implementing unique audio features to solve creative problems such as a music system responding to gameplay mechanics and collaborating between design and engineering teams excite her the most about the role. Besides game audio, Michelle also enjoys food and other creative pursuits like cooking and drawing.

Robert Bantin has been writing audio code for an ever-expanding length of time. While at school, they were an active member of the Amiga demo scene. At Salford University, they studied acoustics and brought their coding experience to their studies in the form of DSP and audio-focused applications. Upon graduating, they were recruited by Philips ASA Labs in Eindhoven in order to join the MPEG technology programme. Robert Bantin has since worked on several AAA games for Activision, Codemasters, and Ubisoft. When they're not programming, they can be found at home cooking, attempting to shred on guitar, and playing video games when the rest of their family are asleep. And the rabbit thinks they are one of the cats.

Stéphane Beauchemin's education pathway could seem quite chaotic. He made several program changes: from music to science, to music, to mathematics, to music technology, and finally to computer science. Given that he now works as an audio programmer in the video game industry, suddenly all that makes sense. Stéphane has been working for more than 15 years as an audio programmer. He began his career at Audiokinetic as a software developer and he is now working as Expert Audio Engineer for That's No Moon. As a lead audio programmer, he went through the complete production cycle of two major AAA games (from pre-production to shipping): *Batman Arkham Origins* and *Gotham Knights.*

Pablo Schwilden Diaz started as a sound designer 8 years ago but gradually became lazy and more interested in audio programming and tools development to spend less time doing redundant tasks. Now leading the team at Demute, he works as a full-time Audio Programmer on many different titles from clients and internal tools for the rest of the team.

Michael Filion has been developing video games for his career of more than 15 years with Ubisoft Québec, with the majority in the world of audio. When explaining his work and passion to friends and family, he often oversimplifies by stating that he is "responsible for ensuring the bleeps and bloops work in the game." He has had the opportunity to work with many talented people from around the world on games such as *Assassin's Creed*, *Tom Clancy's The Division,* and *Immortals: Fenyx Rising.* In between delivering amazing titles, he is known to friends and family for his multitude of different projects, from traveling the world with his daughter to earning his pilot's license to renovating his "haunted" house.

Jorge Garcia started his career in audio in 2001. His passion and curiosity about the potential of audio and music technology to improve people's lives has led him to study sound and music computing and work as an audio engineer, software engineer, and programmer for professional audio brands and game studios on franchises such as *FIFA*, *Skate*, and *Guitar Hero.* Jorge is also experienced in all parts of the interactive audio technology stack across various platforms (desktop, mobile, and console) using proprietary technologies and middleware. He also enjoys working with creatives and thinking on ways of improving their workflows and making their process more efficient and enjoyable. In his spare time, and on top of learning about disparate topics, he likes hiking, reading books, spending time with his family and friends, traveling, and relaxing.

Matias Lizana García is a Computer Engineer and Music Composer, and he mixed his knowledge working as an audio programmer on the video game industry. Based in Barcelona, he made a career starting from indie companies to the AAA industry, as well as teaching audio middleware at university. He is passionate about prog-rock bands, artificial intelligence, and space.

Simon N. Goodwin has designed and implemented advanced audio technology for multi-million-selling games, including two BAFTA award winners and six number 1 hits in the UK and major EU territories. Simon pioneered the interactive use of Ambisonics, co-founded the AES Audio for Games international conferences, lectured at GDC, AES, BBC, and university conferences, advised on AHRC and EPSRC research programs, and has been granted five US and UK patents. Drawing on more than 40 years of experience, Simon now offers professional mentoring for audio programmers and technical sound designers. His book for Focal Press and the Audio Engineering Society, *"Beep to Boom,"* is a deep delve into the development of Advanced Runtime Sound Systems for Games and Extended Reality. Details: http://simon.mooli.org.uk/b2b/BeepToBoom.html

Alex Pappas received her MA in Music Technology from New York University where she built generative music systems, explored procedural sound generation, and researched physical modeling to simulate collision sounds for hollow objects. Since then, she has worked as an audio programmer at Turtle Rock Studios. When she's not making tools for her team or creating systems for managing a cacophony of zombie sounds, she's always looking for an excuse to play classical saxophone or bassoon.

David Su is a musician, engineer, game developer, and researcher interested in creating new musical experiences through technology. He is currently a senior audio programmer at Brass Lion Entertainment, working on an unannounced action-RPG video game title. He is also one of the co-organizers of Game Audio LA. David's game credits include *One Hand Clapping*, *NFL Endzone*, and *Evergreen Blues*. He has also worked on music software at Output, Sunhouse, and Amper Music. David received his MS from the MIT Media Lab and his BA from Columbia University.

Christian Tronhjem, with a diverse background and interests spanning audio design, composition, and music technology, found a way to combine all of these as an audio programmer. After working freelance and in an AI music startup, he decided to move to AAA game development. He is currently working as Lead Audio Programmer for Ubisoft Blue Byte in Düsseldorf, Germany.

Colin Walder has been developing audio technology for games since 2006, with a focus on AAA games. His credits include *GTA V*, *Red Dead Redemption 2*, *The Witcher 3: Wild Hunt*, and *Cyberpunk 2077*, where he was involved in a wide range of audio topics from acoustics and ambisonics to performance and streaming. He currently works as Engineering Director, Management and Audio at CD Projekt RED, where in addition to audio topics, he provides direction for management across the technology department.

I

Game Integration

1

Game Integration

CHAPTER 1

Audio Object Management Techniques

Christian Tronhjem

In this chapter we will look at common techniques to manage objects that emit audio, or as I will refer to them: audio objects. You might find yourself having to improve or optimize an existing middleware implementation or write one from scratch. We often find ourselves dealing with many objects that play back audio or track middleware handles, including handling registering, unregistering, and sending the position updates regularly.

Experienced game audio programmers may not find a lot of new information in this chapter, as many of the topics are fundamental. However, it is meant to serve as a good basis for getting started, thinking about how to deal with a lot of objects and approaches to limiting API calls, memory allocations, and activation and deactivation of audio objects. Every cycle counts when creating detailed audio experiences – particularly on low-end platforms or working under a tight performance budget – and avoiding wasted processing when no audio is heard is especially important.

1.1 AUDIO OBJECTS

As we will see moving forward, we will have a few types of audio classes that share the same traits no matter what audio we are playing. We generally want some method of playing audio and sending an ID for the event to the middleware. Perhaps it needs to be registered with the middleware

DOI: 10.1201/9781003330936-2

before it can be used and its position updated. We can think of this as our general audio object: some functions and data that we can use throughout our game to emit audio. It might not be clear to other programmers that the object needs to be registered in our middleware, so having a `Play()` method in the class for your audio object or a method that takes the audio object as an argument would signal that this is what is needed for correct behavior. Using these affordances enforces using your audio object structure rather than just a normal game entity and gives you more control.

The details of every implementation will be different, but your basic audio object would include ways to at least register and send a play event to your audio object with your middleware and have an update method to take care of any behavior that would have to run while the audio is playing.

```
class AudioObject
{
private:
    // Could also just be the position vector, but you would
    // most likely want to know the rotation as well
    Transform m_Position;
    void Register();
    void DeRegister();

public:
    AudioObject() {}
    int Play(int eventId);
    void Update();
    void SetPosition();
};
```

When talking about calculating the distance, I am referring to the squared magnitude of the vector between the listener's position and the object's position, which we can compare to a distance threshold that is also squared. By operating on squared values, we can avoid several expensive square root calculations.

Most game engines update game entities once per frame, but you should make sure you have access to updates at slower rates – perhaps once every second, or even slower. If these are not available to you, it is worthwhile to set up a system where an object can register itself to receive an update callback at a specified rate. The implementation details will vary based on your game engine, but this is what this chapter refers to when talking about updates at slower rates.

1.2 POOLS

We need ways of supplying our game with audio objects. We want to request these when needed, and not just have game audio emitters assigned to all objects in the game, as this could quickly add up to a lot of redundant objects. Having to allocate and deallocate these in memory every time we want to play audio can be quite costly and quite unnecessary.

Since we most likely won't have 3,000 audio objects active at the same time, we can reuse some pre-allocated objects and shuffle them around when needed. This is where a pool of objects can come in handy. By using the same objects allocated once, we save both memory and CPU cycles. We can simply request a new emitter from the pool, set the position of the emitter at the place we want to play audio from, and return it to the pool when we are done.

We need to select a quantity to start with – let's go with 400 objects for this example. When we want to emit audio, we request a new object from the pool, set the position, and use its ID for playing audio on the object.

```
class PooledAudioEmitter
{
public:
  AudioObject* AudioObject;
  PooledAudioEmitter* Next;
};

constexpr int MAX_POOL_SIZE = 400;
class AudioEmitterPool
{
public:
  AudioEmitterPool()
  {
    m_First = &m_Pool[0];
    for(int i = 1; i < MAX_POOL_SIZE; ++i)
    {
      PooledAudioEmitter* temp = m_First;
      m_First = &m_Pool[i];
      m_First->Next = temp;
    }
  }
```

```
PooledAudioEmitter* GetFreeObject()
{
  assert(m_First != nullptr);

  PooledAudioEmitter* temp = m_First;
  m_First = m_First->Next;
  return temp;
}

void ReturnObject(PooledAudioEmitter* emitter)
{
  PooledAudioEmitter* temp = m_First;
  m_First = emitter;
  m_First->Next = temp;
}

PooledAudioEmitter  m_Pool[MAX_POOL_SIZE];
PooledAudioEmitter* m_First = nullptr;
};
```

Here we have an array in our class which is interpreted as a linked list, and we assume that `PooledAudioEmitter` just needs a default constructor and no initialization. An alternative implementation would be to add a `bool` in `PooledAudioEmitter` to check whether an audio object is free or not. This would work, but every time an object is requested, we would have to iterate through the array to find a free one. Instead, we link all the free objects in a simple linked list. When getting a new object, we get the first element of the list and set the next emitter as the first. When returning an object to the pool, we insert it into the beginning.

This example does not give any solution for what should happen if we run out of emitters, apart from the assert checking for `nullptr`. If possible, the simplest solution is to allocate enough objects or adjust the length of the array to avoid running out of objects. Another approach is to define some rules for emitter stealing and have newly requested objects potentially take over from existing ones. These rules could be to find the emitter farthest away or the one playing at the lowest volume, stop it, and then hand it over to the new request. This functionality could be tied into a voice limiting system with groups, each having its own limit. You will also need to decide if the voice limiting should take place mainly in the middleware or if another system is needed, and with that a pool could work together.

It doesn't matter how many objects are in the pool if they are never put back in the pool.[1] Every game will have different requirements that will inform when to return the objects to the pool. One option could be to return objects to the pool when the audio finishes by registering our ReturnObject() function to a callback when the audio is done playing. However, if audio is emitted from a behavior frequently, such as a footstep, it would be wasteful to request and send back an audio object for every audio event. On top of that, there could be context data that has to be set, such as switched or other game parameters, that would need to be reset every time, which would waste processor cycles. In these cases, it might be worth tying the emitter's lifetime to the lifetime of the object. Alternatively, objects that exhibit this behavior could have a permanent reference to an emitter assigned, rather than request one from the pool.

Another option is to return an audio object after it has not been used by its current game object for a certain amount of time. This solution works, but it comes with the overhead of keeping track of time and when to return the objects. Also, because the audio objects now live for longer on their game objects, the total count of audio objects will need to go up.

One downside to a pool is that the data associated with the specific object must be set every time we want to play audio from that object again, and likewise potentially clean it upon returning, if the objects are not deregistered from the middleware. Features such as switches in Wwise would have to be set every time an emitter is requested from the pool and could add overhead to your "play audio" code. You will need to decide if the cost of memory versus CPU cycles is worthwhile to keep all your emitters in the pool registered with the middleware.

Now that we have allocation and objects out of the way, let us have a look at managing the position updating.

1.3 POSITION UPDATES

For most middleware, we need to send position information back from the game engine to know where our audio object is positioned in the game world. For all objects, this is at least once in the beginning. However, we have sources that are moving and some will never move, so we will need to handle them differently.

1.3.1 Managing Updates

It might seem easy enough to just attach an audio object to an entity or behavior that just sends position information back every frame, but this can become inefficient very quickly. It could seem obvious in an isolated example like this, but I have seen proof of this happening and spent time fixing it more than once. Even at slower update rates, it is still not necessary to update positions every frame. Let us look at why managing position updates for emitters is important.

Consider the following example. You have a marketplace with a lot of NPCs walking around. Let us say we want detailed audio emitting from each NPC, so there's audio for both feet, from the mouth since they are having random barks and dialogue, and a few more for the body to emit some foley on legs and arms and the torso. For each NPC, this means eight position updates for the different emitters. Multiply that by 20 NPCs, and we have 160 position updates called every frame.

The first easy choice here is to not have the audio emitters set position if we have no audio playing. A lot of the audio played would be momentarily only: in this example particularly, voice, footsteps, and foley are all short impulses. Although the sounds play quite often, by only updating while playing, we would have far fewer updates at the same time.

One suggestion would be to keep track of the number of playing sounds on the object. We would increment the counter when we start playing and register our audio object to start receiving update callbacks from the game engine. When receiving the callback for an audio event end, we decrement the count and deregister from the update callback when the count is zero.

1.3.2 Single Position Setting

In some instances, the length of the audio is so short that you can get away with only setting the position once. You could consider this as being another type of `AudioObject` where the `Play()` method only sets the position but does not register an update callback. For something like footsteps, this could work and save some frames of updates, depending on the length of the content for those events and how much detail they contain. The downside to this is that you have yet another audio component to maintain and explain to the audio designers or implementers when and why to use it.

1.3.3 Updates Based on Distance

Another option to consider in terms of updating positions is when the audio objects need to update every frame at all. Depending on the content, having multiple objects' positions set at slower rates based on distance may not be noticeable. An object 20 meters away from the listener moving 2 meters to the left will have less of an impact on the angular offset to the listener than if they were 2 meters in front of the listener moving 2 meters to the left. With that information, we can save more updates by updating at a lower frequency – say every 3rd frame or even every 10th frame.

It could be set up in the following way. Implement a routine that runs if the audio object is active which performs a distance calculation between the object and the listener. You could then categorize an object's distance into buckets of thresholds defined as close, medium, and far, and change the update rate based on the defined thresholds for these categories. For example, lower than 20 meters is close, and the object should update every frame. Between 20 and 40 meters, it could update the position every 5th frame or 3 times a second and so on. This could also be defined as intervals in the object's maximum distance so that it is individual to each audio event.

It is possible that handling the buckets and calculating distance will end up adding more overhead than they end up saving. As with any performance improvement, you should profile to determine whether or not it is worthwhile.

Another option to consider is to completely cull the event if the object is outside of the max distance for the attenuation. This can create issues where an event is looping if it would later come into range. For short-lived audio events, this can be okay, though, as newly triggered sounds will be audible if they are in range. Make sure to communicate this feature to the sound designers in order to avoid confusion – culled sounds will not show up in the middleware profiling tools, which can be surprising if sound designers are not expecting it.

Different rates of updates can act as an effective way to save on API calls. These are suggestions on actions you can take to try and optimize your audio code, especially if the budget is tight. It comes at the cost of having to maintain either more audio object types (and for audio designers to know and understand them) or a more complex audio source that can handle more of these cases. However, implementing this culling can improve your overall performance and give you more milliseconds for other actions.

1.4 GROUPING

Let us build on the previous example of the NPCs in the marketplace. For certain configurations in our game, we know that a group of behaviors will always be close together and never separate. NPCs are a good example of this. Considering the distance calculation to the listener, an approximation of a point centered around these audio sources would be good enough to determine the distance for all these objects, and we can therefore avoid having a distance calculation for each one. A parent object can act as the controller for its children, which can also keep track of the count as well as the distance bucket. When the player character is far away, the events can be played back on one object instead of multiple. The parent object can also switch the audio content to something else as the level of detail gets lower and the object gets further away. We can take advantage of the fact that the parent object needs the distance to the listener to affect the sounds in the group. VO can take the distance into account for different projection levels, and we can likewise use the parent object to check obstruction and occlusion. Since we know these sources will be close to each other, we only need to check once instead of once per sound source.

Grouping does not have to be only a pre-configured setup of objects. At run time, you could identify which objects are close together and define categories and types of events that should group. In its simplest form, this would mean calculating distances between objects of the same defined category, and if close enough, creating a parent object between them to act as an emitter when further away, and when the distance becomes far enough between them again, split from the group.

Grouping can be a performance improvement to limit the amount of active audio objects, but it can also change the content or allowed polyphony of that group and act as a level of detail controller that changes the content of certain configurations when further away. As with all features, there is some overhead, so measure the performance and see whether it is giving a benefit that is worthwhile.

1.5 STATIC SOURCES

With sources that we are certain will never move, we have other options. This could, for example, be trees, torches in a dungeon, windows, audio emitting from inside a house, etc. In the previous examples, we have been talking about managing position updates, but now with static sources, the only management needed is to make sure we set it only once when activated.

If we consider an example of a medieval type of dungeon, we will have quite a few torches on the walls playing a fire crackling sound (for the sake of the example, we assume we do not use one voice with multiple positions, so we have to handle all these voices individually). We also know that the player cannot pick up the torches, so they will stay in that position throughout the game. We are also saving update cycles for all these objects as we just learned we do not need to update positions all at once.

However, we are now facing another problem. There might be over a thousand torches in the dungeon. We want to be able to decide for ourselves when the static source should play and stop and not rely on visual rendering for it to play audio.[2]

Luckily, we do not need to set the position more than once, so one approach could be to just have the sources start playing at the beginning and continue throughout their lifetime. However, when started just in the beginning, we end up with sources that play audio that is not audible to the player. Middleware saves CPU by not processing these audio files usually by making them "virtual," but we can optimize this further since there is no good reason to have thousands of virtual voices playing. To solve this, we can calculate the distance to each object and determine if they are in range. This could mean a lot of redundant checking, as some objects are far away and unlikely to be in range any time soon. Even with slower update rates, evaluating hundreds or even thousands becomes unnecessarily heavy. So, in short, we need a way to find the objects that are close by without having to check all the objects at our disposal.

This is where dividing the space up can help us, also called spatial partitioning.

1.6 SPATIAL PARTITIONING

There are various techniques for spatial partitioning, and we will not go into all available options in this chapter, but we will have a look at a few different techniques. This will also not be a tutorial in implementing some of these approaches yourself, but rather developing an understanding of how to use them.

1.6.1 Grid

Since we know the sources will never move, we can develop a method for knowing what is near to us and what is far away. If we divide the space into chunks, we know that the chunk next to the one the player is currently in is more important to check than a chunk closer to the edge of the map. So, let us consider dividing our game space up into a grid that has a predefined number of cells, where each cell has a fixed size. Each cell has a list of objects that are placed inside that cell. For now, we will assume that the audio objects all have the same size, meaning we will not take different attenuations into account – we will look at this a little later.

With this approach, we now have all sources belonging to some cell in the grid, as well as the listener being in one of these cells. This way we can easily query the cells immediately adjacent to the listener (the eight surrounding cells), to get a list of the objects we should be checking now for starting and stopping the audio. This leaves us with a lot fewer objects to perform distance calculations. One good approach is to remove the audio objects from the grid when we query the grid and add them to an updating list, then start the audio playing on the object. When a source's distance becomes too far from the listener and it is not in an adjacent grid, we remove it again from updating, stop the audio, and insert it back into the grid. Below is sample code of how a simple grid could look.

```
constexpr int NUMBER_OF_CELLS = 50;
constexpr int SIZE_OF_CELLS = 20;

class Grid
{
public:
  Grid(){}

  void Add(AudioObject* audioObject);
  void Remove(AudioObject* audioObject);
  void Get(std::vector<AudioObject*>& queryList,
        const Vector2& position);

private:
  std::array<std::array<std::vector<AudioObject*>,
      NUMBER_OF_CELLS>, NUMBER_OF_CELLS> grid;
};
```

First, we have a method for adding and getting, and a private method for getting from an index, to have the size of the query. Size could either be part of the class or as here defined elsewhere. In this example, the AudioObject is an object that also holds a 2D vector position.

```
void Grid::Add(AudioObject* audioObject)
{
  int xIndex =
    static_cast<int>(audioObject->position.x / SIZE_OF_CELLS);
```

```
int yIndex =
  static_cast<int>(audioObject->position.y / SIZE_OF_CELLS);

grid[xIndex][yIndex].push_back(audioObject);
}
```

When adding, we can find the x and y indices by dividing by the size of the cell and casting to an integer. This example code does not check if the index is within the size of the array and just uses a std::vector as the backing store. Error checking and choice of data structure will be up to your game mechanics.

For removing from a std::vector, we will use std::erase(), which requires C++20. If you are using an older version of C++, the code to use the erase() function with the "erase-remove" idiom is commented out just below.

```
void Remove(AudioObject* audioObject)
{
  int xIndex =
    static_cast<int>(audioObject->position.x / SIZE_OF_CELLS);

  int yIndex =
    static_cast<int>(audioObject->position.y / SIZE_OF_CELLS);

  std::erase(grid[xIndex][yIndex], audioObject);
  // If using an earlier version of C++
  // auto& gridEntry = grid[xIndex][yIndex];
  // gridEntry.erase(
  //   std::remove(gridEntry.begin(), gridEntry.end(), audioObject),
  //   gridEntry.end());
}
```

When we want to query from a position and get the adjacent grids, we pass in a list to put the objects into, as well as a position from where we want to query. We can loop through a 3×3 grid where the cell of the player would be in the middle and get all the objects that were added to those cells. It is up to you what type of container to pass in to get the objects if you want to remove them from the grid if they are playing. When the AudioObject starts playing, you will need to check at some sort of interval if this source is still within range to stop it again.

```
void Grid::Get(std::vector<AudioObject*>& queryList,
               const Vector2& position)
{
  int xIndex = static_cast<int>(position.x / SIZE_OF_CELLS);
  int yIndex = static_cast<int>(position.y / SIZE_OF_CELLS);

  for (int x = xIndex - 1; x < xIndex + 1; ++x)
  {
    for (int y = yIndex - 1; y < yIndex + 1; ++y)
    {
      GetFromIndex(queryList, x, y);
    }
  }
}

void GetFromIndex(std::vector<AudioObject*>& list,
                  int xIndex,
                  int yIndex)
{
  if (xIndex < 0 ||
      xIndex >= NUMBER_OF_CELLS ||
      yIndex < 0 ||
      yIndex >= NUMBER_OF_CELLS)
      return;

  const std::vector<AudioObject*>& gridList = grid[xIndex][yIndex];
  for(AudioObject* obj : gridList)
  {
    list.push_back(obj);
  }
}
```

This should give you an idea of how a basic grid could be implemented. Here, we just allocate everything up front, which could end up with a lot of unnecessary memory spent on empty cells. Looking into implementing a sparse grid could help you save memory by only allocating memory for cells that contain an object. However, search times can become worse over time as we add more objects to it.

Another issue is that, for now, we have not considered that audio sources are rarely just a point in space. They are of varied sizes as we have different attenuations and, therefore, also take up space around the object that determines when we want to activate it. In that sense, the grid is a crude solution. To handle this property, we can add a way to add an `AudioObject` as a box that also checks intersections with adjacent cells and adds itself to those as well. That way, we are able to have a source spanning over multiple cells, but the cost is that we also have to manage multiple cells for querying and removing as well in the implementation. So long as the attenuation range is around the size or not bigger than two cells, we would not run into many problems as we always query the adjacent cells to the one the player is in. Of course, these queries would span over multiple cells, so it would be worth tweaking the cell size and the number of cells.

1.6.2 Quadtree

Another approach to handling objects, and potentially better handling of varied sizes of objects, is dividing the space using a tree structure called a quadtree for 2D or an octree for 3D. As in the example before, we will go over this in 2D, but it can easily be expanded into 3D. We will therefore only be looking at the quadtree here. The octree is based on the same principles, except that it divides into eight octants instead of four quadrants.

The idea of a quadtree is to subdivide spaces into quadrants to find the best possible fit for an object. Instead of dividing our space into equal size grids as looked at previously, we have a more granular defined grid of cells that fit around the objects that are inserted. The algorithm is quite simple. We define a cell size that is our whole game world first. This is our root. Each tree node, including the root, will have four equally sized children, each a quarter of the size of the parent.

When we want to insert an object, we look through the children to see which one can contain the child. When we find one, we go down one level to see if it can fit entirely inside the bounds of the child, and if not, then add it to the level we were at. The process of inserting a square into a quadtree is illustrated in Figure 1.1. In the example, we check if the object is contained within one of the children, and we can see that it is contained in the northwest quadrant (Figure 1.1a), so we can go one level deeper. We subdivide the northwest quadrant into four (Figure 1.1b) and check again if the object can fit fully inside one of the quadrants. We can still fit it, this time in the southeast quadrant. When we go one level deeper, however, it no longer fits fully inside the quadrant (Figure 1.1c). The object overlaps two of the quadrants, and therefore we consider the item to have the best fit two levels down in the southeast quadrant and we can add it to the list.

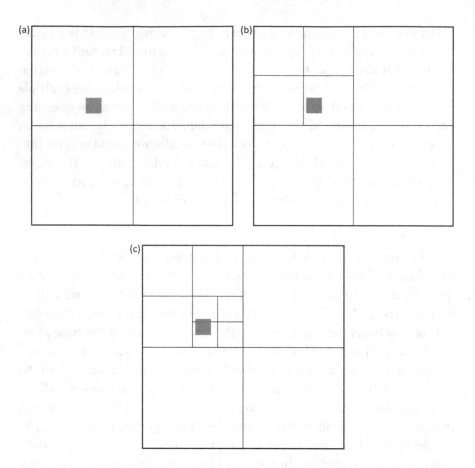

FIGURE 1.1 (a) Quadtree insertion, first step. The object fits into the northwest quadrant. (b) Quadtree insertion, second step. The northwest quadrant is subdivided, and the object fits into the southeast quadrant. (c) Quadtree insertion, third step. The southeast quadrant of the northwest quadrant is subdivided. The object overlaps with two of the subdivisions, so the algorithm stops.

This setup gives the benefit when querying our tree that we can check for overlaps, rather than adjacent cells like we had with the grid. For querying, we check which quadrants overlap with our input box, and potential items that intersect with the query field get returned. In the example (Figure 1.2), we can see that we check all the first big children at level one. Since they have no children in the northeast, southeast, and southwest quadrants, we do not continue into those quadrants. We check each of the four children in the northwest and find that we intersect with the child in

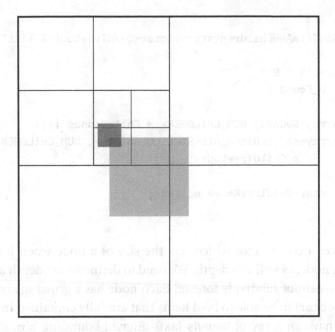

FIGURE 1.2 Quadtree query. The light gray box is passed through the quadtree to find that it intersects the previously inserted object.

the southeast. Here we have an item, and we can see that it also intersects, so we return it.

With this data structure, we have a much more granular approach to querying, and the varying size of objects is handled much more dynamically than in the grid example earlier. Imagine we had objects populated in the other quadrants next to our object here. We would only get the ones that intersect with our box, and it is closer to the objects we are interested in.

Below is some example code to give you an idea of how this could be implemented.

```
constexpr int NUM_CHILDREN = 4;

class QuadTree
{
public:
  QuadTree(const Bounds& nodeBounds, int nDepth = 0);
  void Insert(const QuadTreeNode& audioObject);
  void GetObjects(const Bounds& searchBounds,
            std::vector<QuadTreeNode>& listItems);
```

```
private:
  void AddItemAndChildren(std::vector<QuadTreeNode>& listItems);

  int m_Depth = 0;
  Bounds m_Bounds;

  std::array<Bounds, NUM_CHILDREN> m_ChildBounds {};
  std::array<std::unique_ptr<StaticQuadTree>, NUM_CHILDREN>
          m_ChildTreeNodes;

  std::vector<QuadTreeNode> m_Items;
};
```

We have a constructor which sets the size of a node when it is a new child of a node, as well as a depth. We need to define a max depth as well to ensure we cannot subdivide forever. Each node has a growing array (here a `std::vector`) to be able to hold items that are fully contained in the cell. We also have an array of `Bounds` (axis-aligned bounding boxes) and an array of pointers to each child node. We keep the `Bounds` separate from the child nodes so that we only create a new node when we need a new one, but we can create `Bounds` for each child in the constructor to be able to check if an object can be inserted in that child.

```
constexpr int MAX_DEPTH = 8;

QuadTree::QuadTree(const Bounds& nodeBounds, int nDepth)
{
  m_Depth = nDepth;
  m_Bounds = nodeBounds;

  Vector2 halfSize = m_bounds.Size * 0.5f;
  Vector2 topLeft {m_Bounds.Position.X, m_bounds.Position.Y};

  Vector2 topRight {m_Bounds.Position.X + halfSize.X,
                    m_bounds.Position.Y};

  Vector2 bottomLeft {m_Bounds.Position.X,
                      m_bounds.Position.Y + halfSize.Y};

  Vector2 bottomRight {m_Bounds.Position.X + halfSize.X,
                       m_Bounds.Position.Y + halfSize.Y};
```

```
m_ChildBounds =
{
  Bounds(topLeft, halfSize),
  Bounds(topRight, halfSize),
  Bounds(bottomLeft, halfSize),
  Bounds(bottomRight, halfSize)
};
}
```

We subdivide the root bounds and set the positions of the new children, so each child is now a quadrant. If you are implementing an octree, this is the main point where you would subdivide into eight cubes instead of four quadrants. The rest of the functions would be largely the same, apart from looping over more children.

To insert in the tree, we loop through all children and check whether the new object can fit inside. Many game engines provide this overlap functionality built-in, but if you are implementing it yourself, you will need to check if the x and y coordinates of the object to insert are within the coordinates of the box. If the object is fully contained, we also make sure that the level we reached is not bigger than the max defined depth. We then call **Insert()** recursively to get to the best fit and return.

```
void Insert(const QuadTreeNode& audioObject)
{
  for (int i = 0; i < NUM_CHILDREN; i++)
  {
    if (m_ChildBounds[i].contains(audioObject.Bounds) &&
        m_Depth + 1 < MAX_DEPTH)
    {
      if (!m_ChildTreeNodes[i])
      {
        m_ChildTreeNodes[i] = std::make_unique<QuadTree>(
                              m_ChildBounds[i], m_Depth + 1);
      }

      m_ChildTreeNodes[i]->Insert(audioObject);
      return;
    }
  }

  m_Items.push_back(audioObject);
}
```

To search the tree for objects, we pass in a **Bounds** for the area to search as well as a list to insert items into, here just **std::vector** as an example.

```cpp
void GetObjects(const Bounds& searchBounds,
                std::vector<QuadTreeNode>& listItems)
{
  for (const QuadTreeNode& audioObject : m_Items)
  {
    if (searchBounds.overlaps(audioObject.Bounds))
    {
      listItems.push_back(audioObject);
      // Here you could remove as well if wanted.
    }
  }

  for (int i = 0; i < NUM_CHILDREN; i++)
  {
    if (m_ChildTreeNodes[i])
    {
      if (searchBounds.contains(m_ChildBounds[i]))
      {
        m_ChildTreeNodes[i]->addItemAndChildren(listItems);
      }
      else if (searchBounds.overlaps(m_ChildBounds[i]))
      {
        m_ChildTreeNodes[i]->GetObjects(
          searchBounds, listItems);
      }
    }
  }
}

void AddItemAndChildren(std::vector<QuadTreeNode>& listItems)
{
  for (const QuadTreeNode& item : m_Items)
  {
    listItems.push_back(item);
    // Remove if needed.
  }
```

```
for (const auto& child : m_ChildTreeNodes)
{
  if (child)
  {
    child->AddItemAndChildren(listItems);
  }
}
}
```

It is up to you to decide if you would want to remove the objects when they have been added to the list in the search process and then add them again when the distance between the object and the listener becomes greater than the attenuation range.

We have been using 2D for both examples, mostly for the simpler illustration of the concepts. However, it is worth mentioning that using these as 2D structures can be perfectly valid if you do not care about height information. If your game is in 3D but does not have a lot of height differences, you could save some calculations by implementing the distance checking and query of grids or trees in 2D.

1.6.3 Pros and Cons

In order to decide on the solution for your project, you will have to profile the code and weigh the options available. Quadtrees and octrees are not magical solutions that will just speed up every codebase. If you only have 40–50 objects to go through, you will likely be better off just having objects in a block of memory and iterating over all of them to calculate the distance. The example quadtree presented in this chapter does not optimize for data locality – children are all allocated dynamically, and tree nodes are stored in a linked list. Without extra work, this implementation could easily perform worse than an array or grid with a smaller number of objects.

It is worth noting that we have only looked at the quadtree as a static one, which cannot grow or shrink in size. We could remove items from the list in the query to avoid getting the same objects again with the next query if the player has not moved much, but the child structure would stay the same until the tree is rebuilt. If you are planning to add and remove objects a lot, this is functionality you should consider. This is also the case for moving objects as they would have to be reinserted at regular intervals.

1.6.4 Audio Objects as Rectangles or Cubes

The **Bounds** used in the examples could in theory be a sphere, a circle, or rectangles. A sphere or circle around the object reflects the attenuation of our objects much better. You might find that implementations already exist in your game engine implemented with rectangles. Using rectangles in 2D or cubes in 3D can be a bit easier to deal with, especially when trying to check if an object is contained within another, dealing with intersections, and checking if objects are contained, and can work as a decent approximation.

One thing you should be careful of is how your box is defined and how that impacts the size you want. It is important to make sure that the diameter of your attenuation is within the box. In other words, the distance from the center to an edge should be the radius of the sound's attenuation. If you have the distance from the center to a corner, your attenuation circle will be bigger in some places than the box, and it will not activate your source correctly. This difference can be easy to miss and depends on the way the bounding box class is implemented. Figure 1.3 demonstrates the difference between the two setups.

All these examples should work well as a starting point for how to think about audio objects and their positions and using spatial partitioning to

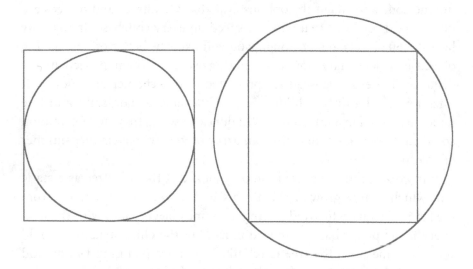

FIGURE 1.3 Left shows the radius defined as an extent. Right shows twice the radius as width and height.

aid you in managing a lot of objects. You will find that this is a deep topic and there is much room for improvement, and this is just the beginning of techniques to help you solve these problems.

NOTES

1 "A cache with a bad invalidation policy is another name for a memory leak." This statement is from Raymond Chen, who is quoting Rico Mariani. https://devblogs.microsoft.com/oldnewthing/20060502-07/?p=31333 – Ed.

2 One might also argue that all these torches or even just the sources should not be loaded in all at the same time, but that is a discussion for another time. For the sake of the example, let us assume that they are all loaded at once.

CHAPTER 2

State-Based Dynamic Mixing

Colin Walder

Dynamic mixing is one of the key topics that separates game audio from audio in other industries. Audio mixing techniques are well known from a long tradition in linear media: how to change the sound volume, processing, or even selection of specific sounds to support the narrative. In interactive media, these techniques are made more challenging by the nonlinear nature of the medium. Typically, we will have a base mix for the game, sometimes called the static mix, that will shape the overall audio aesthetic, and then elements of dynamic mixing that will adjust or superimpose upon that mix as the situation changes in the game. Even in a game with a linear narrative structure, the exact timing of events will be flexible and can change based on the decisions of the player. In some games, the narrative itself might change dramatically based on those decisions and actions. When we know the course of events in the game ahead of time, changes can be described using existing systems such as scripting, visual scripting, quest graphs, etc. If the game is nonlinear or requires narrative changes tied to moment-to-moment gameplay, then these techniques can be impossible or impractical to implement. Not to mention that the people who are best positioned to be making the creative decisions often don't have technical skills, experience, or perhaps inclination toward scripting and similar implementation methods.

We can't ship a sound designer or mixing engineer with each copy of the game to stand behind the player and make creative decisions as the player makes their way through the game, but we still desire and aspire to be able

DOI: 10.1201/9781003330936-3

to creatively use sound in the same ways that are available to our linear peers. Indeed, we could argue that in games there is potential for even more creative impact from sound! Leveraging such techniques from linear media to evoke emotions in a player or direct their attention and focus could affect their decisions and actions, which in turn results in changes in the action and narrative in the game, bringing about a positive cycle.

In order to be able to apply such techniques in an interactive context, we can build a system that is responsible for directing the dynamic audio mix. Such a system (sometimes called a Director System) needs to have a broad overview of - and ability to - affect the game audio, as well as knowledge of the context of the game It then needs a way to bridge that context and capability with decisions about what should be done with the audio in a specific situation. There are different approaches that could be taken with this: a common and effective one is to use a state-based decision machine. In the case of dynamic mixing, each state is a mixing state representing the creative choice (i.e., effect) or choices that are being made, and the transitions between those states represent the act of making that choice. While this chapter will focus mainly on the state-based system, we will also touch on other approaches and see in our examples that the Director System can be viewed also as a collection of interconnected systems. Conceptually (and to some extent practically), we can approach our Director System(s) by dividing it into three concerns: *selection*, *decision*, and *action*.

- **Selection** is the process of choosing what things should be affected by the dynamic mixing. In order to make a creative mix, we need to be able to highlight, focus, or change specific elements; for example, reducing the volume of a specific sound or group of sounds, or modifying the audio for a specific entity or entities. When a sound is played, we need to know whether or not we need to apply some effect based on the current state.

- **Decision** is the core function of the state machine and can be the most complex to set up since it needs to be able to reproduce and/or stand in for (to some extent) the human who makes creative choices. Offline, the designer sets up the states that represent the choices they would like to make in different situations. These states will contain the selection and action information that combine to provide the creative effect of the choice. These states might also be called mixing patches (since they are applied or patched on top of the base mix) or audio scenes (since we will often use them with the intention of creating a cinematic effect). Transitions between the states happen based on conditions that the designer sets up as part of designing the state machine. The conditions can be highly varied, and for this reason the Director System needs to have access to context about the game and the current state of the audio, as well as to maintain some internal state such as timers and a history of previous audio states.

- *Action* refers to the actual effects that we want to have on the audio (or potentially beyond that!). Usually, there will already be some groundwork done on this front – for example, the features used for the static mix – and if you are using a middleware such as Wwise, there will already be a lot of control exposed through switches, states, and RTPCs. With a system that is closely integrated into the game engine, however, we can go even further.

For each of the three elements of the dynamic mixing system, a key factor will be the user experience. Such a system can easily become highly complex, and it doesn't matter how sophisticated the technology is; if it's difficult to use, it won't be used! At each stage of building the system, we need to pay special attention to making it convenient to use. It is also worth keeping in mind that while we consider the elements separately here, in practice the boundaries may not be so clear-cut. Some elements will be better to implement separately in order to provide flexibility of combinations, and some will make sense to implement as a combined solution. There can be a temptation to try to adhere to ideals that appear elegant in theory, but this should always be tempered by pragmatism, considering the specific environment and context.

The exact implementation and even specific features will vary a lot depending on the engine and game that you are working in. I will give examples of features we implemented on Cyberpunk 2077 using REDengine 4 with Wwise as an audio middleware. Some things may fit your own context, some may not – but hopefully they will still act as an inspiration for finding and designing your own features.

2.1 SELECTION

For selection, we consider a variety of Action Types, where each Action Type describes a selection condition that we use to decide if an action should be applied or not. Some Action Types have a local context that allows for finely targeted mixing, while others have a global context.

It is important to note that in Cyberpunk there are several tiers of cinematic Scenes ranging from free gameplay to a fully restricted cutscene, so the use cases go beyond traditional cutscenes. Scenes are a key system in the setup of Cyberpunk and are a distinctive feature of REDengine. Your game likely has a different setup in terms of scenes, but there are likely parallels in your own codebase. Find the key systems in your game that will provide the opportunity to have the most relevant selection for dynamic mixing.

2.1.1 Sound Tags

Perhaps the most obvious thing to be able to select is the sound or category of sound, which begins with categorizing the sounds to enable the selection. Sometimes we want to affect a specific sound event; this we get for free from the event name, but often we want to affect types or categories of sounds. To do this, we need to assign or tag the sounds with categories. Where possible, we can avoid labor-intensive manual setup by reusing the existing data. In Cyberpunk 2077, we found that the folder hierarchy in our Wwise events was already a good representation of the granularity and categories that we wanted to have control of. For example, in the folder structure `devices/drones/signals`, we already had a format that would allow us to select all sounds related to devices, as well as to go more fine-grained and target drones specifically.

As part of our pipeline, we already had a post-soundbank generation process that logs the events and metadata about them so that we could look up the Wwise ID from our engine's native hash and have fast access to the maximum attenuation distance. To this, we added the tags based on the event folder structure in Wwise.

From this data, we can directly detect and select sound events belonging to a specific category, but we also get a second mode of selection. When each event plays, we apply the tags from that event to the emitter and entity that the sound was played on. At first glance, applying the tags like this may seem similar to selecting directly on the sound by tags, but in practice it is even more powerful. Consider a simple example of selecting player sounds. It's usually simple to detect which entity is the player; however, there are occasionally emitters that are conceptually associated with the player but not from a technical point of view, such as weapons that are separate entities with their own emitters. In this case, we can have a situation where we know that the weapon belongs to the player for the purpose of firing, but perhaps not from other systemic sound triggers such as animation or physics. Now we have an easy way to detect this situation without needing additional code to handle each case: if an entity or emitter has had a player sound played on it, we consider it to be associated with the player from the perspective of audio and can now select it as such, including for non-player sounds.

2.1.2 Emitter Tags

In addition to tags that are applied from sounds, it is also convenient for us to add support for applying tags directly to emitters from code and script. In RedEngine 4, an `AudioEmitter` is an object that is roughly analogous to a manager of `GameObject`s in Wwise. These tags function the same as Sound Tags in terms of selection. In practice, we found that they were more or less redundant, given the existence of sound tags (which are more natural to sound designers with their root in the Wwise project), but as it is almost free to support the existing tags selection, it's worth having as an option.

2.1.3 VO Context

In Cyberpunk, we had three categories of voiceovers (VO): *quest, gameplay,* and *community.* These categories were used primarily for mixing and selecting different attenuations and also gave us some valuable information and context about the line being played. A *community* line is usually unimportant: something that can almost be considered part of the ambience. A *gameplay* line is usually something combat related, with medium importance to be heard. A *quest* line is likely to be an important VO that is part of the narrative scenes that we definitely want to hear. As with the sound tags, this information can be applied to both the emitter and the entity so that we can use the context for VOs as well as other sounds. From the VO context, we can also know if an entity is just in the crowd, is relevant to gameplay (usually combat), or is an active participant in the quest.

2.1.4 Actor Name

Including the Actor Name in the context is as straightforward and useful as it seems. When an entity is registered in a narrative Scene, we log it so that we can perform selection on important characters we are likely to want to be involved with dynamic mixing.

2.1.5 Global

In addition to a selection that is specific to an entity in the game, it can also be convenient to be able to apply some global actions from states.

For example, we have the option to set a global parameter (i.e., a globally scoped RTPC in Wwise) or disable combat VO. These things don't follow the paradigm of the system perfectly, since there is no specific selection. It is possible to implement these actions outside of the state system, but since the states themselves provide relevant mixing context, it's good to take advantage of that.

2.2 ACTION

In addition to specifying the selection conditions, the Action Type is also associated with one or more Mixing Actions that define the actual mixing to be done. Where possible, these Actions can be combined freely with different selection conditions. However, some actions (such as globally applied actions) may have no selection condition or only specific selection conditions that make sense.

2.2.1 Event Override

A simple but effective Action that replaces playback of specific events with different events. The power of this is that the sound designer doesn't need to find the point of implementation or request for custom logic to be added by a programmer or scripter in order to be able to handle specific situations that might only happen occasionally. It's best used in a surgical manner to add final details or fix tricky edge cases, as there is the potential for it to become messy and hard to deal with if used in situations that would benefit from a dedicated system.

2.2.2 VO Event Override

In Cyberpunk, the VO Events differ from standard events in that we use the external events mechanism in Wwise. This works by specifying an event that defines the playback properties (attenuation curves, gain, etc.) paired with a specific audio file of the VO to be played. This is important because there are far too many VO files to be able to manage them individually within the Wwise project. Normally, the event will be selected based on a combination of the VO Context (described above) and the VO Expression, which specifies whether the line is being spoken, is internal dialogue, is being played through a speaker, etc. The VO Event Override will then replace the procedural selection of the event for all VO files that are played on the character. This feature is extremely useful to apply creative effects, as well as in situations where we want to have a specific line of VO be heard by the player, but some particular situation in the game would mean that the procedurally selected audio would be inaudible. It is convenient to have multiple ways to implement this content replacement, which can potentially result in a cascade of overrides; for example, a character may have a permanent override set on the entity level that would then be overridden, in turn, by a Mixing Action.

2.2.3 Set RTPC

RTPCs are the primary way to apply mixing in Wwise, and they are very powerful, with the ability to connect them to almost every dynamic property in Wwise. Adding them as a Mixing Action is a no-brainer. Globally-scoped RTPCs and Wwise States can also be applied, and in these cases no selection criteria are necessary.

2.2.4 Apply dB Offset

This is a specific Action for the common case of adjusting the volume of a sound. In Wwise, this Action is set up using a single RTPC that is mapped to Voice Volume on the Master Audio Bus. This approach has two primary benefits. First, the sound designer does not need to add and set up a new RTPC each time they want to have some dynamic mixing that adjusts the volume. Also, it means that we can present the Mixing Action in dB units, which are more natural for sound designers to use to represent volume adjustment than using a linear factor (they are resolved through addition rather than multiplication when stacking multiple actions). The volume adjustment is an offset from the base volume – this property falls out naturally with this approach, but it is worth mentioning as a feature since we want it to stack with other volume adjustments.

This Action is an example of finding the most common situations that will be handled by dynamic mixing and providing custom solutions to improve the workflow, even when generic solutions already exist. You may have different situations that you want to apply this principle to in your game.

2.2.5 Distance Rolloff Factor

This Action also has the effect of adjusting volume and can often feel more organic than a simple dB offset, although it is also more involved to set up. The approach is to virtually reposition the sound by a multiplication factor specified in the Action with the effect that a factor greater than 1.0 will push the sound directly away from the listener, while a factor less than 1.0

will pull the sound directly toward the listener. This requires maintaining two positions for the sound: the true position, which is updated by the game, and the virtual position, which is computed from the true position before passing it to the middleware.

Although this feature is not as simple to set up as the Actions above, you may already have access to the functionality. In Cyberpunk, we already had a repositioning pipeline in place as part of our acoustics system, so we were able to piggyback on the repositioning logic from that feature. Listener handling in third person games also often uses this technique, so if you have such a system in place, check if you can also use it for dynamic mixing. By manipulating the 3D position, we make use of all the distance-based functionality that we have already set up, including distance attenuation curves, low-pass filtering, and reverb. If we consider the situation where we want a specific sound to fade into the background, it becomes clear how much more effective using the distance rolloff factor can be than adjusting volume alone. The fact that it's using the existing distance setup also means that the adjustment has a natural and organic sound, in common with the base audio experience of the game.

2.2.6 Adjust Panning

Where Distance Rolloff Factor uses sound repositioning to artificially manipulate the distance of a sound source from the Listener, Adjust Panning takes the same principle and applies it to the angle. The primary effect we used this for was to either narrow or broaden the sound field, which has both practical and creative applications, in a similar way to changing the field of view of a camera. On the practical side, we can have gameplay situations where the visible field of view changes, for example, a cyberware that allows the player to zoom in the camera, or for player guidance to create space in the sound field for a particularly important sound. On the creative side, we can use it in the same way that we might approach a static mix to highlight specific elements or to change the overall feeling by narrowing and broadening the soundscape. To achieve this, we use a target vector and adjust the position of each sound toward that vector with a linear interpolation:

```
Vector4 startVector = soundEmitterPosition - listenerPosition;
Vector4 targetVector =
  listenerToWorldOrientation.Transform( panningVector );
```

```
Vector4 adjustedPosition = soundEmitterPosition;
if( !areOppositeVectors( startVector, targetVector) )
{
  Vector4 adjustedVector = length( startVector ) *
    normalize( startVector + ( targetVector - startVector ) *
                        panAdjustAmount );
  adjustedPosition = adjustedVector + listenerPosition;
}
```

It would be more technically correct to use a spherical linear interpolation here, but in our case a linear interpolation was sufficient. It is important to keep in mind that the goal is to make something that sounds good; if you're happy with the sound, there's no need to push it further. In this example, we ignore a target vector that is opposite to the start vector; this avoids a divide by zero in the normalize, but also makes sense behaviorally.

If you are also using Distance Rolloff as an Action, then it makes sense to combine the code for both of these "repositioning" actions.

2.2.7 Disable Combat VO

In Cyberpunk, we have a system for Combat VO that responds to gameplay events both to give the player some hints about what the AI is doing and to enhance the atmosphere in combat. Sometimes, however, we can have a situation where the player is in combat, but we are also trying to achieve a certain narrative effect that can be spoiled by the fairly random dialog that enemies can shout. Adding an Action to globally disable the combat VO is a simple and effective solution.

2.2.8 Play Event

Something very straightforward, but effective, to add is the ability to trigger the playback of an event. This Action behaves a little differently than the others since it is fire and forget, so the event is posted once and then has no further effect. A pair of apply and remove events can also be used, for example, to handle a looping sound. Depending on the architecture of your audio system, it may or may not be convenient to play events at the point where you execute the dynamic mixing: in our case, we needed to inject a delegate that would play the event through our standard audio system API, since we wanted it to be treated the same as other audio events.

2.2.9 AI Influence Maps

Going beyond having an effect on the audio, we can also consider having a wider impact on the game itself. One thing that we investigated but ultimately didn't implement was to have the audio feed its state information back into the AI system to affect the behavior of AI agents. Within the AI system, we had an Audio AI Agent that participated in the Squad AI, which gave us access to information that we could use to deduce the state of combat, and also could potentially make requests about squad behavior. An example would be to coordinate the AI to intensify their attacks to coincide with dramatic moments in the music. It's something I hope to come back to in the future!

2.2.10 Interpolation

It is the responsibility of each action to provide interpolation functionality for being added and removed. While there are a variety of curves that can be used to interpolate between different Actions, in practice we found for us that it was enough to use either linear interpolation or immediate transitions depending on the Action.

2.3 DECISION

In Cyberpunk 2077, there are multiple elements that are responsible for making the decision of when and which Mixing Actions to apply. These are key to realizing the "dynamic" part of dynamic mixing.

2.3.1 Mixing Scenes

A Mixing Scene is a data-driven graph consisting of States and Transitions between those states. A Scene represents a specific context within the game and the dynamic mixing that we want to happen within that context. Each State contains the Actions that specify the actual mixing to be performed, and Transitions are the final components that introduce the dynamic element. For some games, it may make sense to have a single scene that covers the majority of the gameplay. For example, in an open world sandbox game, the player typically has a lot of freedom to choose where to go and how to play the game, so the mixing scene needs to be able to transition to many states to reflect this freedom. For a more linear game, it can make sense to have multiple sequential scenes, each with a smaller number of highly specific states. In Cyberpunk, we use a combination of these approaches with a base Scene that covers the dynamic situations faced in open world gameplay and contextual Scenes that are triggered from Quests during narrative sections.

2.3.1.1 Mixing Scene Example

Let's take a look at a case from the Cyberpunk base Scene. Figure 2.1 shows the `tier_3` State; this is a State that is active when we are in a controlled gameplay section like a conversation where the player can make some dialog choices but doesn't have freedom of movement. In this State, we have three Mixing Actions being applied: a VO Context Action that reduces the volume and pushes away community dialog, an Emitter Tag Action that reduces the volume and increases the distance of radio emitters, and a Global Parameter that adjusts some RTPCs to drive mixing in Wwise.

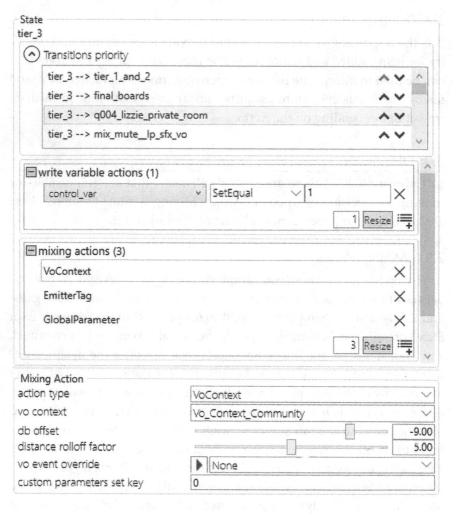

FIGURE 2.1   A Mixing State (`tier_3`) containing three separate mixing actions.

2.3.1.2 Transitions

Another section of the State displays the Transitions priority window. Each state contains a list of Exit Transitions which connect the State to potential next States. The list is sorted by priority so that if there are multiple viable Transitions, we will select the highest priority transition. We can also see in Figure 2.1 the write variable actions array. Rather than a Mixing Action, the write variables provide the possibility to set or modify a value on a variable internal to the Scene which can then be used as a condition on transitions to control the flow. Next, let's see what happens in the `tier_3` to `q004_lizzie_private_room` Transition shown in Figure 2.2.

Inside the Transition, we can set a transition time to control the time taken to interpolate between the first and second scenes, as well as the conditions which will define the dynamic decisions in our system. First, we need to decide if we want the Transition to require all conditions in order to be considered viable or if it can occur with any condition being met. Next, we have

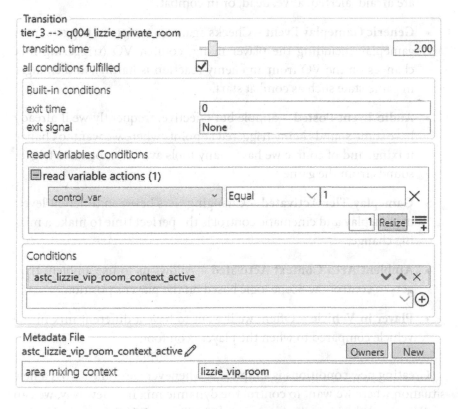

FIGURE 2.2 The Transition from the `tier_3` Mixing State to the `q004_lizzie_private_room` Mixing State.

the built-in conditions which are common across all transitions: we can use the exit time to have States transition after some time or to prevent a transition from happening before that time has elapsed. The exit signal, also known as a Signpost, is the most common way to control Scenes with State logic that follows the progress of a quest; signals are received from Signpost nodes in the quest graph or by Signposts signals resolved from the quest dialog. Using quest dialog as a trigger is convenient because it doesn't require any additional setup on the quest side, and very often we will have some quest dialog in a good moment for us to make a mixing transition. To manage this, we maintain a map of dialog line IDs to mixing Signposts. After the built-in conditions, we have the option to create a condition based on internal Scene variables; in this case, the variable that we set as a write action in the previous State. Finally, we can assign optional conditions based on a variety of contexts:

- **Enemy State Count** – Checks against the number of enemies who are afraid, alerted, alive, dead, or in combat.

- **Generic Gameplay Event** – Checks against a variety of triggers from gameplay including the player firing, combat VO (triggering mix changes on the VO from an enemy reaction is handy), and changes in game state such as combat start.

- **Audio Event Posted** – Simple but effective, frequently we'll already have some sounds being triggered at points where we want to change mixing, and of course we have many tools available for us to trigger sounds from the game.

- **Gameplay Tier Activated** – Changing tiers between different levels of gameplay and cinematic control is the perfect time to make a mixing change.

- **Ambient Area Context Activated** – Allows us to use ambient triggers to control the Scene logic based on the player's position.

- **Player in Vehicle** – Often, we'll want to have a different mix in the vehicle compared to when the player is on foot.

Creating new conditions is simple. So, whenever we come across a new situation where we want to control the dynamic mix in a new way, we can easily extend the logic. In our example in Figure 2.2, the Transition has a condition for the player entering the `lizzie_room_vip` area, at which point the Transition will be activated and the Scene will switch between the `tier_3` and `q004_lizzie_private_room`, interpolating between the Actions over a period of 2 seconds.

Something that we found helpful with the setup of Scenes, especially for the more complex ones, was to introduce a special `any_state` case for Transitions. This allows Transitions to be authored without requiring a specific starting State and instead can be used as a transition from (as the name suggests) any State. This can clean up the graph a lot as well as save on duplicated work when setting up more complex Scenes.

2.3.2 Application to Music

After we had created the State-driven Audio Scene system, we found that it also was a good fit for our needs in driving dynamic music. The inclusion of Play Event Actions provided us with the opportunity to trigger events when entering and exiting a state, which then became the main way that we implemented music throughout Cyberpunk 2077. Figure 2.3 shows a typical Scene used to drive the dynamic music in a combat encounter.

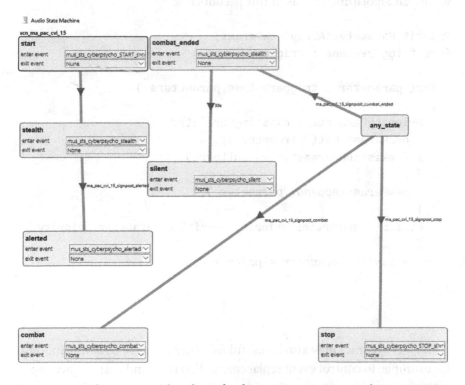

FIGURE 2.3   The Scene used to drive the dynamic music in a combat encounter.

While the State defines the Mixing Actions, the actions triggered, when the State is activated, will be applied on the Scene. The Scene is then responsible for managing the lifetime and updates of the actions, and interpolating and removing them when a Transition occurs.

The combination of Scenes, States, and Transitions allows us to craft powerful dynamic mixing Decisions, but it comes with a certain level of complexity. In order to help the sound designers use it to its fullest potential, it is worth spending time and energy making a polished and expressive user interface to make it as easy as possible to set up the dynamic mixing data.

2.3.3 Trigger Volumes

As we look outside of the state-based system, one tool worth mentioning in the context of dynamic mixing is the humble trigger volume. Setting RTPCs from volumes is a simple but effective way to apply dynamic mixing, especially if we use a priority system. With priorities on the trigger volumes, designers can have a lot of control over RTPCs by placing multiple overlapping trigger volumes. In the update for our trigger volumes, we use an algorithm such as in this pseudocode:

```
PriorityParametersArray newParams;
for( triggerVolume : triggerVolumes )
{
  for( parameter : triggerVolume.parameters )
  {
    PriorityParameter* existingParameter =
      newParams.Get( parameter );
    if( existingParameter == nullptr )
    {
      newParams.Append( parameter );
    }
    else if ( parameter.priority > existingParameter.priority )
    {
      *existingParameter = parameter;
    }
  }
}
```

Trigger volumes may also be useful for other forms of dynamic mixing, for example, to control event replacement. You may find many other applications since player location is such a useful selection mechanic.

2.3.4 Mix Bus Volume

Another interesting Decision mechanism that can be applied either globally or – with some extra effort – locally is mix bus volume. In Wwise, there is the possibility to register to receive callbacks that provide measurements of the audio levels on a specific bus (e.g., RMS, peak) using `AK::SoundEngine::RegisterBusVolumeCallback()`. Details on how to work with bus volume callbacks in Wwise can be found in the online documentation at audiokinetic.com. This volume information opens up some interesting possibilities such as applying game-side mixing actions based on the actual sound levels. However, since each individual case requires coding to set up the bus callback, and the most commonly useful situations (e.g., attenuating one bus by the level of another bus) can be handled by sound designers within the Wwise Authoring tool using meter effects, this isn't a common technique to use in practice.

2.4 CONCLUSION

We've seen how to build a state-based dynamic mixing system based around the concepts of Action, Selection, and Decision, as well as other elements of dynamic mixing that operate in tandem with the state-based system. In examples from the mixing systems developed for Cyberpunk 2077, we've seen both features that could be applied generically to different types of games, as well as features that are more useful to specific contexts in this game, and that we should consider closely the context of the game that we are working on in order to build the system best suited to our needs. While we can gain a lot of value from a powerful bespoke mixing system, we should reuse and adapt existing systems and look for ways to make the system more convenient to use for designers.

As a final word, I want to say a big thank you to the members of our Audio Code team who brought these systems to life in Cyberpunk 2077: Giuseppe Marano, Marek Bielawski, and Mateusz Ptasinki, as well as the awesome Sound Design and Music teams at CD Projekt Red who continue to use these tools to add dynamic mixing and music into the game.

CHAPTER 3

Timed ADSRs for One-Shot Sounds

Guy Somberg

3.1 INTRODUCTION

Consider a long looping sound – say, the crackle of an electric beam weapon or the mechanical motor of a drill. These sounds are usually important and triggered by the player and should therefore be loud, exciting, and dynamic. But what happens if the player holds down the button that fires the electron gun or that triggers the drill for a long time? These sounds can't be the most important thing in the game the entire time that they're playing.

Enter the AHDSR envelope – short for its components of *Attack*, *Hold*, *Decay*, *Sustain*, and *Release*. The *Hold* parameter is a more modern addition to the envelope and is not always present, so the curve is typically abbreviated as ADSR.[1] In this chapter, we'll examine the ADSR curve and its component pieces, look at its applications and where it breaks down, and then discuss a system that we call Timed ADSRs to apply ADSRs to one-shot sounds.

3.1.1 A (Very) Brief History

The first commercially available synthesizer was the Hammond Novachord, which entered production in 1938.[2] It featured an "Attack Control" knob with seven hard-coded preset envelope curves, making it the first documented use of an ADSR-like curve. The next evolution was an envelope generator with custom parameters, developed by American engineer Robert Moog in the 1960s.[3] Although their operation and terminology were originally more complex, they were in spirit and function the same as the modern ADSR curve.

                    DOI: 10.1201/9781003330936-4

3.2 THE ADSR CURVE

The ADSR curve is a generic function of value over time that can be applied to modulate any parameter. The easiest way to think about it is to dive into its functionality.

3.2.1 Parameter Description

Although the AHDSR acronym has five components, the curve itself consists of eight controllable parameters:

- **Initial** – The starting point of the curve. This is the value at time zero.

- **Attack** – The time that it takes the curve to transition from the *Initial* value to the *Peak* value.

- **Peak** – The value that will be reached after the *Attack* time has passed and which is maintained for the duration of the *Hold* time.

- **Hold** – Once the value has reached the *Peak*, it is held for this length of time.

- **Decay** – The time that it takes the curve to transition from the *Peak* value to the *Sustain* value.

- **Sustain** – The value that is maintained while the sound is playing, after the *Attack*, *Hold*, and *Decay* times have passed.

- **Release** – Once a stop has been triggered, how long it takes to reach the *Final* value.

- **Final** – The final value at the end of the curve, after the stop has been triggered and the *Release* time has elapsed.

3.2.2 Curve Behavior

There is a lot of implied behavior in those descriptions, so let's take another look at the behavior of the curve from the perspective of a sound's timeline.

- **T = 0** – The value is set to *Initial*. We begin to fade the value up or down, targeting the *Peak* value.

- **T = *Attack*** – The value has now reached the *Peak* and stays there.

- **T = *Attack* + *Hold*** – We have reached the end of our *Hold* time, so we begin to fade from our *Peak* value to our *Sustain* value, over the *Decay* time.

- **T = *Attack* + *Hold* + *Decay*** – The value has now reached the *Sustain* and stays there until the sound gets untriggered.

- **T = X** – (X is some later time.) The sound is untriggered by a timeline or game event. We begin to fade from the *Sustain* value to the *Final* value over the *Release* time.

- **T = X + Release** – The value has reached the *Final* value, and the sound is stopped.

These descriptions of the ADSR curve are vague as to the actual effect that the curve has and just refer to a nonspecific "value." This is on purpose because the curve can actually be applied to modulate any value. When applied to volume, it will describe how the sound's volume will change over time. When applied to a filter cutoff, it will describe how the cutoff value changes over time. The specific shapes of the curve for these parameters will be different, but the behavior of the curve is the same. Figure 3.1 shows two common curves as they might apply to volume and filter cutoff frequency.

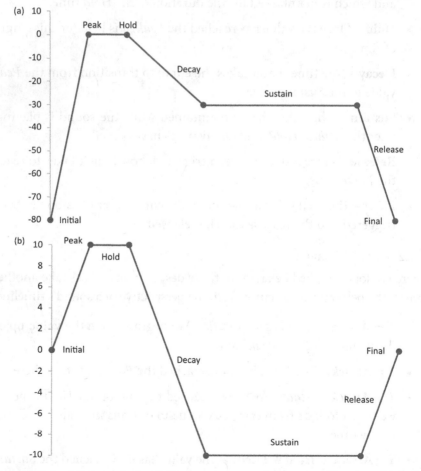

FIGURE 3.1 (a) A typical ADSR curve parameterizing volume in decibels. (b) A typical ADSR curve parameterizing filter cutoff frequency as a percent delta.

3.2.3 Wacky Shapes

The typical AHDSR curve used in games exhibits the "couch" or "boot" shape exhibited in Figure 3.1, but there is nothing in the description of the curve's behavior that requires that to be the case. In fact, the only limiting factor is the practical range of the parameter that is being modulated. That is, a volume curve cannot go below silence, and a frequency curve cannot go above the Nyquist frequency. Every parameter will have some minimum and maximum value which will define the effective range of the curve.

However, within the limits of the parameter's range, any shape is technically valid. If your sound designer wants to design a curve that starts at +10 dB, holds at −30 dB, sustains at silence, and then releases at full volume, then that is perfectly valid[4]! Figure 3.2 shows what that would look like.

3.2.4 Nonlinear Curves with Additional Controls

In all of the figures we've shown so far, each of the points on the curve is linearly interpolated with its next value. While that is a reasonable and simple default, there is nothing that requires a linear interpolation. With a little bit of extra data, control point handles can be added that affect the interpolation between each segment of the curve as shown in Figure 3.3.

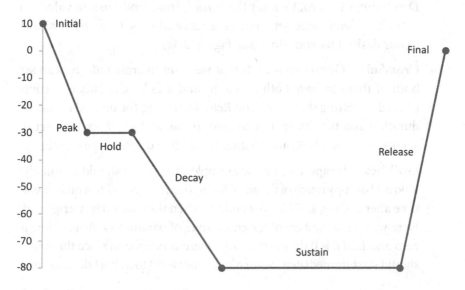

FIGURE 3.2   An ADSR curve with a nontraditional shape.

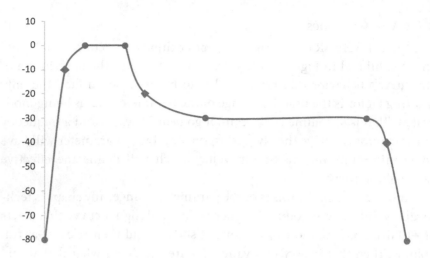

FIGURE 3.3 An ADSR curve with nonlinear interpolation between the various segments.

3.2.5 Common Applications

This chapter opens with a couple of very common – but somewhat more advanced – use cases for ADSR curves. Let's examine in more detail some of the use cases, in increasing order of complexity, and see what the curves would look like:

- **Fadeout** – This is the simplest use of the curve since it only involves one of the features. To implement a fadeout, we set our *Attack* and *Decay* times to zero, then set the *Initial*, *Hold*, and *Sustain* values to 0 dB. The *Final* value gets set to silence, and we set the *Release* time to our desired fadeout time (see Figure 3.4a).

- **Crossfade** – Given two sounds that we want to cross fade, we can set both of them to have both a fade in and a fade out. This is accomplished by setting the *Attack* and *Release* times to the desired crossfade duration and the *Decay* time to zero. *Initial* and *Final* are both set to silence, and then *Hold* and *Sustain* are set to 0 dB (see Figure 3.4b).

- **Drill/Beam Weapon** – In these examples, the sound should be initially loud and occupy much of the aural focus, then fade down to a quieter volume after a while, and fade out entirely when the weapon is untriggered. Here we take advantage of the entire suite of parameters. *Attack* time is zero and *Initial* is 0 dB in this case – there is no fade in since the sound should start immediately. Similarly, *Release* is set to a short duration and

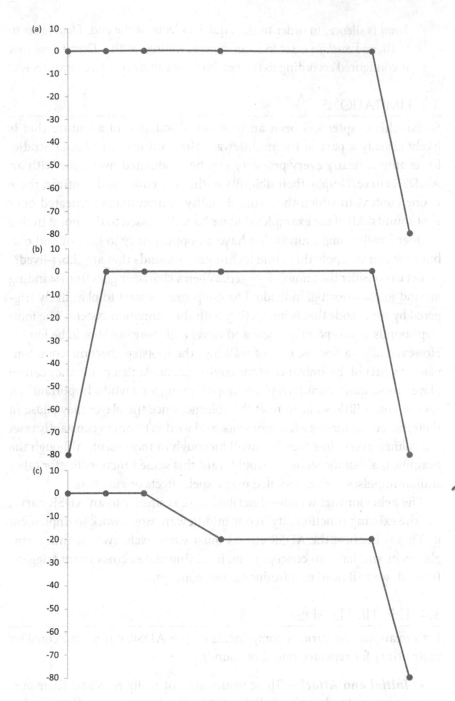

FIGURE 3.4 (a) A simple fadeout implemented with an ADSR curve. (b) A cross-fade implemented with an ADSR curve. (c) A more complex ADSR curve with an instantaneous *Attack*, followed by a *Hold*, *Decay*, *Sustain*, and *Release* to silence.

Final is silence, in order to do a quick fadeout at the end. *Hold* is set to 0 dB, and *Sustain* is set to some quieter volume, with a *Decay* time that is configured according to the needs of the game's mix (see Figure 3.4c).

3.3 LIMITATIONS

So far, this chapter has been an in-depth discussion of a feature that is likely already a part of the middleware that you use. In FMOD Studio, for example, nearly every property can be modulated over time with an AHDSR curve. Despite their ubiquity within the editor and runtime, there is one context in which their functionality is unavailable: repeated one-shot sounds. All of the examples that we have discussed to this point in this chapter involve long sounds that have an opportunity to fade in and out, but how can we apply this same technique to sounds that are short-lived?

Let us consider the humble footstep. When a character goes from standing around idle to moving, individual footstep sounds start to play, likely triggered by some code that is interacting with the animation system. The footstep sounds at this point are new and novel and therefore should be louder. However, after a few seconds of walking, the footsteps become commonplace – a part of the ambiance of the environment. At that point, they can be played more quietly until the player stops moving for a while. Importantly, it should take a little while to reset the volume, since the player may pause in their movement for just a few moments, and we don't want to constantly reset the volume every time there's a small hiccough in movement. Although the example is about footsteps, we would want this same functionality for other similar impulses such as repeated magic spell effects or gunshots.

The behavior that we have described here is similar to an ADSR curve, but the existing functionality in our middleware won't work to implement it. This is because the ADSR curves must work exclusively within a single Event and have no concept of maintaining state across Event triggers. Instead, we will need to introduce a new concept.

3.4 THE TIMED ADSR

Let's examine the various components of the ADSR curve and consider their utility for repeated one-shot sounds.

- *Initial* and *Attack* – These values are not really relevant. Their purpose is to implement a fade-in of the property over time, but one-shot sounds won't benefit from a fade-in. There's nothing to fade in – either they're playing or they aren't.

- **Peak** and **Hold** – These values will be our starting point for our repeated one-shots. We'll start at the *Peak* value and hold it there for the *Hold* duration.

- **Decay** and **Sustain** – Once again, these values map directly to one-shot sounds in the same way that they apply to looped sounds. After the *Hold* time, we fade down to the *Sustain* value over the *Decay* time and then hold it there.

- **Release** and **Final** – Similar to *Initial* and *Attack*, these values have no meaning for one-shot sounds. They're used to implement a fadeout, but one-shot sounds have nothing to fade.

This leaves us with just *Peak*, *Hold*, *Decay*, and *Sustain* as the values left to construct our curve, which results in a curve that looks like Figure 3.5. However, there is one last piece of the puzzle that remains to be implemented: we need some way of knowing when to reset the curve back to its starting point. In our example, this value would map to how long the player should be standing still in one spot before the footsteps get loud again. We'll refer to this value as the *Reset* time.

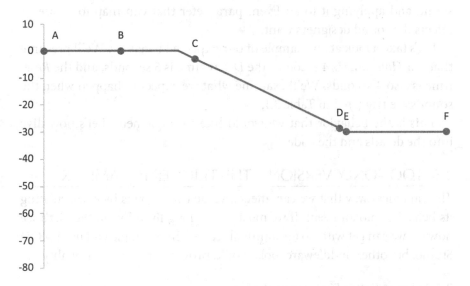

FIGURE 3.5 The Timed ADSR curve used for repeated one-shot sounds. The markers on the curve match the entries in Table 3.1.

TABLE 3.1   Example Sequence of Timed ADSR Values at Various Times. The entries match the markers in Figure 3.5.

Trigger Time	Figure 3.5 Marker	Notes
0 s	A	Our initial playback at time zero starts at the *Peak* value.
2.3 s	B	We are still within the *Hold* time, so remain at *Peak*.
4.5 s	C	We have passed our *Hold* time, and we're 0.5 seconds into our *Decay* time. We start fading from *Peak* to *Sustain*.
8.8 s	D	Same story as 4.5 seconds, except that we're now 4.8 seconds into our 5 second decay time. Our fade continues, except that we are now near the end of it and the value nears *Sustain*.
9 s	E	We've reached the *Sustain* portion of the curve, where the value stays until it resets.
12 s	F	Same as above.
17 s	A	Our *Reset* time has elapsed since the last trigger, so the value is reset to the *Peak*.
19 s	B	Still on the *Hold* time again.
21.5 s	C	Starting into our *Decay* time again.
25 s	A	Even though we haven't finished the *Hold* and *Decay* times, we haven't played since the *Reset* time, so the parameter's value is reset to *Peak*.

Our resulting curve has three sections, parameterized by five values, and we'll refer to it as the Timed ADSR curve. We apply this curve by evaluating it at the beginning of the playback for each repeated one-shot sound and applying it to an Event parameter that can map to whatever effects the sound designers want.

Let's take a look at an example of our expected behavior. We'll presume that our *Hold* time is 4 seconds, the *Decay* time is 5 seconds, and the *Reset* time is also 4 seconds. We'll examine what we expect to happen when the sounds are triggered in Table 3.1.

This is the behavior that we would like to implement. Let's now dive into the details and the code.

3.5 TOOL-ONLY VERSION – THE TRIGGER PARAMETER

The canonical way that we can affect a value over time is by encapsulating its behavior into an Event. If we must have a long-lived Event, then let's see how far we can get with no (or minimal) code. This example will use FMOD Studio, but other middleware tools should provide similar functionality.

3.5.1 Event Setup First Attempt

First, we will set up the desired curve for the Event's master volume[5]: start loud (*Peak* and *Hold*), then fade down (*Decay*), and then stay at the desired volume (*Sustain*) until the end. The sustain section will be implemented with a looping region. That implements the curve itself, but now we must have some way to trigger the sound. We'll add a discrete parameter called *Trigger* to trigger the sound whenever its value goes from zero to one. In order to make sure that the value resets automatically, we'll give it a negative velocity. Figure 3.6 shows how all of the parameters and timeline are set up.

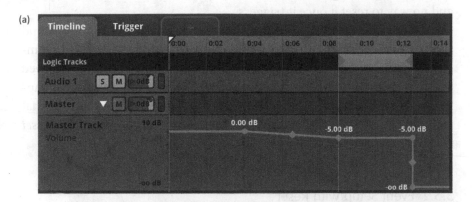

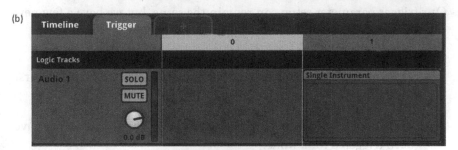

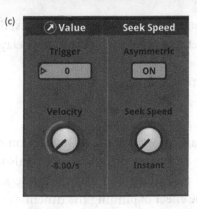

FIGURE 3.6 (a) Event timeline for a first-pass attempt at implementing the desired behavior. (b) The Trigger parameter sheet. (c) Velocity setup for the Trigger parameter.

That wasn't too bad – just a few straightforward items to set up. Let's take a step back now and see how much of our Timed ADSR setup we've managed to implement with this Event so far. The Event starts loud then fades out over time into a sustained value, and each trigger of the sound respects this volume curve – there's our *Peak*, *Hold*, *Decay*, and *Sustain*. Great! But this still leaves us with no automatic way to guarantee that the volume starts at full volume immediately when the first sound triggers, and no way to reset it once it triggers.

One way to implement this reset is to do it by hand. Keep the sound stopped until we're ready to play it and immediately set the *Trigger* parameter to a value of 1 on start. We track how long it's been since we last played and then stop the sound once it's been long enough. All of this must happen in native code, but we're looking to minimize the amount of code that we have to write for this solution. Is there any way to implement *Reset* without having to leave the tool?

3.5.2 Event Setup with Reset

Our trigger parameter setup can remain the same, but we have a few new requirements in order to implement the *Reset* value properly:

- The timeline must stay at the beginning of the Event until the first time the Trigger parameter is hit.

- The timeline should reset back to the beginning if no sounds have been triggered for a while.

- Every time a sound is triggered during the sustain interval, the timeline should reset to a point that defines the delay time.

Let's take these one at a time.

3.5.2.1 Timeline Pinned at Beginning

To implement the waiting, we will put a Destination Marker at the beginning of the timeline and name it *Beginning*. We also add a Transition to that marker that we just added and place it at the same moment on the timeline. This has the effect of pinning the timeline cursor at time zero. In order to free the timeline cursor to move past the beginning of the timeline, we add a condition to the Transition, such that it is only active if the

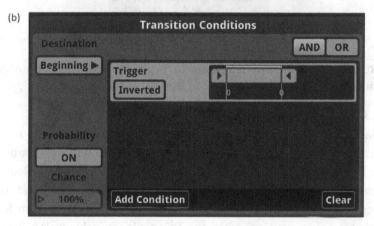

FIGURE 3.7 (a) Destination Marker and Transition at the beginning of the timeline. (b) Transition condition setup.

Trigger parameter is off (zero). With this setup in place, the timeline cursor is freed as soon as we play our first sound. Figure 3.7 shows this setup.

3.5.2.2 Timeline Resets

To implement the timeline move after the sound has not been triggered for the *Reset* time, we'll remove our Loop Region from the Event. Instead, we place an unconditional Transition at the end of the time that we expect it to reset, which will end up being the *Hold* time plus the *Decay* time plus the *Reset* time. In our example, our sustain region started at 9 seconds (4 seconds *Hold*, 5 seconds *Decay*), and our *Reset* time is 4 seconds, so the unconditional Transition is set at 13 seconds on the timeline. This setup is demonstrated in Figure 3.8.

FIGURE 3.8 Unconditional Transition to Beginning marker after sufficiently long sustain.

3.5.2.3 Reset Sustain on Trigger

Our last bit of functionality that we need to include is a way to reset the sustain time every time the sound is triggered. We will do this by adding a Destination Marker at the beginning of the sustain called *Begin Sustain* and then adding a Transition Region over the entire *Reset* time to the beginning of the time. We add a condition to the Transition Region such that it only transitions when the Trigger is set (value of 1).[6] Figure 3.9 shows the setup for the sustain region.

3.5.3 Tool-Only Approach Verdict

With these extra features implemented, we now have a working ADSR curve that we can apply to one-shot sounds. It implements all of the functionality that we want, but it has a few problems that make it less desirable.

- **Weird Trigger** – In order to have one of these Events, it must be started and attached to the target even though it is not playing any audio. Then, in order to actually have it trigger, it further subverts the normal sound playback flow by requiring that the *Trigger* parameter be set instead of playing an Event.

- **Volume Changes during Playback** – Although the volume curve moves in the way that we want, it also changes while the sounds are

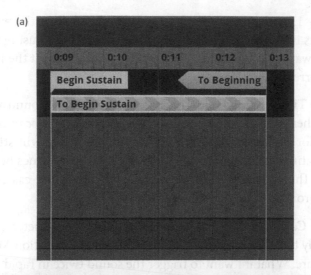

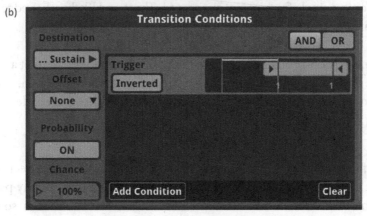

FIGURE 3.9 (a) Event Timeline showing the sustain region. (b) Transition region condition setup.

playing. For a short impulse-like sound such as a footstep, this isn't a problem because the sound is so short that any volume adjustment during playback will be undetectable. However, for a longer sound such as a spell effect, the volume adjustment will be noticeable and likely undesirable.

- **Complex Setup** – Setting an Event up like this requires creating two Destination Markers, two Transition Markers and a Transition Region along with their conditions, and an Event parameter. That's a lot of stuff to get wrong or forget. In fact, if any of these components of the Event is missing or set up incorrectly, then the entire setup breaks in subtle and difficult-to-debug ways. When using this setup, we'll want to write an auditing script[7] to validate that the Event is set up correctly.

- **Reset Time during Hold/Decay** – If we trigger the sound a few times and then stop at some point during the *Hold* or *Decay* times, then stop for the duration of the *Reset* time, the Event will still wait for the entire duration of the *Hold*, *Decay*, and *Reset* times before resetting. This may be acceptable depending on the use case, but it is a compromise.

- **Edge Cases** – What happens if the Trigger parameter gets set on exactly the same frame as the "To Beginning" Transition Marker? I'm not sure. What if I want to trigger the sound twice in rapid succession (or in a single frame)? Not supported. These and likely other edge cases are either unsupported or will have unpredictable behavior.

None of these problems is fatal to using this setup to implement a Timed ADSR, but all together they make it a much less attractive option. We will have to see if we can do better driving the functionality with code.

3.6 CODE-DRIVEN APPROACH

One of the advantages of the tool-driven approach described in Section 3.5 is that the curve itself can be fully customized and applied to any parameter that can be automated on the timeline. Our code-driven solution should provide this same flexibility, and the most straightforward way to provide this flexibility is by encapsulating it into an Event Parameter.

3.6.1 The TimedADSR Parameter

Our design will use a continuous parameter that we will call *TimedADSR*, which will range from 0 to 1. The rest of the Event can be set up as normal, whether it is a timeline or an action sheet, and the *TimedADSR* parameter can then be hooked up to anything that can be automated on a parameter. Each time we trigger the Event, the code will select a value for the parameter and hold it there for the duration of the playback. During the *Hold* period the parameter's value will be zero, during the *Decay* it will linearly interpolate from zero to one, and thereafter it will remain at a value of one. Using a parameter like this allows us to simplify the parameterization

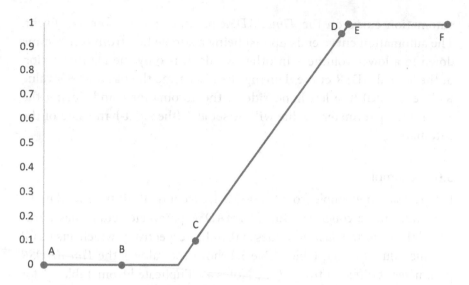

FIGURE 3.10 Curve driving the *TimedADSR* parameter. The markers correspond to Table 3.2.

since the *Peak* and *Hold* values are effectively hard-coded to zero and one, respectively. The shape of this curve is shown in Figure 3.10.

Note that Figure 3.10 represents the value of the parameter rather than the parameter curve itself, and the parameter can then adjust any property that can be automated. Figure 3.11 shows an example of an

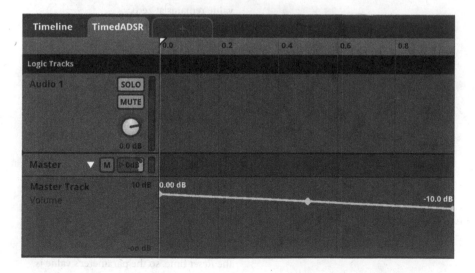

FIGURE 3.11 An example *TimedADSR* parameter automation curve for a footstep event.

automation curve on the *TimedADSR* parameter for a footstep Event. The automation curve ends up just being a simple line from full volume down to a lower volume – in other words, it is only the *Decay* portion of the Timed ADSR curve. During the *Hold* time the parameter's value will be set at 0 (the left-hand side of the automation), and during the *Sustain* the parameter's value will be set at 1 (the right-hand side of the automation).

3.6.2 Example

Let's revisit our example from Section 3.4, except that this time we'll make the values more concrete. Our *TimedADSR* parameter curve has hard-coded the *Peak* and *Sustain* values at 0 and 1, respectively, which lets us fill specific values into our table. Table 3.2 shows the value of the *TimedADSR* parameter at different times. (The Notes are duplicated from Table 3.1 for convenience, with the specific values included.)

TABLE 3.2   Example Sequence of *TimedADSR* Values at Various Times

Trigger Time	Figure 3.10 Marker	*TimedADSR* Parameter Value	Notes
0 s	A	0	Our initial playback at time zero, played with a value of zero.
2.3 s	B	0	We are still within the *Hold* time, so the value remains at zero.
4.5 s	C	0.1	We have passed our *Hold* time, and we're 0.5 seconds into our *Decay* time. The *Decay* time is 5 seconds, so 0.5/5 = 0.1.
8.8 s	D	0.96	Same story as 4.5 seconds, except that we're now 4.8 seconds into our 5 second decay time.
9 s	E	1	We've reached the *Sustain* portion of the curve, where the value is at 1 until it resets.
12 s	F	1	Same as above – we stay at 1 until reset.
17 s	A	0	Our *Reset* time has elapsed since the last trigger, so the value is reset to zero.
19 s	B	0	Still on the *Hold* time again.
21.5 s	C	0.1	Starting into our *Decay* time again.
25 s	A	0	Even though we haven't finished the *Hold* and *Decay* time, we haven't played since the *Reset* time, so the parameter's value is reset to zero.

Note: The markers are at the same times as in Table 3.1 and are mapped in Figure 3.10.

It is worth noting that Figure 3.10 and Table 3.2 are exactly the same as Figure 3.5 and Table 3.1, except with the specific values of 0 and 1 for *Peak* and *Sustain*. With this in mind, we can now dive into our implementation.

3.6.3 Implementation Details

Our Event design must now have three configuration values which we'll implement as User Properties, in addition to the *TimedADSR* parameter:

- **HoldTime** – The time to keep the Event at a value of zero.

- **DecayTime** – How long after the *Hold* time to linearly interpolate from zero to one.

- **ResetTime** – How long after the last trigger of the Event before the curve is reset.

There are three other considerations that we must keep in mind:

1. We must track our Timed ADSRs per Event for each actor in the game. Consider two player characters in a multiplayer game casting the same spell at the same time – each one will need to track the Timed ADSR status independently.

2. Most Events will not be set up with Timed ADSRs, so our design must not pay a memory or CPU cost for Events that do not use the system.

3. For those Events that do use Timed ADSRs, we must avoid any kind of operation happening on a tick for performance reasons.

3.6.4 The Code

We will split our implementation into three components:

- A `TimedADSR` structure, containing the instigator (that is, the actor with which it is associated), the start time of the current curve, and the last trigger time. We will use the timing information to determine the correct parameter value to assign.

- A `TimedADSRContext` structure, containing cached values for the *Hold*, *Decay*, and *Reset* times, along with an array of `TimedADSRs`.

- A mapping between Events (we'll use `FMOD::Studio::ID` here) and `TimedADSRContexts`.

When we play an Event, first we'll check that it has all of the required parameters, and then we'll look up the correct parameter value. In order to find the value, we look up the `TimedADSRContext` in the mapping based on the Event that we're playing and then do a linear search through the array of `TimedADSRs` to find the one that matches the actor that we're attached to.

Let's put this all together:

```cpp
struct TimedADSR;
struct TimedADSRContext
{
  float HoldTime;
  float DecayTime;
  float ResetTime;
  std::vector<TimedADSR> TimedADSRs;
};

struct TimedADSR
{
  std::weak_ptr<Actor> Instigator;
  float StartTime;
  float LastTriggerTime;
};

class AudioEngine
{
  // ...
  std::unordered_map<FMOD::Studio::ID, TimedADSRContext> TimedADSRs;
};
```

A quick note on the types used in these examples: for the purposes of this book, we are using the C++ standard library, but the types may need to be changed based on your game engine. For example, when using Unreal engine, the instigator would need to be a `TWeakObjectPtr<AActor>`, and the `TimedADSRs` map would use a `TMap<>`. Either way, the types used will have some requirements about how they are implemented. For example, to properly use `FMOD::Studio::ID` in a `std::unordered_map`, there will need to be a specialization of `std::hash` and `operator==` for `FMOD::Studio::ID`. For the purposes of this book, we will assume that these operations exist and are implemented properly.

Now that we have the structures in place, we can start to put together functionality. Let's start with the code that actually evaluates the curve:

```cpp
// Get the current value of the curve
float TimedADSR::GetValue(
  const TimedADSRContext& Context,
  float CurrentTime) const
{
  // How long has it been since we started this TimedADSR.
  auto TimeSinceStart = CurrentTime - StartTime;

  // If we're less than the Hold time, then the parameter
  // value is zero.
  if (TimeSinceStart < Context.HoldTime)
    return 0.0f;

  // We're past the Hold time, so adjust the time so that the
  // zero value is at the beginning of the Fade time.
  TimeSinceStart -= Context.HoldTime;

  // We've adjusted our zero to be at the beginning of the Decay
  // time, so if the current time is less than the Decay time,
  // then we must linearly interpolate.
  if (TimeSinceStart < Context.DecayTime)
    return TimeSinceStart / Context.DecayTime;

  // We've passed the Hold and Decay times, so the current value
  // is 1.
  return 1.0f;
}

bool TimedADSR::IsExpired(
  const TimedADSRContext& Context,
  float CurrentTime) const
{
  // How long has it been since the last time we played.
  auto TimeSinceLastPlay = CurrentTime - LastTriggerTime;

  // If our last play time is past the reset time, then this
  // TimedADSR has expired.
  return TimeSinceLastPlay < Context.ResetTime;
}
```

These two functions describe the entire operation of the Timed ADSR curve described in Section 3.4, and they meet all of the technical requirements outlined in Section 3.6.3. The rest of the work that we have to do is to hook up these new structs. The API that we will expose from the audio engine is a single function that returns the current value for the Timed ADSR given an Event ID and instigator. This function will find or add a `TimedADSRContext`, find or add a `TimedADSR` for the given instigator, reset the `TimedADSR` if it has expired, and then return the current value.

In order to implement that function, we'll need a few straightforward helper functions:

```
TimedADSRContext::TimedADSRContext(
  float HoldTime, float DecayTime, float ResetTime) :
  HoldTime(HoldTime), DecayTime(DecayTime), ResetTime(ResetTime)
{}


TimedADSR* TimedADSRContext::FindADSR(const Actor& Instigator)
{
  // Linear search to find the TimedADSR for the Instigator
  auto FoundTimedADSR =
    std::find_if(
      TimedADSRs.begin(), TimedADSRs.end(),
      [&Instigator](const TimedADSR& TimedADSR)
      {
        return TimedADSR.Instigator.lock().get() == &Instigator;
      });

  // There was no TimedADSR with that Instigator
  if (FoundTimedADSR == TimedADSRs.end())
    return nullptr;

  // FoundTimedADSR is an iterator, so we dereference it to
  // turn it into a TimedADSR&, then we take the address of that
  // to return.
  return &(*FoundTimedADSR);
}


TimedADSR* TimedADSRContext::AddTimedADSR(float CurrentTime)
{
  // emplace_back returns a reference to the newly-constructed
  // entry, so we can just return the address of the result.
  return &TimedADSRs.emplace_back(CurrentTime);
}
```

```
TimedADSR::TimedADSR(float CurrentTime)
{
  Reset(CurrentTime);
}


void TimedADSR::Reset(float NewStartTime)
{
  // We reset the TimedADSR by setting all of its time entries to
  // the new start time, which has the effect of resetting the
  // curve to zero at the current time.
  LastTriggerTime = StartTime = NewStartTime;
}
```

Note that the `TimedADSRContext` member functions must be declared and defined separately rather than inline with the struct because the declaration order of the structures means that we do not have the definition of the `TimedADSR` struct at that point. The `TimedADSR` functions are shown out of line, but they can be defined inline with the struct if desired.

We are now ready to write our function that gets the Timed ADSR value:

```
float AudioEngine::GetTimedADSRValue(
  const FMOD::Studio::ID& EventId, const Actor& Instigator,
  float HoldTime, float DecayTime, float ResetTime)
{
  // First, either find the existing TimedADSRContext
  // for the given Event or add a new one.
  auto [FoundContext, NewlyAdded] =
    TimedADSRs.try_emplace(EventId, HoldTime, DecayTime, ResetTime);

  // Sanity-check.  try_emplace() should always return a valid
  // iterator.
  assert(FoundContext != TimedADSRs.end());

  auto CurrentTime = GetCurrentTime();

  // Next we find the TimedADSR for the Instigator
  auto* FoundADSR = FoundContext->second.FindADSR(Instigator);
  if (FoundADSR == nullptr)
  {
    // If we fail to find it, then we'll add a new one
    FoundADSR = FoundContext->second.AddTimedADSR(CurrentTime);
  }
```

```
// Another sanity check.  We have either found an existing
// entry or added a new one, so we expect that FoundADSR
// will always be valid.
assert(FoundADSR != nullptr);

// Reset the TimedADSR if it has expired.
if (FoundADSR->IsExpired(FoundContext->second, CurrentTime))
{
  FoundADSR->Reset(CurrentTime);
}

// Finally, we can get the value.
return FoundADSR->GetValue(FoundContext->second, CurrentTime);
}
```

Now that we've written this code, the final piece of the puzzle is to actually use the `AudioEngine::GetTimedADSRValue()` when starting to trigger our Event. We will write a function that can be called on Event playback, in the `ToPlay` state[8]:

```
void PlayingEvent::SetupTimedADSR()
{
  // Get the user properties for the Hold, Decay, and Reset times.
  FMOD_STUDIO_USER_PROPERTY HoldTimeProperty;
  FMOD_STUDIO_USER_PROPERTY DecayTimeProperty;
  FMOD_STUDIO_USER_PROPERTY ResetTimeProperty;
  auto HoldTimeResult =
    EventDescription->getUserProperty(
      "HoldTime", &HoldTimeProperty);
  auto DecayTimeResult =
    EventDescription->getUserProperty(
      "DecayTime", &DecayTimeProperty);
  auto ResetTimeResult =
    EventDescription->getUserProperty(
      "ResetTime", &ResetTimeProperty);

  // Make sure that all three values have been read properly
  if (HoldTimeResult != FMOD_OK
      || DecayTimeResult != FMOD_OK
      || ResetTimeResult != FMOD_OK)
    return;
```

```
// Verify that the values are all set up properly.
auto IsNumber = [](const FMOD_STUDIO_USER_PROPERTY& Prop)
{
  return Prop.type == FMOD_STUDIO_USER_PROPERTY_TYPE_INTEGER
    || Prop.type == FMOD_STUDIO_USER_PROPERTY_TYPE_FLOAT;
};
if (!IsNumber(HoldTimeProperty)
    || !IsNumber(DecayTimeProperty)
    || !IsNumber(ResetTimeProperty))
  return;

// Get the property values as floats
auto GetValue = [](const FMOD_STUDIO_USER_PROPERTY& Prop)
{
  if (Prop.type == FMOD_STUDIO_USER_PROPERTY_TYPE_INTEGER)
    return static_cast<float>(Prop.intvalue);
  else
    return Prop.floatvalue;
};
auto HoldTimeValue = GetValue(HoldTimeProperty);
auto DecayTimeValue = GetValue(DecayTimeProperty);
auto ResetTimeValue = GetValue(ResetTimeProperty);

// Check that the values are all valid.
if (HoldTimeValue <= 0.0f
    || DecayTimeValue <= 0.0f
    || ResetTimeValue <= 0.0f)
  return;

// We now have the correct setup for a TimedADSR, so query the
// engine for the value.
auto TimedADSRValue =
  Engine.GetTimedADSRValue(
    EventId,
    Instigator,
    HoldTimeValue,
    DecayTimeValue,
    ResetTimeValue);

// Finally, we can set up the Event Parameter.
EventInstance->setParameterByName("TimedADSR", TimedADSRValue);
}
```

We have avoided any sort of ticking code, but now we have a different problem: old `TimedADSRContext`s stick around indefinitely. We have a few options:

- We can accept the memory leak under the expectation that it will be small and the memory cost is manageable.

- We can add a ticking function that runs at some slow rate to clean up any expired `TimedADSR`s. Despite our determination to do otherwise, this will end up being a minor cost that we may be willing to accept.

- We can select a specific moment in time (such as loading a new game map) to clean up the expired `TimedADSR`s.

- We can schedule a timer to run only when we expect that there will be at least one `TimedADSR` to clean up. There are a few options for selecting when to trigger the timer:

  - Schedule one timer for each `TimedADSR` at the moment of its expiration. The benefit is that there will never be any wasted space, and each `TimedADSR` will be cleaned up immediately when it expires. However, we do have to keep track of potentially many timers.

  - Schedule one timer only, for the time of the nearest `TimedADSR` expiration. This is a lot more efficient in space and time (fewer timers, fewer timer handles, fewer callbacks), but it can still have a lot of callbacks, as we will need to hit each `TimedADSR`. Also, the function to calculate this value is more complex, since it needs to iterate over all of the `TimedADSR`s.

  - Schedule one timer only, for the time of the latest `TimedADSR` expiration. This has all of the same benefits and drawbacks as the previous option, but it collects several `TimedADSR` expirations into one callback trigger. So long as we're okay holding onto the `TimedADSR`s for a few seconds, this is my preferred option.

Which option we pick depends on the game requirements, but the code for doing the actual cleanup is straightforward.

```
void TimedADSRContext::CleanupExpiredTimedADSRs(float CurrentTime)
{
    // Remove any expired TimedADSRs from the context.
    std::erase_if(
```

```
    TimedADSRs,
    [=](const TimedADSR& Entry)
    {
        return Entry.IsExpired(*this, CurrentTime);
    });
}

void AudioEngine::CleanupExpiredTimedADSRs()
{
    // Clean up any expired TimedADSRs from each context
    for (auto& [ID, Context] : TimedADSRs)
    {
        Context.CleanupExpiredTimedADSRs(GetCurrentTime());
    }

    // Remove any empty contexts
    std::erase_if(
        TimedADSRs,
        [](const auto& Entry)
        {
            return Entry.second.TimedADSRs.empty();
        });
}
```

3.6.5 Code Approach Verdict

For all that we've written several pages of code, this system is not very complex. Despite its simplicity, this system implements the Timed ADSR functionality correctly and even improves on the tool-only approach in many ways. Let's take a look at the drawbacks from Section 3.5.3 and see how this approach stacks up:

- **Weird Trigger** – With the tool-only approach, we had to attach a looped Event to the instigator and then set a *Trigger* parameter in order to play the sound, which subverts normal Event playback. With this code-driven approach, Events with Timed ADSRs can trigger and play back in exactly the same way as every other Event.

- **Volume Changes during Playback** – Because the parameter's value is evaluated only once just before Event playback, the value is fixed for the duration of the Event, which eliminates aural artifacts resulting from the curve moving during playback.

- **Complex Setup** – Without any sort of built-in mechanism for implementing a Timed ADSR, there will be some level of complexity implied in Event setup. Both approaches require a parameter to be set up, but this approach has no particularly complex components beyond that. Other than the parameter, we require three user properties to be set up, which one could argue is much less complex than the timeline markers required for the tool-only setup. With both approaches, it's a good idea to implement an auditing script to check for the correct setup.

- **Reset Time during Hold/Decay** – The code-driven approach will reset the parameter correctly when the *Reset* time has passed, even if it is during the *Hold* or *Decay* times.

- **Edge Cases** – Although I don't know of any as I write this chapter, there are likely some edge cases that remain unhandled. However, because this is all our code, we can fix any issues that arise.

3.7 CONCLUSION

ADSRs are a massively useful tool in the hands of sound designers, but they are limited to looped sounds. The Timed ADSR concept introduced in Section 3.4 extends the ADSR to one-shot sounds. In this chapter, we have examined two different approaches for implementing the Timed ADSR: a tool-only approach and a code-driven approach. Although both approaches function well, the code-driven approach has fewer caveats and a simpler setup (once the code has been written, of course).

NOTES

1 Both ADSR and AHDSR are the sort of unfortunate acronyms that aren't actually pronounceable. That is, you don't typically hear people refer to them as "add-ser" curves, but rather as "aiy dee ess ar" curves.

2 Cirocco, Phil. "The Novachord Restoration Project," CMS 2006, http://www.discretesynthesizers.com/nova/intro.htm

3 "Envelope (music)," Wikipedia, Wikimedia Foundation, June 3, 2022, https://en.wikipedia.org/wiki/Envelope_(music)

4 Valid, but, y'know, weird... However, we're coming into this with the assumption that the sound designer knows what they want, and that this is it.

5 This example uses volume, but can be applied to any parameter that can be automated.

6 This is in contrast to the pinning that we did in Section 3.5.2.1, where the transition was set when the value is 0.

7 See Game Audio Programming: Principles and Practices Volume 2, Chapter 8 "Advanced FMOD Studio Techniques", section 8.3.2 by Guy Somberg, published by CRC Press.

8 See Game Audio Programming: Principles and Practices Volume 1, Chapter 3 "Sound Engine State Machine" by Guy Somberg, published by CRC Press.

CHAPTER 4

Systemic Approaches to Random Sound Effects

Michael Filion

4.1 INTRODUCTION

Large open-world games, where the world is one of the fundamental elements of the player experience, need to feel alive, vibrant, and detailed so that players do not get bored of seeing the same blade of grass or the same tree for the 100th time. Systemic implementation of random sound effects (RFX) in video games adds a level of realism and unpredictability to what can easily become a repetitive backdrop. A systemic approach can allow for a greater diversity of sound with less repetition and give the impression to the player of a full-fledged dynamic world simulation without requiring huge computational resources and development time.

This chapter will discuss the fundamentals of RFX and walk through the implementation of a complex and flexible system that allows for greater creative control.

4.2 WHAT ARE RFX

Imagine yourself standing in a grassy clearing of the forest, surrounded by a thick dense forest. What sounds would you expect to hear? Often, we will hear small insects in the grass, perhaps small animals scurrying around in the field, and larger animals breaking the underbrush while moving through

DOI: 10.1201/9781003330936-5

the densely packed forest – even when they are not easily visible. While in reality the reason why a given sound is produced at any given moment in this scene is not random and is the reaction to a given event, as a simple observer in this environment each of these sounds will be indistinguishable from random background noise. This perceived randomness is what systemic RFX systems attempt to recreate in the virtual game environment.

For the purposes of this chapter, we will define RFX as any random sound effect not triggered as part of player or NPC actions. This means that any sound triggered for any animations, gameplay events from interaction (such as opening a door or a chest), looping ambience sounds, etc. will not be included as part of the discussion. This category of sound will often attempt to imitate the randomness of the natural world.

4.3 PSEUDORANDOM NUMBER GENERATORS

One of the fundamental tools that drive RFX is the pseudorandom number generator. The C standard library provides **rand()** and **srand()** functions to generate and seed a global random number generator, respectively. However, the use of those functions is discouraged for a number of reasons. First, their state is global – that is, there exists only one random number state in the whole program, so we cannot have independent generators running. Second, the quality of the generator is inconsistent and often poor – the algorithm that it uses is not defined and may be inconsistent (and of inconsistent quality) across compilers or environments. Finally,[1] the distribution of values is not guaranteed, only the range – 0 to **RAND_MAX**, which may be inconsistent on different implementations, and is often relatively small for the range of values that we want to generate.

The C++11 standard rectified these problems by providing a separate API for generating random numbers using different well-defined algorithms, as well as APIs for selecting numbers with particular distributions. The canonical example of a simple program that uses this API looks like this:

```cpp
#include <random>
#include <iostream>

int main()
{
    std::random_device rd;
    std::mt19937 gen { rd() };
    std::uniform_real_distribution<> dis { 0.0f, 1.0f };
```

```
    std::cout << dis(gen) << std:endl;
    std::cout << dis(gen) << std:endl;
    std::cout << dis(gen) << std:endl;

    return 0;
}
```

Those three lines will output different values each time the code is run. This code uses a `random_device` to select a seed for the `mt19937` generator and then feeds that generator to a `uniform_real_distribution` to select uniformly distributed random values between 0 and 1.

Extending this functionality to a useful game context is outside the scope of this chapter, but it can be encapsulated without too much effort into a function with an interface similar to `float GetRandomNumber(float Min, float Max)`, which is what we will use in this chapter as a proxy for a fuller random number interface.

4.4 DISCONTINUITY BETWEEN VISUAL AND AUDIO CUES

Because RFX attempt to imitate the real world, it is important to ensure that players do not hear something that cannot be associated with something visually. Imagine being in an urban environment in the middle of a road and hearing a dog barking relatively close to your location within that environment without seeing anything that corresponds visually to the sound. This breaks the immersion of our virtual environment and leads to an overall feeling of a lack of quality in the world.

The simplest way to eliminate this effect is with a judicious choice of assets. In an interior space, wood creaks and other generic structural movement sounds can be played relatively close to the player without any issues. However, it is important that the sound of wind hitting a pane of glass does not come from a brick wall without any openings.

Another method is to create a cone around the player where RFX sounds are forbidden to play. While this will not entirely solve the discontinuity problem, it will help to reduce it. However, this can have the effect of making the world seem further away, creating a cone of silence around the player.

4.5 DATA-DRIVEN SYSTEM PROTOTYPE

Whatever your choice of sound engine, it should be possible to implement a simple implementation rather quickly. There are a few elements that are required: a method to play a random sound from a given list, an option to

FIGURE 4.1 A basic data-driven example using Wwise. The Sequence Container is set to continuous, and the Silence is randomized between 1 and 5 seconds.

play silence with a randomizable duration, and the ability to loop between these two methods.

While the basic example shown in Figure 4.1 does not provide any interesting results, we can use it as a baseline for discussions around a more complex system. For example, we can randomize the position of the sounds to create some more variety.

4.6 BASIC PROGRAMMATIC APPROACH

Starting from the basic data-driven approach described in Section 4.5, we will define a few requirements for a basic programmatic approach. Our system must contain the following:

- An array of different sound events to trigger
- A minimum and maximum delay between the end of one sound and the start of another
- The minimum and maximum distance from the player

We will start by defining a simple class to represent the data for our RFX.

```
struct RandomSoundEffect
{
  bool IsPlaying() const;
  Time GetNextTriggerTime() const;

  SoundEffect soundEffect;
  float minDistance;
  float maxDistance;
  Time lastTriggerTime;
  Duration triggerDelay;
};
```

This information should be provided by the sound designer in whatever format that the game engine allows. The minimum distance should be at least the distance that a player can travel while the sound is playing plus a little bit extra "safety" distance, so as to not create any issues of visual discontinuity with the sound. The maximum distance is the maximum audible distance of the sound in order to avoid playing inaudible sounds.

With the data structure for RandomSoundEffect in hand, we will define a small class to handle playing and keeping track of all the current instances.

```
class RandomSoundEffectPlayer
{
public:
  void Update();

private:
  void PlayRandomSoundEffect(
    const RandomSoundEffect& rfx, const Vector3& pos) const;
  Vector3 GetRfxPosition(const RandomSoundEffect& rfx) const;

private:
  std::vector<RandomSoundEffect> rfxs;
};
```

With the above prototype, we have the beginnings of a system that can provide a level of perceived randomness to the world, making it feel dynamic and alive. While the definitions are simple, we are still providing a lot of flexibility to allow for artistic creativity for the sound designers.

The Update() function is quite straightforward: we iterate through all the sound effects in rfxs and validate whether or not they are playing. If the sound is not playing and enough time has elapsed, determine a new position and play the sound.

```
void RandomSoundEffectPlayer::Update()
{
  const Time now = GetCurrentTime();
  for(auto& rfx : rfxs)
  {
    //Has the RFX finished playing?
    //Has enough time passed since the last trigger?
```

```
if(!rfx.IsPlaying() && now > rfx.GetNextTriggerTime())
{
  //Get a position and play the RFX
  Vector3 pos = this->GetRfxPosition(rfx);
  this->PlayRandomSoundEffect(rfx, pos);

  //Update the RFX information
  rfx.lastTriggerTime = now;
 }
 }
}
```

This loop plays an RFX if necessary, then updates the random sound effect with the fact that it has been played. We have left out the implementations of a few of the helper functions referenced in this code. `GetCurrentTime()` returns the current time, and `GetNextTriggerTime()` returns a value indicating the next time that the RFX can be played, calculated as: `lastTriggerTime` + (duration of the RFX) + `triggerDelay`.

Another important function is the `GetRfxPosition()`, which requires the player's position and the min/max distance from the player (from the `RandomSoundEffect` data structure). Because we want to provide a position around the player, we will generate three random float values between −1 and 1, assign each one to an axis of a 3D vector, normalize the vector, generate a random float value between the min and max distance, then multiply that by the normalized vector. That will give us an offset vector that we can add to the player's position to return.

```
Vector3 RandomSoundEffectPlayer::GetRfxPosition(
  const RandomSoundEffect& rfx) const
{
  const Vector3 playerPos = GetPlayerPosition();

  //Create the Vector3 with random values
  Vector3 rfxOffset;
  rfxOffset.x = GetRandomNumber(-1.f, 1.f);
  rfxOffset.y = GetRandomNumber(-1.f, 1.f);
  rfxOffset.z = GetRandomNumber(-1.f, 1.f);

  //Normalize the vector
  rfxOffset.Normalize();
```

```
rfxOffset *= GetRandomNumber(rfx.minDistance, rfx.maxDistance);

return playerPos + rfxOffset;
}
```

There are other algorithms for generating a more uniformly random vector,[2] but this algorithm has the benefit of being simple and straightforward. Depending on the game's mechanics, selecting a random position in the sphere may not be appropriate. For games where the player can move around in 3D by climbing buildings, trees, or other environmental elements, a sphere selection (which includes an elevation component) is more likely to be appropriate. For games that do not provide such flexibility in movement, consider whether having sounds with elevation could lead to visual discontinuity – if so, then you can select a vector in the unit circle around the player instead of the unit sphere.

The result of this basic system is that the player will end up with random sound effects placed around them in random directions. The shaded area from Figure 4.2 shows a visual representation of where the sounds will be played in relation to a stationary player. The inner non-shaded area is the minimum distance specified with `RandomSoundEffect::minDistance`. As a reminder, this area should also represent the maximum amount of

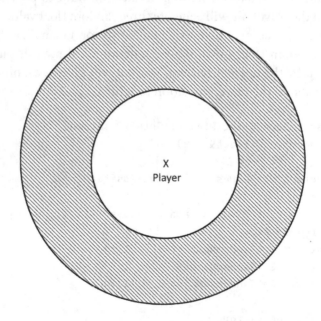

FIGURE 4.2 The shaded area where random sound effects will play.

distance the player can traverse given the length of a random sound effect to avoid any discontinuity issues.

4.7 REMOVING THE MINIMUM DISTANCE

The simple system that we covered in the previous section is a great starting point, but it does have some limitations. If we want to represent the world closer to the player and avoid any discontinuity issues, we need to make a few modifications. We would also like to add sound categories in order to allow the RFX system to integrate more cleanly with the game's state.

To create a category of random sound effects, we will take the previously defined RandomSoundEffect, modify it, and add a new data structure to define a category:

```
struct RandomSoundEffect
{
  bool IsPlaying() const;

  SoundEffect soundEffect;
  float maxDistance;
};

struct PlayingRandomSoundEffect
{
  Time GetNextTriggerTime() const;

  Time lastTriggerTime;
  RandomSoundEffect rfx;
};

struct RandomSoundEffectCategory
{
  //Configuration Data
  unsigned int maxConcurentRfxs;
  Duration triggerDelay;
  std::vector<RandomSoundEffect> rfx;

  //Runtime Data
  std::vector<PlayingRandomSoundEffect> playingRFXs;
  std::vector<std::pair<OwnerID, Vector3>> positions;
};
```

Let's go through these structures and describe their purpose:

- `RandomSoundEffect` is the basic information for a given RFX. It has a maximum distance that it can be played from the player and the similar functions that were provided in the base system.

- `PlayingRandomSoundEffect` is responsible for providing information about a given instance of a playing RFX. The last trigger time is stored in this data structure because we will have an arbitrary number of playing RFX (defined as `maxConcurrentRfxs` in `RandomSoundEffectCategory`).

- `RandomSoundEffectCategory` contains most of the configuration information in addition to runtime tracking information. The maximum number of concurrent RFX is defined there, which we can use to initialize `playingRFXs`. Additionally, the positions that are possible to select are provided in a pair to allow for adding/removing of positions as needed. These positions should be provided by instances of entities/game objects in the world that represent the visuals where we want the RFX to be played from. This would include entities such as trees, bushes, doors, crates, etc. The method for providing this information will differ based upon the game engine and the way the world is constructed.

There are several functions in the previous `RandomSoundEffectPlayer` that will need to be modified for our new system to work. The first that we will start with is providing the position.

```
Vector3 RandomSoundEffectPlayer::GetRfxPosition(
  const RandomSoundEffect& rfx,
  const RandomSoundEffectCategory& category) const
{
  const Vector3& playerPos = GetPlayerPosition();
  const unsigned int maxCatPos = category.positions.size();

  Vector3 pos;
  do
  {
    const unsigned int idx = GetRandomNumber(0, maxCatPos);
    pos = category.positions[idx].second;
  } while((playerPos - pos).Length > rfx.maxDistance);

  return pos;
}
```

The function now requires both the RFX and the category it is associated with. Because each RFX can have a different maximum distance, the function enters a loop to continuously select a random position, ensure that it is close enough to the player, and repeats if that is not the case. One assumption that this algorithm makes is that there are enough positions that eventually a valid position will be found. This function can quickly become a performance bottleneck if there are too many positions provided that are not close enough to the player's position. If that is the case, then there are other algorithms that will find appropriate positions quickly.

The next function that is required is an update per category. With this function, the algorithm needs to iterate on all the playing RFX, validate if they are currently playing, and play a new instance if enough time has elapsed after the previous one has finished.

```cpp
void RandomSoundEffectPlayer::Update(
  RandomSoundEffectCategory& category) const
{
  const Time now = GetCurrentTime();
  const unsigned int maxCatRFXs = category.rfx.size();
  for(auto& playingRFX : category.playingRFXs)
  {
    //Has the RFX finished playing?
    //Has enough time passed since the last trigger?
    if(!playingRFX.rfx.IsPlaying() &&
       now > playingRFX.GetNextTriggerTime())
    {
      //Determine the new RFX to play & assign it
      const unsigned int idx = GetRandomNumber(0, maxCatRfxs);
      playingRFX.rfx = category.rfx[idx];

      //Get a position and play the RFX
      Vector3 pos = this->GetRfxPosition(category, playingRFX.rfx);
      this->PlayRandomSoundEffect(rfx, pos);

      //Update the RFX information
      playingRFX.lastTriggerTime = now;
    }
  }
}
```

Looking at the algorithm for the RFX category, we notice that it shares the same basic structure as the original implementation. The differences here are that the algorithm now assigns the RFX in `PlayingRandomSoundEffect` and stores information in that structure rather than the `RandomSoundEffect`. The number of playing RFX can be increased or decreased globally or based upon a given game context.

We have left off a few implementation details in this chapter, such as initialization of the arrays and any runtime resizing given a specific context. We also haven't shown some game-specific details, such as updating, adding, and removing positions as appropriate for the specific game engine used. Finally, the global `RandomSoundEffectPlayer::Update()` function needs to be modified to iterate on the categories and call the `Update()` function with the category as a parameter.

The level of control that sound designers have has increased substantially with these added features. The amount of time to add these additional features is more than worth the improvements.

4.8 DEBUGGING FEATURES

Now that we have a functional system, it is important to add debugging features so that the sound designers (and audio programmers!) can understand what is happening. These features need to allow both programmers and artists to use the system, gather useful information, and be efficient.

One useful piece of information to report is the value that was used to seed the pseudorandom engine. Exposing it can be as simple as outputting the value to a log somewhere, then you can implement a feature that allows the user to set the seed manually rather than using the default implementation. If the system uses a global pseudorandom number generator, then this seed will be less useful because other calls into the generator will cause inconsistent behavior, so the RFX system should store its own random number generator context.

Being able to visually see the information related to the current RFX will be useful as well, beyond the information that the sound engine can provide for any given sound. Providing a 3D visual representation of the sound in the world, and the fact that it has been triggered by the RFX system, can be useful to visually validate what is being heard. A simple icon or other graphical primitive can be used to provide this visual indication.

Logging textual information about the state of the RFX system can give a good overview of how the system is currently operating and allow for a quick overview of erroneous behavior. A snapshot of the current system can be provided to a console. Commercial game engines generally provide such functionality – in Unity it is `Debug.Log()` and in it is Unreal `UE_LOG`. If a button is pressed or a console command has been issued, we can add logs to (for example) the `RandomSoundEffectPlayer::Update()` function to output the state to the console.

Snapshots of the current state of the system are useful, but sometimes continually updated debugging information is necessary. The implementation details change depending on the game engine, but the basic principle is the same. Rather than outputting the information to a console, we will update a debug view each frame containing the runtime information of the system.

4.9 CONCLUSION

Helping a game world come alive with an added level of sound that mimics what we know from the real world is an effective tool for player immersion. Both the simplest and more complicated implementations can be memory and CPU efficient while respecting an artistic vision. Starting with the most basic implementations can provide a level of realism to the world with very little investment. With the basic version in place, iterating on the basic algorithm and modifying the behavior to be more appropriate for the given game context can be done over time. The resulting implementations will often be still quite simple, allowing for easy debugging and testing in a multitude of scenarios and also imitating the real-world easily with great results.

NOTES

1 At least, finally for this chapter. The failings of `rand()` could fill many, many more pages of text. It's an awful function and you shouldn't use it. - Ed

2 https://mathworld.wolfram.com/SpherePointPicking.html

CHAPTER 5

The Jostle System

A Baked Solution to Environmental Interaction Sounds

Alex Pappas

5.1 INTRODUCTION

5.1.1 Establishing the Problem

Early on in the development of *Back 4 Blood*, our sound design team was struggling to implement a system for shrubbery sounds. Their solution at the time was to hand-draw and place volumes throughout every gameplay map at locations where shrubbery had reached a critical density. Each time a character would move while inside this shrubbery volume, it would trigger a traversal sound determined by parameters assigned per volume. The end result would simulate the sounds of leaves and branches pulling at the clothes of players, NPCs, and enemies alike as they passed through overgrown foliage and brambles.

Most of the game's foliage relied heavily on static meshes, a type of mesh that is capable of conveying a great amount of detail, though it can't be deformed through vertex animations. Thus, these shrubbery volumes added a great deal of life to the game, even though the meshes themselves remained stationary and unmoving. We could heighten immersion for players as they crashed through the undergrowth or reward a keen ear with the subtle rustlings of a "Ridden" as it ambled through a cornfield.

DOI: 10.1201/9781003330936-6

It soon became clear that the shrubbery system was highly impractical. At this stage in the project, every gameplay map was undergoing iteration, and there were more maps, level designers, and environment artists than any single sound designer could keep up with. Often shrubbery volumes drawn by a sound designer on Monday would need to be entirely reworked before the end of the week because maps were changing with such velocity. Also, organic foliage is seldom so neatly placed that a single volume will properly capture its shape. The sound designers would often grapple with fields of tall grass that would dissolve into sparse clumps at the edges. Deciding to draw a volume only over the densest parts of the grass would risk having inconsistent behavior; the sparser clumps not included within the volume wouldn't trigger the expected traversal sounds. On the other hand, drawing a volume to encompass everything would result in erroneous foliage traversal sounds in locations where there was no tall grass.

This was not the only system that suffered from these issues. Two other systems – one designed to handle sounds for bumping into objects and another to trigger rattle sounds in response to explosions – also required the team to draw volumes around ever-changing chain link fences and alleyways full of debris. The maintenance work was endless.

5.1.2 Other Solutions

If you have worked with a game engine like Unreal Engine, you may be wondering why this problem cannot simply be solved by creating a new static mesh asset that includes logic for handling these sonic behaviors. The problem could be solved by using an Actor Component to encapsulate this behavior that can then be attached to the placed static mesh actors as they are added to the map. Unfortunately, audio implementation comes late in the game development pipeline, often long after other departments have already established their workflows and toolbelts. In these cases, often the "correct" answer is not the best answer if it would require other departments to redo perhaps months of work. Sometimes a solution needs to work within both the limitations of your hardware and the pre-existing circumstances of your development cycle.

Performance concerns may also shape your solution. Collision could be enabled on every one of these static mesh actors, and trigger sounds from character overlaps. However, if your game features a large world or many moving characters (or both), the sheer volume of overlap events may strain your physics engine. Additionally, if all the logic for identifying and playing these sounds is distributed across disparate actors or components, the run-time cost of your system is fragmented and difficult to control as several events could stack up on the same frame.

5.2 DESIGN REQUIREMENTS AND CONCEPTUAL TOUCHSTONES

Let's outline some touchstones to keep in mind as we work to create a system that can reproduce the sonic behavior desired by our sound designer and also works within the limitations described above. We need to:

1. Provide the sound designer with a tool that they can use to dictate a static mesh's sonic behavior when acted upon by nearby characters and/or explosions.

2. Develop a process for associating these behaviors with placed static mesh actors without changing the nature of, or adding on to, the meshes themselves.

3. Generate and store this data such that it can gracefully handle map iteration.

4. Identify valid character and explosion interactions at run-time without relying on overlap or trigger events.

5. Create a run-time manager to process all the incoming interaction requests during gameplay, house any performance optimizations, and play the appropriate sounds.

5.3 THE JOSTLE SYSTEM

Together, these features create what we called a Jostle System, a unified pipeline for handling shrub, bump, and rattle sounds in response to external stimuli – in response to being *jostled*, if you will. This pipeline is meant to assist sound designers in their quest to quickly and accurately mark up maps with proper jostle sounds, as well as assume responsibility for playing these sounds back at run-time.

Figure 5.1 shows a bird's-eye view of the whole process. To begin, sound designers will add a static mesh asset to the Jostle System's database and set up its unique sonic behavior. Afterward, an automated build process will iterate over all placed static mesh actors in each gameplay map. For each jostleable mesh it identifies, it will package its world position, transform data, and

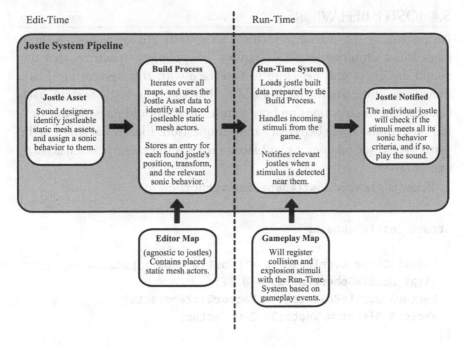

FIGURE 5.1   An overview of our Jostle Pipeline, outlining the primary responsibilities and functions of each step.

the appropriate sonic behavior together. These are saved to an array for each gameplay map. At run-time, this packaged data will be loaded in with the map and then interpreted by the Jostle System's Run-Time Manager. The manager uses this data to determine when an external stimulus should trigger a jostle sound based on the stimulus's nature, world position, and the unique sonic behavior of the nearby static mesh actors.

5.3.1 Use Cases

Jostle sounds themselves are not a novel concept; they are common to many genres of games including open world games, stealth games, first person shooters, and many more. This chapter isn't here to sell you on the idea of adding jostles to your game, but instead to provide an alternative way of thinking about and implementing such a feature while working around some common constraints. It provides a less invasive solution to this problem that might otherwise require alteration to – or intimate knowledge of – other departments' assets. This type of solution can also empower small but ambitious teams in which your designers' time is at a premium.

5.4 JOSTLE BEHAVIORS

No jostles can be placed, and thus no sounds are generated, without some input from our sound designers. The primary structures that our sound designers will be using to interface with this system are Jostle Behaviors. These are the basic building blocks of the Jostle System; each one contains instructions on how a static mesh should respond to external excitations. These behaviors answer questions like: What shape is the jostle? What sound does it play? How easy is it to excite? Is it sensitive to explosions?

Below is a sample `JostleBehavior struct`:

```
struct JostleBehavior
{
  EJostleShape OverlapShape = EJostleShape::Sphere;
  float JostleSphereRadius = 0.0f;
  Vector3 JostleBoxExtent = Vector3::ZeroVector;
  Vector3 Offset = Vector3::ZeroVector;
};
```

This structure currently has no audio-related content. Instead, its few member variables offer the API through which sound designers will adjust the jostle's size and shape, ensuring that it closely fits the basic shape of the static mesh it will later represent. We can use an `enum EJostleShape` to let our user choose the jostle's basic shape. For our sample implementation, we will allow the sound designer to select between a sphere and a box shape. When `EJostleShape::Sphere` is selected, the designer can adjust its size using the `JostleSphereRadius`. When `EJostleShape::Box` is selected, the box dimensions can be specified using the `JostleBoxExtent`. The `Offset` provides a solution for handling static meshes that are not centered about their origin.

5.4.1 Types of Jostles

There are several different ways a static mesh could respond to being jostled, each with slightly different criteria that need to be tracked. For now, we will look at three sample jostle behaviors: *Shrubs*, *Bumps*, and *Rattles*. For each of these jostle types, we will create a child **struct** of **JostleBehavior** to house the unique audio properties for each jostle type as shown in Table 5.1.

TABLE 5.1   Summary of the Three Basic Jostle Types and How They Respond to Collision and Explosion Events

Jostle Type	Properties	Collision Behavior	Explosion Behavior
Shrub	ShrubSound	Always play ShrubSound	NA
Bump	BumpSound Probability SpeedThreshold	Play BumpSound if the source of the excitation is moving faster than SpeedThreshold with a likelihood of Probability	NA
Rattle	RattleSound	Same behavior as *Bumps*	Always play RattleSound

5.4.1.1 Shrub Behavior

The *Shrub* is the simplest of the Jostle Behaviors. It will always play its jostle sound when a character moves past or through it. It is ideal for simulating the sonic behavior of its namesake, shrubbery. The only additional parameter we need to add is the sound to play when the jostle is triggered.

```
struct ShrubBehavior : public JostleBehavior
{
   SoundAsset* ShrubSound = nullptr;
};
```

5.4.1.2 Bump Behavior

Bumps are similar in functionality to *Shrubs* and also have an additional Probability and SpeedThreshold. These variables can be quite powerful as they provide the designers the ability to specify playback behavior based on a character's movement speed. This is ideal for breathing life into parts of the game littered with detritus that characters may be able to kick or bump into while running, as shown in Figure 5.2. With a player walk speed of 250 units/s and a sprint speed of 500 units/s, we can tune some jostle SpeedThresholds such that they only trigger when the player is sprinting through, while the Probability maintains variety. For example, the glass bottle in Figure 5.2 is easily excitable, as it can be triggered when the player is walking or running. But because its Probability is only 50%, it will only sometimes be "kicked" by a character passing through.

```
struct BumpBehavior : public JostleBehavior
{
   SoundAsset* BumpSound = nullptr;
   float Probability = 1.0f;
   float SpeedThreshold = 0.0f;
};
```

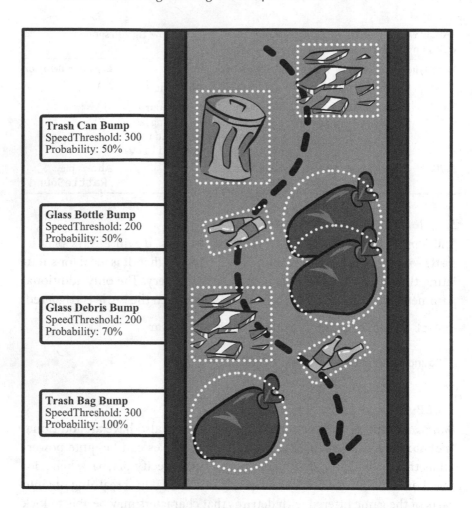

FIGURE 5.2 An alleyway full of trash has been decorated with Bump Behaviors (visualized by the dotted white outlines around various meshes). By including a speed threshold, we may reward cautious players with more stealthy navigation, while less aware players may noisily knock over discarded bottles as they sprint through.

5.4.1.3 Rattle Behavior

Rattles share all the same functionality as *Bumps*, but they are also sensitive to nearby explosions. An additional rattle sound is added so it may play a different sound in response to a remote explosion than to a character overlap. This makes them ideal for objects like chain link fences which characters may bump up against when close, but should also rattle in response to grenade explosions.

```
struct RattleBehavior : public BumpBehavior
{
  SoundAsset* RattleSound = nullptr;
};
```

5.4.2 Jostle Behavior Asset

Now it is time to associate our new Jostle Behaviors with appropriate static mesh assets. Our asset class below will function as our data entry tool for sound designers, housing the mappings of Jostle Behaviors to static mesh assets. This class will also need an API for querying and returning the associated Jostle Behavior for a given static mesh asset. These will be used in Section 5.5.1.

```
class JostleBehaviorsAsset
{
public:
  ShrubBehavior* GetShrubBehavior(const StaticMeshAsset* Mesh) const;
  BumpBehavior* GetBumpBehavior(const StaticMeshAsset* Mesh) const;
  RattleBehavior* GetRattleBehavior(
    const StaticMeshAsset* Mesh) const;

private:
  std::map<StaticMeshAsset*, ShrubBehavior> ShrubBehaviors;
  std::map<StaticMeshAsset*, BumpBehavior> BumpBehaviors;
  std::map<StaticMeshAsset*, RattleBehavior> RattleBehaviors;
};
```

5.4.2.1 A Note on Referencing Static Mesh Assets

If you attempt a direct translation of the above C++ standard library code into Unreal Engine's code base, you may (rightfully) balk upon discovering that our keys in the ShrubBehaviors, BumpBehaviors, and RattleBehaviors maps are hard references to static mesh assets. Once completely filled out, the Jostle Behaviors Asset will potentially reference hundreds of static mesh assets. I would highly recommend using Soft Object Pointers (or your engine's equivalent) to reference these assets instead. Otherwise, loading the Jostle Behaviors Asset will cause all of the referenced static mesh assets to load as well. This can slow down your sound designers, lead to some less than ideal cascading references, and is generally not desirable.

5.5 AUTOMATING MAP MARKUP

You may have noticed that our Jostle Behaviors Asset stores the linkages between Jostle Behaviors and their corresponding static mesh assets, but it is agnostic to the placement of these meshes in our gameplay maps. Without the location, rotation, and scaling data unique to every static mesh actor, the run-time portion of the Jostle System will be unable to accurately determine when to play a jostle sound.

In order to prepare this data for run-time use, we will create a build process responsible for associating the information in our Jostle Behaviors Asset with the unique transform data of every jostleable mesh placed in every map. Our build process will perform automated map markup, which is crucial for a successful pipeline because it removes the burden of manually maintaining this feature for all maps from our sound designers' shoulders. The build process can quickly and accurately update jostle data in response to changes from environment artists, as well as to any tweaks to the Jostle Behaviors Asset. Rather than trying to draw the best fitting volume over several static mesh actors, the system can instead draw individual trigger shapes for every mesh. With this process in place, the system is responsive and precise, and the sound design team has more time to focus on other features.

5.5.1 Sample Jostle Build Process

Let's start building up our framework for our Jostle Builder, which will be responsible for identifying jostleable static mesh actors and storing their positions alongside their associated Jostle Behavior. Below is some pseudo-code for the function `GenerateJostlesForWorld()` which will populate the jostle data for a single gameplay map.

```
void JostleBuilder::GenerateJostlesForWorld(
  JostleBehaviorsAsset* Behaviors)
{
  // Clear out old jostle data
  JostleEmitterNodes.clear();

  // Evaluate all static mesh actors for Jostle Behaviors
  GenerateForSMActors(Behaviors);

  // Evaluate all instanced foliage actors for Jostles Behaviors
  GenerateForInstancedFoliage(Behaviors);

  // ...
}
```

First, we discard any old jostle data that may have been generated from previous builds. Calling `GenerateForSMActors()` and `GenerateForInstancedFoliage()` should repopulate this data as they iterate over all static mesh actors and instanced foliage actors, respectively. If your team is using any custom systems for placing static meshes in maps, you will want to expand `GenerateJostlesForWorld()` to accommodate those systems as well. With access to the world, it is trivial to iterate over all placed static mesh actors to check if any of their static mesh assets are referenced by the Jostle Behaviors in our Jostle Behaviors Asset.

```
void JostleBuilder::GenerateForSMActors(
  const JostleBehaviorsAsset* Behaviors)
{
  // Iterate over all static mesh actors in the world
  for (const auto& SMActor : GetAllStaticMeshActorsForWorld())
  {
    // Get the static mesh asset used by the static mesh actor
    StaticMeshAsset* Mesh = SMActor->GetStaticMeshAsset();

    Transform ActorTransform = SMActor->GetTransform();

    // Check the found mesh against the list of shrub, bump, and
    // rattle behaviors stored on the Jostle Behaviors Asset
    AddPotentialShrubBehavior(Behaviors, Mesh, ActorTransform);
    AddPotentialBumpBehavior(Behaviors, Mesh, ActorTransform);
    AddPotentialRattleBehavior(Behaviors, Mesh, ActorTransform);
  }
}

void JostleBuilder::AddPotentialShrubBehavior(
  const JostleBehaviorsAsset* Behaviors,
  const StaticMeshAsset* Mesh,
  const Transform& ActorTransform)
{
  // Retrieve the Shrub Behavior in our Jostle Behaviors Asset, if
  // an association has been made
  const ShrubBehavior* ShrubPtr = Behaviors->GetShrubBehavior(Mesh);

  if (!ShrubPtr)
    return;
```

```
// Create a Shrub Emitter Node for the placed static mesh actor
// and Shrub Behavior
ShrubEmitterNode* ShrubNode =
  CreateAndInitializeNewShrubNode(ShrubPtr, ActorTransform);

// Add this new Shrub Emitter Node to our list containing
// all jostles for the current map
JostleEmitterNodes.push_back(ShrubNode);
}

// AddPotentialBumpBehavior() and AddPotentialRattleBehavior() have
// similar implementations...
```

In `AddPotentialShrubBehavior()`, we check our Jostle Behaviors Asset for the passed-in static mesh asset. If found, we create a new `ShrubEmitterNode` which will be responsible for storing both the static mesh actor's transform data and the Shrub Behavior returned by the Jostle Behaviors Asset. We will circle back around to this class later, but for now, we store the new `ShrubEmitterNode` in the array `JostleEmitterNodes`. This contains a Jostle Emitter Node for every jostleable static mesh actor in the current world. We can house our logic from the previous section on an actor, giving us easy access to the world and every static mesh actor in it. Any map with this actor will have its jostle data generated.

5.5.2 When to Run the Builder

Any changes made to either the Jostle Behaviors Asset or these placed static mesh actors will dirty the generated data and require it to be built all over again. It is important to ensure this build process can be run as part of a sound designer's workflow so that they may properly assess their work. I would recommend exposing it through a console command or as a button on the Jostle Behaviors Asset itself. Additionally, it should run automatically when identifying changing environments and shifting levels. Running the builder every time navigation meshes are dirtied and rebuilt is a good start, as this is often in response to changing level design. Depending on the size of your maps, building this jostle data should be relatively quick. Additionally, having the process run as part of your game's packaging process will ensure that the generated jostle data in every package build is always current and correct.

5.6 JOSTLE EMITTER NODES

The Jostle Emitter Nodes created by the Jostle Builder are the basic building blocks of the Jostle Run-Time System. It couples the transform data of
the placed static mesh actor with the appropriate Jostle Behavior. It will
also handle the jostle's unique run-time responsibilities, which are: detecting character overlaps, evaluating incoming jostle requests against its
assigned Jostle Behavior, and finally playing the appropriate sound. Below,
we can see the basic outline of our base class.

```cpp
class JostleEmitterNode
{
public:
  // World position of the jostle including actor
  // transform and any offset present in the Jostle Behavior
  Vector3 Position = Vector3::ZeroVector;

  // Initialize the proper world position of the jostle
  virtual void Init(
    const Transform& ActorTransform,
    const JostleBehavior* Info)
  {
    ReferencedActorTransform = ActorTransform;
    Position =
      TransformUtils::TransformLocation(
        ReferencedActorTransform, Info->Offset);
  }

  // Run-time behavior in response to character collisions
  virtual bool TryExciteNodeCollision(
    const Vector3& ExcitationLocation,
    const Vector3& Velocity)
  {
    return false;
  }

  // Run-time behavior in response to nearby explosions
  virtual bool TryExciteNodeExplosion(
    const Vector3& ExcitationLocation,
    float ExplosionRadius)
  {
    return false;
  }
```

```
protected:
  Transform ReferencedActorTransform = Transform();

  // Utility function for detecting overlaps
  bool IsWithinRange(
    const JostleBehavior* Behavior,
    const Vector3& ExcitationLocation);

private:
  // Utility function for detecting sphere overlaps
  bool IsWithinRangeSphere(
    const float Radius, const Vector3& ExcitationLocation);

  // Utility function for detecting box overlaps
  bool IsWithinRangeBox(
    const Vector3& BoxOrigin,
    const Vector3& BoxExtent,
    const Vector3& ExcitationLocation);
};
```

Our Init() function should be called right after the Emitter Node's creation during the Build Process (AddPotentialShrubBehavior() in Section 5.5.1). Looking at the internals of this function, we see how the static mesh actor's transform is used to properly set the Jostle Emitter Node's world position. TryExciteNodeCollision() and TryExciteNodeExplosion() will handle our run-time behavior in response to different types of excitation. For now, these functions both return false. You may have also noticed that JostleEmitterNode is agnostic to its Jostle Behavior. Much like we created *Shrub*, *Bump*, and *Rattle* versions of our Jostle Behavior, we will also create *Shrub*, *Bump*, and *Rattle* child classes of JostleEmitterNode and override each of our virtual functions to reproduce the unique sonic behavior of each jostle type.

5.6.1 Exciting Jostle Emitter Nodes

Referring back to our Jostle Behavior criteria outlined in Table 5.1, we see that there are two primary ways a jostle can be excited: in response to character collisions (used by all three jostle types) and in response to explosive events (used only by *Rattles*).

Below, we can see how each child class of JostleEmitterNode should override the relevant excitation functions and interpret its associated Jostle Behavior in response to these collision and explosion jostle events.

```cpp
bool ShrubEmitterNode::TryExciteNodeCollision(
  const Vector3& ExcitationLocation, const Vector3& Velocity)
{
  if (!IsWithinRange(&ShrubInfo, ExcitationLocation))
    return false;

  PlaySound(ShrubInfo.ShrubSound, ExcitationLocation);

  return true;
}

bool BumpEmitterNode::TryExciteNodeCollision(
  const Vector3& ExcitationLocation, const Vector3& Velocity)
{
  if (!IsWithinRange(&BumpInfo, ExcitationLocation))
    return false;

  const float ThresholdSqr =
    BumpInfo.SpeedThreshold * BumpInfo.SpeedThreshold;

  if (Vector3::SizeSqr(Velocity) < ThresholdSqr)
    return false;

  if (JostleMathUtils::GetRandomFloat() > BumpInfo.Probability)
    return false;

  PlaySound(BumpInfo.BumpSound, ExcitationLocation);

  return true;
}
```

Both the *Shrub* and the *Bump* first check to make sure the ExcitationLocation falls within the range of the jostle's collision shape. ShrubEmitterNode goes on to play its jostle sound immediately while BumpEmitterNode performs additional work using the excitation's Velocity and the Jostle Behavior's Probability. Only after an incoming excitation exceeds the SpeedThreshold and passes the probability test will the sound be triggered.

By making `RattleEmitterNode` a child of `BumpEmitterNode`, it can share the *Bump*'s response to any collision events. Thus, it needs only to override `TryExciteNodeExplosion()`. Here, we check to see if the `RattleEmitterNode`'s `Position` falls within the `ExplosionRadius`, and if so, play the rattle sound.

```
bool RattleEmitterNode::TryExciteNodeExplosion(
  const Vector3& ExcitationLocation, const float ExplosionRadius)
{
  const float DistSqr =
    Vector3::DistSqr(Position, ExcitationLocation);

  // Check that our Rattle is within range of the explosion
  if (DistSqr > (ExplosionRadius * ExplosionRadius))
    return false;

  PlaySound(RattleInfo.RattleSound, ExcitationLocation);

  return true;
}
```

5.6.2 Overlap Detection

The Jostle System contains its own simple and efficient collision detection so that each Jostle Emitter Node can handle its own logic for detecting character overlaps. The `IsWithinRange()` function is used to determine if incoming jostle collision events actually fall within the jostle overlap shape created by the sound designers. We use the Jostle Behavior's `OverlapShape` to determine whether to use point-in-sphere or point-in-box for our encapsulation check.

```
bool JostleEmitterNode::IsWithinRange(
  const JostleBehavior* Info, const Vector3& ExcitationLocation)
{
  switch (Info->OverlapShape)
  {
    case EJostleShape::Sphere :
      return IsWithinRangeSphere(
        Info->JostleSphereRadius, ExcitationLocation);
    case EJostleShape::Box :
      return IsWithinRangeBox(
        Info->Offset, Info->JostleBoxExtent, ExcitationLocation);
  }
}
```

Inside `IsWithinRangeSphere()` and `IsWithinRangeBox()`, we can use the Jostle Emitter Node's `ReferencedActorTransform` and its Jostle Behavior to check if the `ExcitationLocation` falls within the Jostle Emitter Node's area of influence. These functions will take into account the jostle's offset and any scaling or rotation applied to the static mesh actor.

```
bool JostleEmitterNode::IsWithinRangeSphere(
  const float Radius, const Vector3& ExcitationLocation)
{
  const float TransformedRadius =
    Radius *
      TransformUtils::GetMaxAxisScaling(ReferencedActorTransform);

  // Offset has already been applied to Position during Init()
  const float DistSqr =
    Vector3::DistSqr(Position, ExcitationLocation);

  return (Radius * Radius) > DistSqr;
}

bool JostleEmitterNode::IsWithinRangeBox(
  const Vector3& BoxOrigin,
  const Vector3& BoxExtent,
  const Vector3& ExcitationLocation)
{
  // Convert ExcitationLocation from world space to local.
  const Vector3 TransformedExcitationLocation =
    JostleMathUtils::WorldToLocal(
      ReferencedActorTransform, ExcitationLocation);

  // Now we can use our jostle's original box origin and extent
  // to create an axis-aligned bounding box and check if the
  // excitation occurred within our jostle's area of effect.
  const AABBox JostleBox = AABBox(BoxOrigin, BoxExtent);

  return JostleBox.Contains(TransformedExcitationLocation);
}
```

5.7 JOSTLE SYSTEM AS A RUN-TIME SYSTEM

Our Jostle Run-Time System will handle all character collision and explosion event requests generated during gameplay. When received, it will notify all nearby Jostle Emitter Nodes of the incoming jostle event request.

If the request is within the range of the Jostle Emitter Node and passes the criteria specified by its Jostle Behavior, the excited Jostle Emitter Node will play its jostle sound.

5.7.1 Using a Grid

Iterating over our entire array of Jostle Emitter Nodes for every jostle event request would be incredibly costly and slow. Instead, we can leverage spatial partitioning to limit the number of relevant Jostle Emitter Nodes to evaluate for each jostle event request. For this example, we will be using a 2D grid container. When loading into a new map, the Jostle Emitter Nodes stored on our Jostle Build Actor should be inserted into a grid container used by the Jostle Run-Time System.

```
class JostleSystem
{
public:
  // Register our list of Jostle Emitter Nodes, and insert them into
  // our EmitterGrid when the gameplay map loads
  void RegisterEmitters(
    const std::vector<JostleEmitterNode>& Emitters);

  // Remove our list of Jostle Emitter Nodes from our EmitterGrid
  // when the map unloads
  void UnregisterEmitters(
    const std::vector<JostleEmitterNode>& Emitters);

  // ...

private:
  // 2D Grid which contains all currently active Jostle Emitter Nodes
  TGridContainer<JostleEmitterNode*> EmitterGrid;

  // List of collision requests to handle this update
  std::vector<JostleCollisionRequest> CollisionRequests;

  // List of explosion requests to handle this update
  std::vector<JostleExplosionRequest> ExplosionRequests;

  // ...
};
```

In `RegisterEmitters()`, the grid will use the Jostle Emitter Node's `Position` to place it into the proper grid cell with other Jostle Emitter Nodes that represent nearby static mesh actors as illustrated in Figure 5.3a. Since all Jostle Emitter Nodes represent unmoving static mesh actors, we do not have to worry about updating any of their positions in the grid over the course of play. Just as we can sort Jostle Emitter Nodes into cells using their `Position`, we can also identify the cell in which a jostle event took place. With this knowledge, we can retrieve that cell's constituent Jostle Emitter Nodes and only check this specific subset for overlaps as shown in Figure 5.3b.

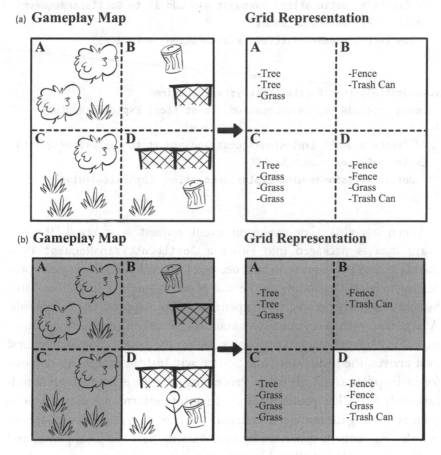

FIGURE 5.3   (a) We partition our gameplay map into four quadrants, each corresponding to a cell in our (incredibly coarse) grid container. (b) When a character moves through Quadrant D, we only need to evaluate the four Jostle Emitter Nodes in the corresponding Grid Cell D for overlaps, rather than evaluating all Jostle Emitter Nodes for the entire map.

5.7.2 Jostle Event Request Handling

In addition to our registration/unregistration logic for Jostle Emitter Nodes, we will want to extend our API to handle our primary ways of exciting the Jostle System: collisions and explosions. We will add the two public functions below to our Jostle System Run-Time Manager to receive incoming jostle event requests.

```
void JostleSystem::ExciteJostleSystemCollision(
  const Vector3& CollisionLocation, const Vector3& Velocity)
{
  // Create a JostleCollisionRequest and add it to CollisionRequests
  CollisionRequests.push_back(
    JostleCollisionRequest(CollisionLocation, Velocity));
}

void JostleSystem::ExciteJostleSystemExplosion(
  const Vector3& ExplosionLocation, const float ExplosionRadius)
{
  // Create a JostleExplosionRequest and add it to ExplosionRequests
  ExplosionRequests.push_back(
    JostleExplosionRequest(ExplosionLocation, ExplosionRadius));
}
```

When a collision or explosion event request is received, the relevant data is packaged into either a `JostleCollisionRequest` or a `JostleExplosionRequest` to be processed later. Why should we defer processing to later? Depending on the size of your game, the Jostle Run-Time System can easily become very expensive without appropriate safeguards. A large map with many characters and explosions can generate huge numbers of jostle event requests to process. Rather than evaluating each request as it arrives, the Jostle Run-Time System will instead process all requests for each update as a single batch. Processing all jostle event requests simultaneously will allow you to make a variety of performance optimizations such as limiting the number of collision and explosion requests each frame, prioritizing requests generated by or occurring near the local player, and scaling the number of allowable jostle requests per platform.

5.7.3 Processing a Single Collision Event Request

When the Jostle Run-Time Manager processes jostle event requests, it uses the location of the request to determine within which cell(s) to search.

Let's look at a sample implementation for retrieving Jostle Emitter Nodes from our **EmitterGrid** in response to a single collision event request.

```
void JostleSystem::EvaluateCollisionRequest(
  const JostleCollisionRequest& Collision,
  const Vector3& ListenerPosition)
{
  std::vector<JostleEmitterNode*> CandidateEmitters;

  const Vector3 ExcitationLocation = Collision.ExcitationLocation;

  const Vector3 SearchExtent(
    CollisionSearchRange, CollisionSearchRange, CollisionSearchRange);

  // Create a box centered about the collision request, this is the
  // area we will be searching over
  AABBox SearchBox(ExcitationLocation, SearchExtent);

  // Get all Jostle Emitter Nodes for all grid cells that overlap
  // with our search box
  EmitterGrid.GetElements(&SearchBox, CandidateEmitters);

  for (auto& Node : CandidateEmitters)
  {
    bool Result = Node->TryExciteNodeCollision(
      ExcitationLocation,
      Collision.ExcitationVelocity);

    // For clarity of mix, we only trigger the first valid jostle
    // though this is a matter of preference
    if (Result)
      break;
  }
}
```

A **SearchBox** is passed into **EmitterGrid.GetElements()** to identify overlapping grid cells and return all the Jostle Emitter Nodes contained within them via the **CandidateEmitters** array. We iterate over all **CandidateEmitters** and call **TryExciteNodeCollision()**. As we saw in Section 5.6.1, **TryExciteNodeCollision()** will ensure the current Jostle Emitter Node encompasses the **ExcitationLocation** and that the current

`JostleCollisionRequest` fulfills the Jostle Behavior criteria. If these tests pass, the Jostle Emitter Node will play its assigned sound.

5.7.4 Processing a Single Explosion Event Request

An implementation of `EvaluateExplosionRequest()` will share much of the same structure as `EvaluateCollisionRequest()`. Looking back, we can see that our `SearchExtent` in `EvaluateCollisionRequest()` is easily tunable, and thus we can drive its size using the `ExcitationRadius` of the `JostleExplosionRequest` currently being evaluated.

When evaluating collisions, we chose to only excite the first valid Jostle Emitter Node. For `EvaluateExplosionRequest()`, you will want to iterate over and excite all `CandidateEmitters`. If we only excite one or two Rattles in the vicinity, the Jostle System's response may sound sparse and unnatural.

5.8 PARTING THOUGHTS

We have created a Jostle System that fulfills all of our touchstones listed in Section 5.2. It meets the sonic expectations of our sound design team, respects the workflow and toolsets of our fellow departments, and is capable of adhering to the performance requirements of our game. There is still so much more to add, such as debugging tools, toggleable jostles, and custom propagation delays for explosions. New features aside, the system we've built in this chapter is quite flexible; you should be able to modify or add new Jostle Behaviors depending on your game's unique needs, expand the build process to handle any number of ways your environment artists have decided to decorate your gameplay maps, tweak the run-time behavior to help your sound designers manage the mix, and so much more.

CHAPTER 6

Background Sounds

Guy Somberg

6.1 INTRODUCTION

Creating the feeling of being in a realistic environment is one of the challenges of game audio. There are many individual aural components that make a player feel as though they are in a space. The room tone – the sound of the space itself – is just the first component of this soundscape. Once the room tone is established, the sound designers will want to layer on more elements, including both loops and randomized one-shot sounds. In a space like the tunnels of a subway, there will be a light breeze, the creaks of the tunnel walls settling, and maybe a ghost train moving around in the distance. In a forest, we'll hear wind, trees rustling, birds chirping, and a stream burbling in the distance. One sound designer I worked with immediately wanted to add the sound of children crying in the distance.

All of these layers could be added to a single looped sound or middleware event, but without any sort of systemic randomness, players will quickly notice the repetition inherent in the sounds. I call the collection of these sounds and layers as well as the system that plays them "Background Sounds," but they go by other names in different games: ambiences, environmental effects, etc. Depending on how much fine-grain control we want to provide the sound designers, we can either implement a system that allows the sound designers to create these soundscapes or use the tools that the middleware provides to do similar work. Either way, first we'll need to break the sounds down into their component parts and figure out how we want to handle them.

DOI: 10.1201/9781003330936-7

6.2 COMPONENTS OF BACKGROUND SOUNDS

There are two broad categories of sounds that make up background sounds: loops and one-shot sounds, which we will need to handle separately.

6.2.1 Background Sound Loops

When you are in a space with many different sounds, you are not usually aware of all of them at once. Different sounds come to your consciousness at different times, and the world is rarely so neat as to provide a constant stream of unchanging sound. Sound designers can isolate these sounds (room tone, wind, etc.) into loops to play individually, but if we just triggered all of the layers at once, we would fail to capture this nuance. Our handling of looped sounds, therefore, needs to account for randomization in duration and volume at least, and optionally other properties (such as panning or effects) as well.

- **Duration** – We would like our sound to be audible for a certain length of time, fade out to silence for a while, and then fade back up. This fading scheme will let us capture the idea of the sounds coming in and out of the player's attention.

- **Volume** – Similar to duration, when the looped sound is playing, we would like its volume to ramp up and down. These volume changes will provide variety to the mix and make it less predictable.

- **Other Effects** – Just adjusting the volume is unlikely to satisfy the modern sound designer. They will want to expose one or more parameters that the game can control to adjust the effects, panning, or other properties of the event. Once we have a scheme for selecting and ramping volume over time, it is easy to adapt it to control an event parameter, then run both controls independently.

6.2.2 Background Sound One-Shots

In a real environment, there are always short sounds that make up part of the ambiance – bird chirps, creaks, drips, etc. These sounds do not occur in a regular pattern or on a regular beat, so – similar to the looped sounds – we need some sort of system to replicate this arrhythmic property. We will also want to encode a few properties of the triggered sounds:

- **Grouping** – Similar sounds often come in groups. A bird will chirp a few times in a row, or a few drops of water will drip in rapid succession. We'll want to have a mechanism to play a randomized count of sounds.

- **Timing** – Each group of sounds will need both a randomized length of time between individual sound triggers and a randomized length of time between groups.[1]

- **Volume** – Each sound played will need to be played at a randomized volume. While we can implement a complex system for selecting volumes within a group, it turns out not to be worth the energy.

- **Panning** – One-shot background sounds can have several different panning models:

  - Nonspatial sounds that are coming from the environment at large. These sounds won't need any sort of pan randomization, since they're played as 2D.

  - Sounds that appear to be coming from a particular location in the world. These sounds can be placed in 3D to create the illusion of spatialization.

  - Sounds that are coming from a particular direction relative to the player. These sounds can have their pan randomized through an event parameter that is controlling the event panning.

- **Other Effects** – As with the looping sound, the sound designers are going to want to adjust other properties of the sounds exposed through parameters, and a system similar to the volume control can be used to control the parameters.

6.3 USING BUILT-IN TOOLS

Before we dive in to write a bunch of code, let's see how close we can get with the tools built into our middleware. In this chapter, we'll use FMOD Studio,[2] but similar tools should be available in any middleware.

6.3.1 Looping Sounds

There are two components that we need to handle for looping sounds: duration and volume. Once we have those, we can adapt the solutions to apply to other effects. The first thing that we'll do is add an audio track with a sound to play and a loop region, as shown in Figure 6.1.

This setup is unremarkable so far; with the basic playback configured, let us first tackle how to have the sound play and stop over time. We can use an LFO oscillator to turn the volume of the track on and off, as

FIGURE 6.1   A multi-sound instrument playing with a loop region.

shown in Figure 6.2. However, if we just adjust the volume of the track or the instrument using this modulator, we will end up with potentially undesirable effects. If we use a square wave, then the volume changes abruptly, and we have no way to change it over time.[3] If we use a sine

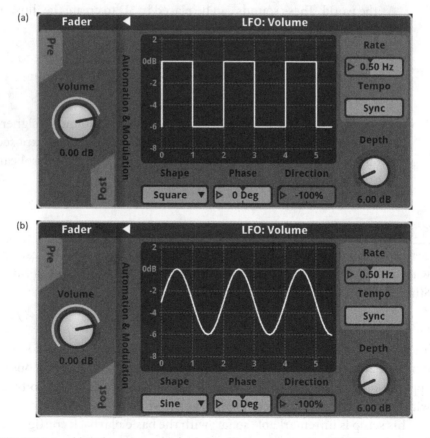

FIGURE 6.2   (a) Volume control modulated by a square wave. (b) Volume control modulated by a sine wave.

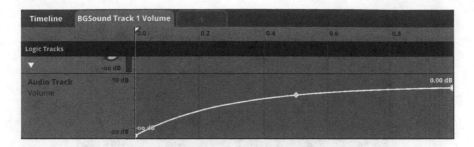

FIGURE 6.3 Track volume automation curve for the `BGSound Track 1 Volume` event parameter.

wave, then the volume will change smoothly, but it won't hold at a particular volume over time.

Instead, we will solve this problem by adding an event parameter, which we will call `BGSound Track 1 Volume`. First, we'll add an automation curve to the parameter for the track volume and give it a nice smooth curve,[4] as shown in Figure 6.3. With that curve in place, we can give the parameter a seek speed and then apply a square wave LFO modulation to the parameter value (Figure 6.4). Using a square wave in this way does not provide a random time for the on-off cycle, but with a slow enough LFO, it shouldn't be noticeable. Although we won't show it in this chapter, you can use a similar scheme to adjust event parameters.

Now that we have the duration set up, we must handle the volume. We'd like the volume to be randomized over time as the sound itself is playing,

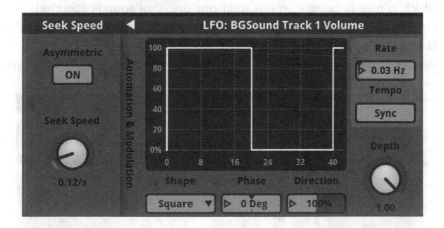

FIGURE 6.4 Event parameter configuration showing parameter seek speed and LFO modulation.

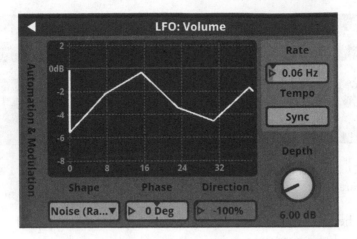

FIGURE 6.5   Instrument volume with Noise (Ramped) LFO modulator applied.

which we will do by applying an LFO configured as "Noise (Ramped)" to the instrument as in Figure 6.5. The "Noise (Ramped)" LFO selects random values, then linearly interpolates between them over time. By applying the volume LFO to the instrument volume and the automation curve to the track volume, we get a smooth ramp.

All of this setup gets one of our tracks configured. We will have to perform the same configuration steps for each looping audio track that we add.

6.3.2 One-Shot Sounds

FMOD Studio provides an instrument called a scatterer for these purposes, which is nice because it lets us treat our one-shot sounds effectively the same as we do looping sounds. We'll create a scatterer instrument over the same range as the main loop, as shown in Figure 6.6. Scatterer instruments already contain much of the functionality that we're looking for. They have

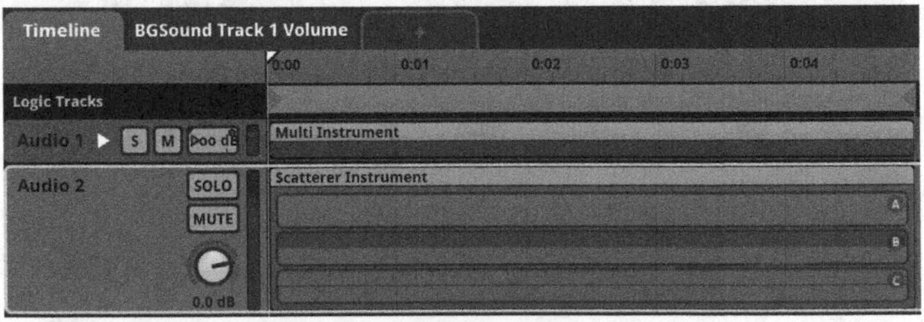

FIGURE 6.6   A scatterer instrument on the timeline.

FIGURE 6.7   Scatter configuration showing the minimum and maximum distances configured for nonspatial sounds.

volume and pitch randomization, as well as randomized 3D position and timing. We can apply effects by using referenced or nested events in the scatterer instrument playlist, but there is no grouping functionality.

The last piece to discuss is the panning control. We have three options:

- Nonspatial sounds are handled either by selecting a value of zero for the minimum and the maximum scatter distance or by using nested or referenced 2D events for all of the sounds. The zero-distance configuration is shown in Figure 6.7.

- World sounds are the default case for scatterer instruments. They're placed in the world around the listener and pan and attenuate in the manner that we expect.

- Fixed-pan sounds will have to be implemented by using nested or referenced events in the playlist (Figure 6.8) and applying a Random modulator to the value parameter controlling the panning in the event (Figure 6.9).

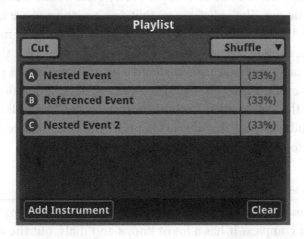

FIGURE 6.8   Scatterer instrument playlist showing nested and referenced events.

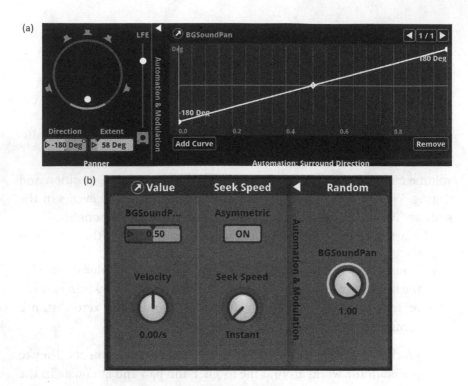

FIGURE 6.9 (a) Event parameter curve controlling event panning. (b) Random modulator on the event parameter value.

6.3.3 Built-in Tools Overview

Now that we've set up our looping and one-shot sounds in an event, it turns out that we've been able to get pretty close to the design goals we originally laid out. The only features that aren't supported are randomized duration and fixed volume for looping sounds, and grouping functionality for one-shot sounds. This is great! If we're willing to accept these limitations, then playing a background sound really is as simple as just triggering a single event. However, if your sound designers want more control or really want the features that the built-in systems can't provide, or if you're using an audio engine that doesn't support the necessary features, then you'll have to build a system to implement the functionality.

6.4 FROM-SCRATCH IMPLEMENTATION

The functionality that we'd like to implement for this system is not, ultimately, that complex. It has a lot of knobs and dials, but the actual work that we're doing amounts to rolling some dice 🎲 🎲 and triggering changes based on those rolls. In this section, we'll build a data- and event-driven system to implement the desired behavior.

6.4.1 Description of the Functionality

Let's go through some examples to see how we want the system to work, which will help us to understand what we need to build.

6.4.1.1 Looping Sound Algorithm

We start by rolling our dice 🎲🎲 and checking against the chance that this sound will play. If the dice roll is lower than the play chance, then we choose to play. We will need to select random volume and pitch, as well as any other event parameters that the sound designers have configured. Ordinarily, when transitioning from not playing to playing, we would fade in, but since this is the first play, we will just start playing the sound with the selected parameters. We also need to know how long to play the sound or to be silent before we check again. The play time may be different from the silent time, so we pick the direction from different configuration settings.

After our duration has passed, we roll the dice again 🎲🎲. Our universe now branches into four possibilities, enumerated in Table 6.1.

From here on out, the algorithm remains the same: wait for the chosen duration, roll the dice, and then select the appropriate action from the table.

6.4.1.2 One-Shot Sound Algorithm

Similar to the looping sounds, we start by rolling the dice 🎲🎲 and comparing against our play chance. If we choose to play, then we select a group count and trigger the sound playback. When a sound plays, we

TABLE 6.1 Possibilities for Dice Rolls after the First One

	Currently Playing	**Currently Not Playing**
Choose to Play	Select new playback parameters, then fade to those new values. Play duration selected from "Play Time" setting.	Select new playback parameters. Pitch and event parameters set instantly, and volume fades up from silence. Play duration selected from "Play Time" setting.
Choose Not to Play	Volume fades down to silence. Silent duration selected from "Silent Time" setting.	Remain silent. Silent duration selected from "Silent Time" setting.

select the volume, pitch, 3D position, and event parameters, then decrement the group count and select a time for the next roll of the dice. The next roll time is selected by the group delay if we have any more sounds left in the group or by the trigger delay if this is the last sound in the group.[5]

The only other item of note here is that we want to force the first roll of the dice to fail. If we allowed the initial playback to trigger, then we would occasionally get a cacophony of sounds immediately as the player enters a new environment.

That is it! These algorithms should be fairly straightforward to implement. Let's go through the process.

6.4.2 Data Definition

We will presume that there is some mechanism for storing data and allowing sound designers to configure it. In this chapter, we'll avoid markup that is specific to an engine and just use plain old data structures that you can adapt to work within your game engine environment.

We'll start with the looping sounds, which need the following parameters in addition to the event to play:

- **Play Chance** – Every time we roll the dice, this is the chance that we'll choose to play a sound.

- **Play Time and Silent Time** – If we choose to play, then we'll pick a random duration within the Play Time range before rolling the dice again. If we choose not to play, then we pick a random duration within the Silent Time range before rolling the dice again.

- **Fade In Time, Fade Out Time, Fade To Time** – When fading in from silence, we'll fade the volume over a random value in the Fade In Time range. When fading out to silence, we'll fade the volume over a random value in the Fade Out Time range. And, when we're already playing the sound and choose to continue playing the sound, but at a different volume, then we'll fade the volume over a random value in the Fade To Time range.

- **Volume Control** – There are two ways that we can configure volume. We can allow the sound designers to provide decibel values and adjust the event volume explicitly. Alternatively, if the sound designers would like a custom curve, then we can have them set up an event parameter with a known name that the code will drive. Our example code will support both options.

- **Pitch Control** – Very simple: the pitch is adjusted over time in the same way that volume is controlled. We allow the sound designers to configure the pitch range in cents.

- **Event Parameters** – Sound designers can configure event parameters that the system controls. We will select a value in the range 0..1 in order to keep this simple, but the ranges can be whatever you would like, or even read the range of the value from the event description and select from that range at runtime. Because the range is fixed, we only need to know the name of the parameter to control.

Here is the data structure that holds all of that information:

```
namespace BackgroundSoundData
{
  enum class VolumeControlType
  {
    Decibels,
    Parameter,
  };

  struct LoopingSoundData
  {
    EventDescription Event;
    float PlayChance;
    FloatRange PlayTime;
    FloatRange SilentTime;
    FloatRange FadeInTime;
    FloatRange FadeOutTime;
    FloatRange FadeToTime;
    VolumeControlType VolumeControl;
    FloatRange Volume;
    FloatRange PitchCents;
    std::vector<std::string> Parameters;
  };
}
```

One-shot sounds will have a similar configuration. They also need an event to play, play chance, and volume, pitch, and parameter control in exactly the same way as the looping sounds. However, they also have their own set of configuration data:

- **Group Count** – A range of how many sounds will be triggered in a row.

- **Group Delay** – When triggering a group of sounds, a range of how long to wait between each sound in the group.

- **Trigger Delay** – In between groups of sounds, a range of how long to wait before potentially triggering the next group.

- **Pan Style** – An indication of whether the 3D sounds are nonspatial (played as-is), world sounds (played in 3D), or fixed-pan sounds (set a known event parameter).

Here is the configuration data for the one-shot sounds:

```
namespace BackgroundSoundData
{
  struct OneshotSoundData
  {
    enum class PanStyle
    {
      None,
      Surround,
      Fixed,
    };

    EventDescription Event;
    float PlayChance;
    IntRange GroupCount;
    FloatRange GroupDelay;
    FloatRange TriggerDelay;
    VolumeControlType VolumeControl;
    FloatRange Volume;
    FloatRange PitchCents;
    std::vector<std::string> Parameters;
    PanStyle Panning;
  };
}
```

The last piece of data is to describe an ambiance as a collection of looping sounds and one-shot sounds:

```cpp
namespace BackgroundSoundData
{
  struct Ambiance
  {
    std::vector<LoopingSoundData> LoopingSounds;
    std::vector<OneshotSoundData> OneShotSounds;
  };
}
```

There are a couple of useful helper functions that are used in the implementation that we will present here. These functions are used when setting the volume in order to support the dual-mode volume control.

```cpp
namespace BackgroundSoundData
{
  inline float GetSilenceValue(VolumeControlType VolumeControl)
  {
    if (VolumeControl == VolumeControlType::Decibels)
    {
      return SILENCE_DB;
    }
    else
    {
      return 0.0f;
    }
  }

  float LoopingSoundData::GetSilenceValue() const
  {
    return BackgroundSoundData::GetSilenceValue(VolumeControl);
  }

  float OneshotSoundData::GetSilenceValue() const
  {
    return BackgroundSoundData::GetSilenceValue(VolumeControl);
  }
}
```

6.4.3 Instance Data

With our definition data described and hooked up to the game's data description format, we are now ready to start implementing the actual runtime behavior of the system. Let's first see the class interfaces and what data they're going to be storing:

```cpp
// Context for playing a collection of looping and oneshot ambiences
class BackgroundSoundContext
{
public:
  BackgroundSoundContext(const BackgroundSoundData::Ambiance& Data);

  // Update all currently-fading looping sounds
  void Tick(float DeltaTime);

private:
  // Context for playing a single looping sound
  class LoopingSoundInstance
  {
  public:
    LoopingSoundInstance(
      BackgroundSoundContext& Owner,
      const BackgroundSoundData::LoopingSoundData& Data);
    ~LoopingSoundInstance();

    // Are we currently fading up or down
    bool IsLerping() const;
    // Update the fade volume and parameters
    void Tick(float DeltaTime);

  private:
    // Roll the dice and pick what to do
    void Roll();

    // Pointers back up to the owner and configuration data
    BackgroundSoundContext& Owner;
    const BackgroundSoundData::LoopingSoundData& Data;

    // Our playing sound
    PlayingEventHandle PlayingEvent;

    // Timer for our next roll of the dice
    TimerHandle NextRollTimer;
```

```
  // Time tracking for fades
  float RemainingFadeTime = 0.0f;
  float TotalFadeTime = 0.0f;

  // Fade contexts
  LerpContext VolumeFade;
  LerpContext PitchFade;
  std::vector<LerpContext> ParameterFades;
  bool IsPlaying = false;
};

// Context for playing oneshot sounds
class OneshotSoundInstance
{
public:
  OneshotSoundInstance(
    const BackgroundSoundData::OneshotSoundData& Data);
  ~OneshotSoundInstance();
private:
  // Roll the dice
  void Roll();
  void RollHelper(bool ForceNoPlay);

  // Pointers back up to the owner and configuration data
  const BackgroundSoundData::OneshotSoundData& Data;
  std::vector<PlayingEventHandle> PlayingEvents;

  // Our playing sound
  TimerHandle NextRollTimer;

  // How many triggers are left in this group
  unsigned int RemainingGroupCount = 0;
};

// Configuration data
const BackgroundSoundData::Ambiance& Data;

// Instances of looping sounds and oneshot sounds
std::vector<LoopingSoundInstance> LoopingSounds;
std::vector<OneshotSoundInstance> OneshotSounds;

// Pointers to currently-fading oneshot sounds.
std::vector<LoopingSoundInstance*> FadingLoopingSounds;
};
```

Our `BackgroundSoundContext` contains a reference to its configuration data and a list of looping sounds and one-shot sounds. It also stores a list of pointers to looping sounds that are currently fading, which will be used in the `Tick()` function. In the `LoopingSoundInstance` class, we have configuration data about how we're playing the sound encapsulated in `LerpContexts`, as well as information about the fades. The `OneshotSoundInstance` only needs to store information about the current group count, since sound playback parameter information is used immediately and doesn't change over the lifetime of the sound.

Let's take a look at the `BackgroundSoundContext` constructor before we dive into the implementation details of the looping and one-shot sounds. The constructor is straightforward since it just has to create the instance data for the looping and one-shot sounds.

```
BackgroundSoundContext(const BackgroundSoundData::Ambiance& Data) :
  Data(Data)
{
  LoopingSounds.reserve(Data.LoopingSounds.size());
  for (const auto& LoopingSoundData : Data.LoopingSounds)
  {
    LoopingSounds.emplace_back(*this, LoopingSoundData);
  }

  OneshotSounds.reserve(Data.LoopingSounds.size());
  for (const auto& OneshotSoundData : Data.OneShotSounds)
  {
    OneshotSounds.emplace_back(OneshotSoundData);
  }
}
```

6.4.4 Implementation Details – Looping Sounds

The `LoopingSoundInstance` class has two primary workhorses: the `Roll()` function and the `Tick()` function. `Roll()` encodes the behavior of Table 6.1, so it takes the form of a sequence of conditions.

```
void LoopingSoundInstance::Roll()
{
  // We will schedule the next roll at this time. Unininitialized
  // because all codepaths should fill it.
```

```
float TimeToNextRoll;

// Determine whether or not we should play this time
bool ShouldPlay = (GetRandomValue() < Data.PlayChance);
if (ShouldPlay)
{
  if (!IsPlaying)
  {
    // We have decided that we want to play, but we are not
    // currently playing, so start the sound playing.
    PlayingEvent = AudioEngine.PlayEvent(Data.Event);
    IsPlaying = true;

    // Select the fade in time from the FadeInTime range.
    TotalFadeTime =
      RemainingFadeTime = Data.FadeInTime.RandomValue();

    // Pitch and event parameters can just be set - no need to fade
    // them.  We set volume to silence, then start the fade later
    // on in this function.
    VolumeFade.Set(Data.GetSilenceValue());
    PitchFade.Set(Data.PitchCents);
    auto NumParameters = Data.Parameters.size();
    for (size_t i = 0; i < NumParameters; i++)
    {
      ParameterFades[i].Set(FloatRange::ZeroOne);
    }
  }
  else
  {
    // We have decided to play, and we are already playing, so
    // continue playing, but select new random parameters.

    // Select the new fade time from the FadeToTime range.
    TotalFadeTime =
      RemainingFadeTime = Data.FadeToTime.RandomValue();

    // Start fading the pitch and event parameters.
    PitchFade.Start(Data.PitchCents);
    auto NumParameters = Data.Parameters.size();
    for (size_t i = 0; i < NumParameters; i++)
    {
```

```
        ParameterFades[i].Start(FloatRange::ZeroOne);
    }
}

// Fade the volume to the selected range
VolumeFade.Start(Data.GetVolumeRange());

// Tick zero seconds of time to force the parameters to be set
// on the playing sound.
Tick(0.0f);

// Our time to the next roll of the dice is selected from the
// PlayTime value.
TimeToNextRoll = Data.PlayTime.RandomValue();
}
else
{
    if (IsPlaying)
    {
        // We have decided to stop playing, but we are currently
        // playing.

        // Select the new fade time from the FadeOutTime range.
        TotalFadeTime =
            RemainingFadeTime = Data.FadeOutTime.RandomValue();
        // Fade out to silence
        VolumeFade.Start(Data.GetSilenceValue());
    }
    // There is nothing to do for the else case - in that case we
    // are currently not playing and would like to continue not
    // playing

    // Our time to the next roll of the dice is selected from the
    // SilentTime value.
    TimeToNextRoll = Data.SilentTime.RandomValue();
}

// If we're lerping, then add this object to the list of fading
// looping sounds.
if (IsLerping())
{
    // We're using C++20 ranges here, but you can use the std::find()
```

```
  // algorithm if you're using using an older version of C++.
  if (std::ranges::find(Owner.FadingLoopingSounds, this) ==
      Owner.FadingLoopingSounds.end())
  {
    Owner.FadingLoopingSounds.push_back(this);
  }
}

// Schedule the next roll.
NextRollTimer =
  Game.ScheduleTimer([this]() { Roll(); }, TimeToNextRoll);
}
```

There are two extra details of note here. The first is that we call different functions on the **LerpContext**s for the pitch and event parameters if the sound is starting play (**Set()**) than if it is already playing (**Start()**). This difference is because the pitch and other parameters will start with the correct values immediately when the sound is starting from nothing – there is no need to fade those values from a previous value. The other item of note is that we store this object on a list of fading looping sounds when the volume is changing value over time so that we know which ones we need to tick. Let's take a look at how that works:

```
bool LoopingSoundInstance::IsLerping() const
{
  return RemainingFadeTime > 0.0f && TotalFadeTime > 0.0f;
}

void BackgroundSoundContext::Tick(float DeltaTime)
{
  // Tick any looping sounds that need it
  for (auto& LoopingSound : FadingLoopingSounds)
  {
    LoopingSound->Tick(DeltaTime);
  }

  // Erase any looping sounds that are finished looping.
  std::erase_if(FadingLoopingSounds,
    [](const LoopingSoundInstance* LoopingSound)
    { return !LoopingSound->IsLerping(); });
}
```

The only other details that we need to cover are the `Tick()` function to set the parameters of the playing sound, and the constructor and destructor:

```
LoopingSoundInstance::LoopingSoundInstance(
  BackgroundSoundContext& Owner,
  const BackgroundSoundData::LoopingSoundData& Data) :
    Owner(Owner), Data(Data)
{
  // Get the parameter fades to the correct size.
  ParameterFades.resize(Data.Parameters.size());

  // Roll the dice.
  Roll();

  // If the roll indicated that we're playing, then force the sound
  // to start playing immediately with no fade in.
  if (IsPlaying)
  {
    TotalFadeTime = 0.0f;
    RemainingFadeTime = 0.0f;
    Tick(0.0f);
  }
}


LoopingSoundInstance::~LoopingSoundInstance()
{
  Game.CancelTimer(NextRollTimer);
}


void LoopingSoundInstance::Tick(float DeltaTime)
{
  // Update remaining time.
  RemainingFadeTime = std::max(RemainingFadeTime - DeltaTime, 0.0f);

  // Figure out our percentage of the way through the fade, making
  // sure to mind an invalid fade time.
  float TimeValue =
    (TotalFadeTime <= 0.0f)? 1.0f :
      (TotalFadeTime - RemainingFadeTime) / TotalFadeTime;
```

```
// Update volume either by setting the volume or a parameter value.
auto VolumeValue = VolumeFade.GetValue(TimeValue);
if (Data.VolumeControl ==
    BackgroundSoundData::VolumeControlType::Decibels)
{
  PlayingEvent.SetVolumeDecibels(VolumeValue);
}
else
{
  PlayingEvent.SetParameterValue("BGSoundVolume", VolumeValue);
}

// Set pitch and event parameters.
PlayingEvent.SetPitchCents(PitchFade.GetValue(TimeValue));
auto NumParameters = Data.Parameters.size();
for (size_t i = 0; i < NumParameters; i++)
{
  PlayingEvent.SetParameterValue(
    Data.Parameters[i], ParameterFades[i].GetValue(TimeValue));
}

// If we're done fading to silence then stop the event.
if (!IsLerping())
{
  if (VolumeValue == Data.GetSilenceValue())
  {
    IsPlaying = false;
    PlayingEvent.Stop();
  }
}
}
```

Most of the Tick() function is given over to applying the volume, pitch, and event parameters, although it does also stop the sound when it's done fading out to silence. The constructor initializes some data, rolls the dice, and then immediately forces the fade to end if the sound was played.

6.4.5 Implementation Details – One-Shot Sounds

One-shot sounds do not have a tick, which makes them simpler than looping sounds in many ways. Almost all of the logic is encapsulated in the

Roll() function – or, more precisely, the RollHelper() function. We use RollHelper() so that we can pass a flag indicating whether we want to force the play roll to fail, which we do in the constructor to avoid a cacophony of one-shots when the ambiance starts. Some tick scheduling systems support capturing function parameters to send to the scheduled method, but we are not presuming that that exists here, so we add the extra layer of abstraction.

This time we'll start with the constructor, destructor, and Roll() functions since they're trivial:

```
OneshotSoundInstance::OneshotSoundInstance(
  const BackgroundSoundData::OneshotSoundData& Data) : Data(Data)
{
  RollHelper(true);
}

OneshotSoundInstance::~OneshotSoundInstance()
{
  Game.CancelTimer(NextRollTimer);
}

void OneshotSoundInstance::Roll()
{
  RollHelper(false);
}
```

Simple enough: they're just wrappers for RollHelper() with different parameters, which we'll take a look at next:

```
void OneshotSoundInstance::RollHelper(bool ForceNoPlay)
{
  if (RemainingGroupCount == 0)
  {
    // We're not currently in the middle of playing a group of sounds,
    // so we need to ask whether or not we should play.
    bool ShouldPlay = ForceNoPlay? false :
      (GetRandomValue() < Data.PlayChance);
    if (ShouldPlay)
    {
```

```
    // If we decide that we want to play then, perforce, we are now
    // playing a group of sounds.  Set up the data for the group,
    // then recurse into this function.  In the recursion we'll have
    // RemainingGroupCount > 0, so we'll go into the else case and
    // play a sound.
    RemainingGroupCount = Data.GroupCount.RandomValue();

      // Got to check for infinite recursion!
      if (RemainingGroupCount > 0)
        RollHelper(false);
      return;
    }
    // If we decided not to play, then we'll jump to the bottom where
    // the next roll of the dice is scheduled.
  }
  else
  {
    // We're in a group!  Play the sound.
    auto NewEvent = AudioEngine.PlayEvent(Data.Event);

    // Set the sound volume.
    auto VolumeValue = Data.GetVolumeRange().RandomValue();
    if (Data.VolumeControl ==
        BackgroundSoundData::VolumeControlType::Decibels)
    {
      NewEvent.SetVolumeDecibels(VolumeValue);
    }
    else
    {
      NewEvent.SetParameterValue("BGSoundVolume", VolumeValue);
    }

    // Set pitch and event parameters.
    NewEvent.SetPitchCents(Data.PitchCents.RandomValue());
    for (const auto& ParameterName : Data.Parameters)
    {
      NewEvent.SetParameterValue(
        ParameterName, FloatRange::ZeroOne.RandomValue());
    }
```

```cpp
// Set the event panning based on the mode.
switch (Data.Panning)
{
using enum BackgroundSoundData::OneshotSoundData::PanStyle;
case None:
default:
  // Nothing to do for no-pan mode.
  break;
case Fixed:
  // Fixed pan modes need to set a parameter from zero to one.
  NewEvent.SetParameterValue(
    "BGSoundPan", FloatRange::ZeroOne.RandomValue());
  break;
case Surround:
{
  // For surround, we'll pick a location in the circle a fixed
  // distance from the listener.  (Your code might need different
  // logic here.)
  float Angle = FloatRange::ZeroTwoPi.RandomValue();
  auto ListenerPosition = AudioEngine.GetListenerPosition();
  Vector3 Direction{ cosf(Angle), sinf(Angle), 0.0f };
  constexpr float Distance = 100.0f;
  NewEvent.Set3DPosition(ListenerPosition + Direction * Distance);
}
break;
}

// Track the playing event, and reduce the remaining group count.
PlayingEvents.push_back(std::move(NewEvent));
--RemainingGroupCount;
}

// Clean up finished events
std::erase_if(PlayingEvents,
  [](const PlayingEventHandle& PlayingEvent)
  { return !PlayingEvent.IsPlaying(); });

// Select the time to next roll of the dice based on whether we're
// currently in a group.
float TimeToNextRoll;
if (RemainingGroupCount > 0)
```

```
{
    TimeToNextRoll = Data.GroupDelay.RandomValue();
}
else
{
    TimeToNextRoll = Data.TriggerDelay.RandomValue();
}
NextRollTimer =
    Game.ScheduleTimer([this]() { Roll(); }, TimeToNextRoll);
}
```

As with the looping sounds, much of this function is occupied with playing and configuring the playing sounds, although this code also includes special behavior for adjusting the panning of the event. There is also a little bit of logic for tracking playing sounds, even though this code doesn't make use of them. You may need the playing events for debugging or for implementing some features in the future, so it is worthwhile and does not incur much overhead to track the playing sounds. The only other clever bit worth calling out here is the case where we start playing a group of sounds – in that case, we select a new group count, then recurse into the same function, which will take the else case and trigger the sound immediately.

One improvement to this code that we could add would be to cache the panning information for sounds in a group so that they are all played in a way that appears to be close to each other. After all, a bird chirping in a tree won't hop around to three different trees surrounding your player character within a few seconds. Adding this functionality is a three-step process:

- Add a `float` data member to `OneshotSoundData` that stores the percentage change in panning for each trigger of a sound in a group.

- Add a `float` data member to the `OneshotSoundInstance` that stores the selected panning value. When starting a Group, select a value from `FloatRange::ZeroOne` to get a value from 0 to 1.

- When a sound in a group is played that doesn't use the `None` panning mode, pick the panning value from the stored panning value, plus or minus the allowed percentage change (clamped to the range `0..1`). If the panning is `Fixed` mode, this value can be passed directly to the event parameter, and if the panning is `Surround` mode, then it will need to be scaled to an angle in the range `0..2π`.

6.4.6 Implementation Verdict

This implementation will drive the looping and one-shot sounds for a background sound context. All that is needed is to set up the data, create the context (or contexts), and drive the `Tick()` function. Using this system is in some ways more complex than the built-in event described in Section 6.3: each looped sound and each one-shot sound needs to be set up as a separate event, and the data can potentially be less intuitive for a sound designer. We haven't touched on debugging visualizations in this chapter, but with the bespoke code implementation, a good visualization is going to be critical to having the sound designers understand what is going on. Nevertheless, this system is exceptionally powerful and flexible, while at the same time being extremely performant.

6.5 CONCLUSION

A good background sound engine can bring your game environments to life in subtle and wonderful ways. This chapter discussed two methods for building them: using built-in tools to create an event that can be played as normal and creating a bespoke system to implement the feature. Ultimately, which method you choose to use will be a conversation with your sound designers, but they are both effective and powerful techniques.

NOTES

1 Early versions of this technology that I built referred to these as "intraset delays" and "interset delays," respectively, which I thought was very clever. My sound designers eventually rebelled at this nomenclature, and I had to change the names. This chapter will refer to them as group delays and trigger delays, respectively.

2 Version 2.02.13, which is the latest of this writing. Doubtless, a newer version will be available by the time it goes to print.

3 Future versions of FMOD (to be released after this book is written – see previous footnote) are supposed to include per-property seek speeds, which will solve this issue and simplify the entire setup. When they do materialize,

it will be possible to remove the event property and just use the square wave LFO, assuming that the fade characteristics are amenable to your sound designer.

4 This curve is what would be missing from using the property seek speeds mentioned in the previous footnotes.

5 I find it interesting that despite the fact that the one-shot sounds have more configuration complexity, the playback complexity is actually much simpler than the looping sounds.

CHAPTER 7

Data-Driven Music Systems for Open Worlds

Michelle Auyoung

7.1 INTRODUCTION

For vast open world games, there is a lot of space to fill both visually and aurally. To help fill the sonic space, a data-driven and responsive music system can provide a flexible tool to convey evolving gameplay elements of the world by connecting to the emotional experience of the music. With this responsive approach between gameplay and music, the player experience becomes more immersive. The fundamental idea is to parameterize gameplay data to map to music states and other real-time parameter controls. Gameplay systems like combat with varying enemy difficulty and progression of time in the game world can hook into the music system to respond to these events, driving music state changes throughout these encounters. To add variability to the music system, other randomized techniques such as music data controls and other overrides may help. In scenarios with narrative or scripted events, this dynamic music system can be disabled. There is no one music system to handle every gameplay situation, but a data-driven approach can help with faster and more flexible music implementation for large levels with various encounters.

DOI: 10.1201/9781003330936-8

Music systems with multiple layers and looping clips driven by gameplay parameters are a common approach to implementing game music, but this chapter will explore more details on how the data can be driven to help create a more dynamic musical soundscape. Some common game engine features and gameplay systems will be discussed to explain how they can influence music cues. Music data can contain overrides, randomized subsets of higher level music state categories, and variable delay thresholds.

7.2 INTERACTIVE MUSIC SYSTEM REVIEW

Interactive music systems are not a new concept, as they have existed since the first video games were invented. When games evolved to contain more content, music systems also adapted to support a broader range of emergent gameplay features. The music system often depends on the game genre or style, and some music systems may be designed as purely procedural or generative. For most narrative-driven games that have a combination of exploration and combat, an interactive multilayered approach is common. These music systems use a combination of stems and stingers to create ambient and combat music. Global game states can map to music changes by automating the mix or transitions on stems driven by the data an audio designer creates. The foundation of game layer data communicating with the audio engine data setup gives the power and flexibility to generate interactive music with simplified data. This will be the basis for our more in-depth discussion on data-driven dynamic music systems for open world games.

7.3 DYNAMIC MUSIC SYSTEM ARCHITECTURE

At the center of the data-driven dynamic music system is the music manager class, which can interact with any gameplay system. This music manager is responsible for controlling the music tracks streamed by the audio engine. We will do this by using two key continuous game parameters: *Threat* and *Time of Day*, which are commonly utilized in open world games since they relate to combat and time progression in the game world. In Figure 7.1, we can see a high-level view of how these systems interact with each other from the game engine layer to the audio engine. The audio engine shows a simplified version of the interactive music hierarchy, but the goal is to demonstrate how the music manager in the game layer acts as a bridge between the game and audio engines.

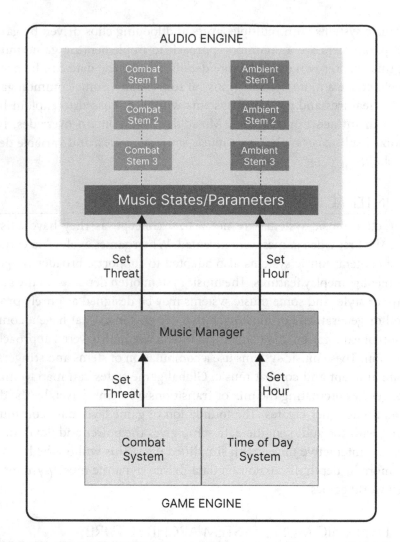

FIGURE 7.1 Diagram of music manager communicating between game systems and audio engine.

A simple music manager class can have functions to get music data, play and stop the music, and set music states, as well as member variables to store the current music data and state that should be playing. Other gameplay systems can then drive the music playback by feeding gameplay data through parameters to control music transitions and fading between different instrument layers. Some of the music manager functions may be exposed so designers can script certain music behaviors when the data-driven dynamic music system is disabled. Here is a basic music manager class definition example to show what kinds of functions and member variables it can have:

```
class MusicManager
{
public:
  void Initialize();
  void Deinitialize();

  void EnableDynamicMusicSystem(MusicData* MusicData);
  void DisableDynamicMusicSystem();

  void PlayMusic();
  void StopMusic();

  void SetMusicState(const MusicState* State);
  void SetCurrentThreat(float ThreatValue);
  void SetCurrentTimeOfDay(float Hour);

  void SetOverrideState(const MusicState* OverrideState);
  void ClearOverrideState();

private:
  MusicSettings* MusicSettings;
  MusicData* AreaMusicData;

  float CurrentThreat;
  float CurrentHour;

  MusicThreshold* GetThreatMusicData();
  MusicThreshold* GetTimeOfDayMusicData();
};
```

The MusicSettings class would have global parameter controls that apply to any music data. The MusicData class may have several MusicThreshold objects that contain the ranges of values corresponding to the different music states representing combat or time of day. A more detailed explanation of the music data will be described in the next section.

To keep the dynamic music system simple, we want to separate the playback of systemic gameplay music from scripted narrative moments like cinematic sequences. The gameplay-driven system can be disabled and enabled by scripting within the current level to allow for predetermined events at crucial story points. With the dynamic music system enabled, separate overrides allow for smaller spaces within a larger level to trigger unique music when inside the bounds of that area. The goal is to provide enough flexibility for controlling music changes without overcomplicating the data and allowing natural gameplay progressions to influence organic music transitions during non-scripted moments.

7.4 ORGANIZING THE MUSIC DATA

Typically, we can associate music data with a single level or map, which the gameplay systems use to drive the audio engine playing back the music streams. An example music data asset can have the basic play and stop events for this level's music, a state for level transitions to begin playing music for this area during a loading screen, and containers of nested arrays representing layered music states within thresholds. These thresholds have varying ranges of float values that map to gameplay data such as threat values for combat music or the hour for time-of-day ambient music. Depending on the game and narrative, anything could be mapped to music data such as player character status, experience points, and other trends in a character's traits commonly used in role-playing games.

Below is a simplified class definition of what the music data could look like along with the structs it uses to represent subcategories of music data. It should contain the major components of what the level or map represents musically. Typically, we have ambient music during exploratory states of play and combat music when engaging with enemies.

```
struct AmbientStateCycle
{
  FloatInterval DelayRange;
  Array<MusicState*> AmbientMusicStates;
};

struct MusicThreshold
{
  FloatInterval Threshold;
  MusicState* MusicState;
  AmbientStateCycle StateCycling;
  bool EnableAmbientStateCycling;
};

class MusicData
```

```
{
  AudioEvent* PlayEvent;
  AudioEvent* StopEvent;
  MusicState* LevelTransitionState;
  Array<MusicThreshold> ThreatMusicStateThresholds;
  Array<MusicThreshold> TimeOfDayMusicStateThresholds;
};
```

Every `MusicThreshold` contains a range of values that makes up the threshold or bucket for a set of music states. If `EnableAmbientStateCycling` is turned on, the `AmbientStateCycle` struct provides an array of music states within the owning threshold. Otherwise, the single `MusicState` will be used within the threshold.

Figure 7.2 shows an example layout of how the music data can be organized visually in multiple containers of data structures that the different

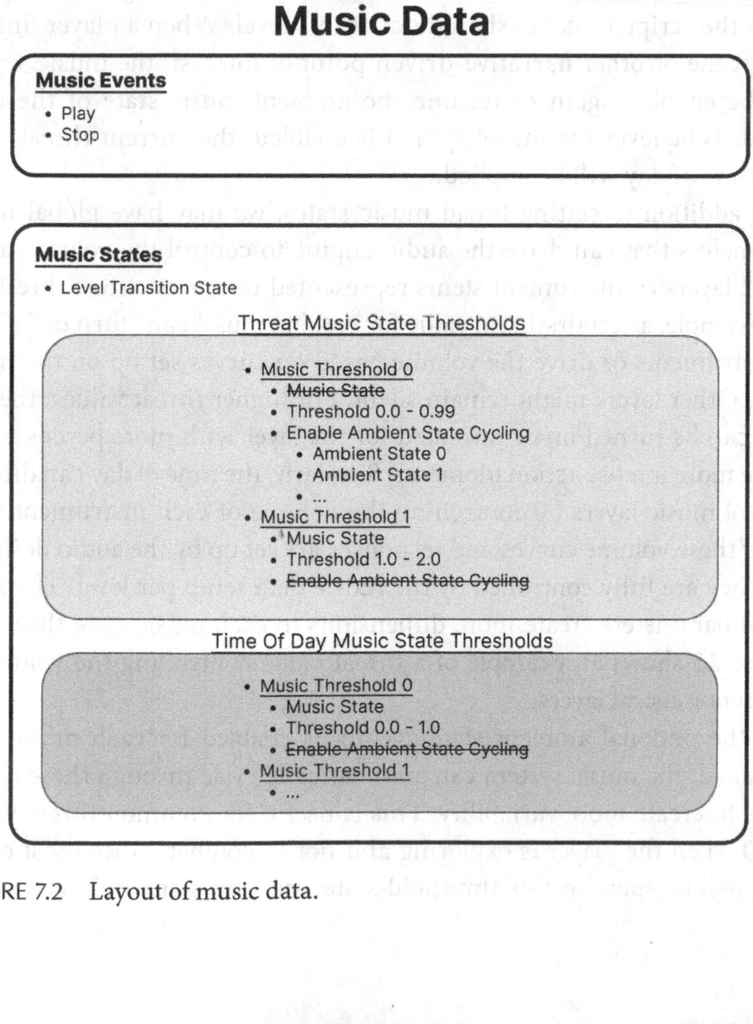

Music Data

FIGURE 7.2   Layout of music data.

gameplay systems can map to. In each container of music data thresholds, an optional nested subset of ambient music states for each threshold range can be randomly cycled through to add more variation to each threshold. To add another layer of variability, a range of delays can be applied to adjust the timing of the music state changes and reduce the abruptness of the transitions during the random cycling.

7.5 CONTROLLING AND DRIVING THE MUSIC SYSTEM

Under ordinary circumstances, we would always want the music system to be enabled throughout most of the level so that it will react to gameplay related to combat and ambience. During certain points in an open world level, we can disable the dynamic music system to script specific narrative scenes. Functions to enable and disable the music system in the music manager class should be exposed for designers to decide when the scripted scenes should occur in a level. When a player finishes a cutscene or other narrative-driven point of interest, the music system can be enabled again to resume the ambient music state of the open world. Whenever the music system is enabled, the current threat value and time of day will be applied.

In addition to setting broad music states, we may have global music parameters that can drive the audio engine to control the volume of the music layers or instrument stems represented in a music state threshold. For example, a certain threat value for combat music can "turn on" a layer of instruments or drive the volume based on curves set up on the music stem. Other layers might remain silent. For higher threat values, the volume can be turned up or unmuted for the layer with more percussion to create more intense action moments. Similarly, the time of day can directly control music layers by controlling the volume of each instrument type. All of these volume curves and responses are set up by the audio designer, and they are fully controlled by the music data setup per level. The additional parameters create more dimensions to each music state threshold. Figure 7.3 shows an example of a threat value controlling the volume of different musical layers.

If the optional ambient state cycling is enabled for each music state threshold, the music system can automatically cycle through these nested states to create more variability. This is useful for common threat values like 0 when the player is exploring and not in combat. Since most of the time will be spent in this threshold state, ambient state cycling is useful

Music Track Volume Control

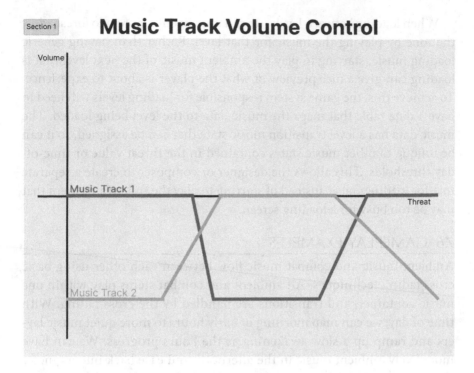

FIGURE 7.3   Simplified example of threat value controlling volume of different music layers.

to reduce the repetition of staying in the same state and looping the same music layers too often. For less common threat values such as combat experiences with more than ten enemies, this threshold may not need to use ambient state cycling since a level would most likely only have one or two encounters with that intensity.

For music specific to certain areas or regions on the map, we can assign music override states to ambient volume actors. When the player enters a volume, the music state can be overridden with the state assigned for that volume to create location-based music. We keep track of the current state in the music manager so that we can resume the music when leaving the volume back to what it was before the override was applied. Many volumes are primarily used to play ambient sound beds, but any volume can trigger a music override state, which would not need to be defined in the level music data itself to function. Therefore, not all volumes need to have an override music state assigned. If an ambient volume does have an override music state assigned, the music system will set or clear that override state when the player enters or exits that volume.

When loading between levels, we can implement a system to foreshadow the tone by playing the music for that level. Rather than having generic loading music, starting to play the ambient music of the next level that is loading can give a nice preview of what the player is about to experience. To achieve this, the game system responsible for loading levels will need to have a data table that maps the music data to the level being loaded. The music data has a level transition music state that can be assigned, so it can be unique to other music states contained in the threat value or time-of-day thresholds. This allows the designer or composer to create a separate mix for loading music instead of starting to play the full arrangement that may be too busy for a loading screen.

7.6 GAMEPLAY EXAMPLES

Ambient music and combat music flow between each other using basic cross fading techniques. All ambient and combat stems play within one music container, and transitions are handled by the cross fading. With time of day, we can map morning or early hours to more quiet music layers and ramp up a slow awakening as the hours progress. We can have more lively ambient music in the afternoon and ease back into a quieter sleepy nighttime ambience. If there is a special area that needs to attract the player's attention, we could assign an override state to an ambient volume encapsulating that area. This could make the aural experience more interesting to trigger special music rather than playing a sound effect or using other visual effects to cue the player to something in the level to investigate.

For combat music, it would depend on how the combat system and enemy artificial intelligence (AI) work. With a simple AI framework, we can assign specific threat values to enemies and sum them up to a total threat value to drive the music system. Lesser enemies could each be assigned a threat value of 1 while more powerful enemies could be assigned a higher value. If many lesser enemies engage the player in combat, the threat value would be high, but it could also happen when fighting only one difficult enemy. Since the combat music can start and stop quickly, we typically would not want to use ambient state cycling for threat music state thresholds greater than 1. Anything less than 1 should mean the player is not in combat and is in an exploratory state in the open world level.

With an open world role-playing game, there are many more gameplay elements that may be mapped to generic music threshold data outlined in this chapter. Rather than just mapping environmental gameplay to music, we could also explore the player character's progression in the game. For example, the character can usually gain experience points throughout the game, slide between good and evil dispositions, and have different party dynamics with diverse companions. The music data should be generic enough that any of these features from the game could utilize it through the music system.

7.7 FUTURE IMPROVEMENTS

As this is a foundational music system that can be extended and built upon further, there is always room for improvement. One of the challenges is related to entering and exiting combat because we do not want the transition to be too jarring. Adding finer control like gating thresholds for threat values between combat and ambient music could help prevent abrupt changes. There could be a transitory music state or additional fine-tuning on the audio engine side to ease in and out of combat. For example, rather than setting the state on combat start and end the same way as any other states are set, we might want to add a little intro and outro for combat music to play on these events to transition more smoothly between combat and ambient music besides simply cross fading these music layers.

This music system can be extended as much as the designer wants, or it can work as simply as it needs to help fill the sonic space with limited time. Depending on the game and music designer, the music data should reflect what the major gameplay systems are. Since combat music is woven into open world ambient music, we need to track the threat value. One possible extension could involve using the music data to influence the gameplay somehow, so the music manager would be a two-way bridge.

7.8 SUMMARY

To summarize, this is just one of many ways to implement a dynamic music system, but we found this to work well with a simple framework that still offers flexibility. The main goal was to fill open world spaces with music that would automatically evolve with the gameplay, driven by the different game systems. This music system is not fully procedural or scripted, but we were able to organize and map the music to game data, so the different gameplay systems could organically orchestrate the music. It should provide a good middle ground for implementing music in large open world games.

I would like to thank Raison Varner for designing and providing the musical framework for me to build the dynamic music system on the game engine side. Also, I am grateful for the opportunity and support from many of my peers at Obsidian Entertainment.

II

Low-Level Topics

CHAPTER 8

Finding the Intersection of a Box and a Circle

Guy Somberg

8.1 INTRODUCTION

In the second volume of this series, Game Audio Programming: Principles and Practices Volume 2, Chapter 12 "Approximate Position of Ambient Sounds of Multiple Sources" by Nic Taylor shows how to determine the contribution of sound with multiple sources to a single event's direction, spread, and magnitude. It shows two solutions: one using a collection of rectangles and the other using a uniform grid or set of points. For the solution using the collection of rectangles, we need to find the intersection of a circle with a rectangle. Figure 8.1 is a duplicate of Figure 12.11 from that volume, which shows how the subdivision would work. Section 12.11 of that volume describes it thus:

> The other detail is how to clip a rectangle with a sphere. Doing this adds many different cases to solve. Instead, a rectangle not fully inside or outside the sphere can be subdivided and each subdivision either subdivided further or solved as an independent rectangle. The process can be repeated within some error tolerance.

That chapter doesn't go into greater detail about how to solve this problem, which is what we will do here.

DOI: 10.1201/9781003330936-10

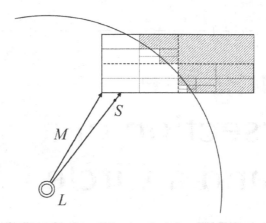

FIGURE 8.1 Subdividing rectangles. This is the same as Figure 12.11 from Game Audio Programming: Principles and Practices Volume 2, Chapter 12 by Nic Taylor.

8.2 PSEUDOCODE

We can build the pseudocode for the solution to this problem with just a couple of observations. First, if the box is fully outside of the circle, then it cannot be part of the output set. Next, if the box is fully within the circle, then it is for sure part of the output set, so it gets added. Finally, we split the box into its four quadrants and recurse into each of them. The only other thing is that we need a way to break the recursion. So, if the box is at a minimum size and intersects with the circle, then we'll add it to the output set without recursion.

Written out, it looks like this:

- If the box is outside the circle
  - Return
- If the box is at minimum size or fully within the circle
  - Add the box to the output
  - Return
- Split the box into its four quadrants and recurse for each one

8.3 BASIC VERSION

Our pseudocode asks two questions about our box: is it fully outside the circle, and is it fully within the circle? We can determine whether a box is fully inside of the circle if all four of its corners are inside of the circle, and we can determine if it is outside of the circle if there is no intersection between the circle and the box. Let's write those two helper functions:

```
static bool DoesBoxIntersectCircle(
  const Box2D& Box,
  const Circle2D& Circle)
{
  // Check if the circle's center is inside of the box. If so, then
  // we can just return early.
  if (Box.IsInside(Circle.Center))
    return true;

  // Check if the closest point on the box is within the circle's
  // radius.
  auto Dist = Box.SquaredDistanceToPoint(Circle.Center);
  return Dist <= (Circle.Radius * Circle.Radius);
}

static bool IsBoxFullyWithinCircle(
  const Box2D& Box,
  const Circle2D& Circle)
{

  // An initializer list containing the list of corners of the box.
  auto Corners = { Box.Min, Box.Max,
                   Vector2D { Box.Min.X, Box.Max.Y },
                   Vector2D { Box.Max.X, Box.Min.Y } };

  // Check to see if all of corners are within the circle's radius.
  auto RadiusSquared = Circle.Radius * Circle.Radius;
  return std::ranges::all_of(Corners, [=](Vector2D Corner)
    {
      return DistSquared(Circle.Center, Corner) <= RadiusSquared;
    });
}
```

Now that we have those two helper functions out of the way, we can write the actual function, which exactly follows the shape of our pseudocode:

```
static void SubdivideBox(
  const Box2D& Box, const Circle2D& Circle,
  std::vector<Box2D>& BoxList)
```

```
{
  // If the box is outside of the circle, then we're done.
  if (!DoesBoxIntersectCircle(Box, Circle))
    return;

  // If the box is at the minimum size or is fully within the circle,
  // then add it to the output.
  if (Box.GetLongestAxis() <= MinAxisLength ||
      IsBoxFullyWithinCircle(Box, Circle))
  {
    BoxList.push_back(Box);
    return;
  }

  // Split the box into four quadrants.
  auto [Center, Extents] = Box.GetCenterAndExtents();

  Box2D BottomLeft{ Center - Extents, Center };
  Box2D TopRight{ Center, Center + Extents };
  auto TopLeft = BottomLeft.ShiftBy(Vector2D{ 0.0f, Extents.Y });
  auto BottomRight = TopRight.ShiftBy(Vector2D{ 0.0f, -Extents.Y });

  // Recurse into this function for each quadrant.
  SubdivideBox(BottomLeft, Circle, BoxList);
  SubdivideBox(TopRight, Circle, BoxList);
  SubdivideBox(TopLeft, Circle, BoxList);
  SubdivideBox(BottomRight, Circle, BoxList);
}
```

Figure 8.2 shows an example output from this algorithm. The non-shaded rectangles are the resulting output, and the shaded rectangles are outside of the output. We could stop here and run the resulting 49 rectangles through the volumetric sound code, but that's a lot of boxes. We should see whether there is anything that we can do to reduce that count.

8.4 RECTANGLE ANALYSIS

If we look specifically at the smallest rectangles on our output, there are a few patterns where there are rectangles that can be combined. Figure 8.3 is the same as Figure 8.2 with the different patterns labeled: **A** for rectangles

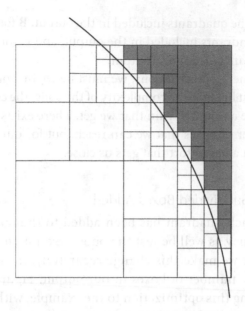

FIGURE 8.2   Example output of the basic subdivision algorithm.

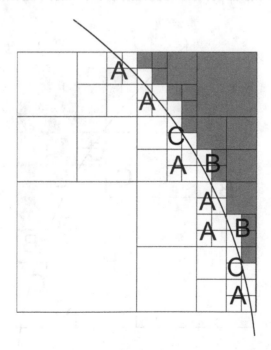

FIGURE 8.3   Circle-box intersection from Figure 8.2, with rectangles labeled **A**, **B**, and **C** depending on how many of the subdivided rectangles are included in the output.

with all four of the quadrants included in the output, **B** for rectangles with two adjacent quadrants included in the output, and **C** for rectangles with three quadrants included in the output.

As we implement optimizations, we must be cognizant of diminishing returns. We must balance the complexity of the code, the complexity of the analysis, and the amount of gain that we get. There exists some optimally minimal number of boxes that we can reach, but for our use case we are willing to accept a best effort that gets us close.

8.4.1 All Four Subdivided Boxes Added

A box where each quadrant has been added to the output (labeled **A** in Figure 8.3) may as well be just the outer box, rather than four individual boxes. If we make this change recursively, then we can drastically reduce the number of boxes in our output. Figure 8.4 shows the result of applying this optimization to the example, with the remaining **B** and **C** subdivisions labeled. Note that we have been able to collapse the entirety of the upper left quadrant of the outer box into a single box

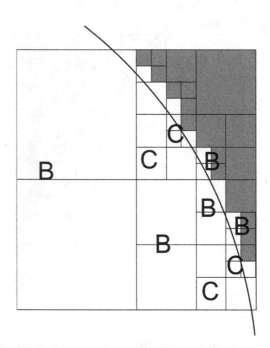

FIGURE 8.4 The result of recursively replacing boxes subdivided into four with the larger box.

by applying the optimization at every level. That is, the smallest boxes get collapsed into a single box, which leaves the next level up with four equal-size boxes all in the output, which get collapsed together until we get to a single large box. After applying this optimization, we are left with just 25 boxes, just over half of what we started with, which is a great success!

In order to implement this optimization, we will make two changes to our code:

- Return a **bool** indicating whether the input rectangle was added to the output.

- Check the result of all four subdivisions and if they all return **true**, then replace them with the input box.

```
static bool SubdivideBox(
  const Box2D& Box, const Circle2D& Circle,
  std::vector<Box2D>& BoxList)
{
  // If the box is outside of the circle, then we're done.
  if (!DoesBoxIntersectCircle(Box, Circle))
    return false;

  // If the box is at the minimum size or is fully within the circle,
  // then add it to the output.
  if (Box.GetLongestAxis() <= MinAxisLength ||
        IsBoxFullyWithinCircle(Box, Circle))
  {
    BoxList.push_back(Box);
    return true;
  }

  // Split the box into four quadrants.
  auto [Center, Extents] = Box.GetCenterAndExtents();

  Box2D BottomLeft{ Center - Extents, Center };
  Box2D TopRight{ Center, Center + Extents };
  auto TopLeft = BottomLeft.ShiftBy(Vector2D{ 0.0f, Extents.Y });
  auto BottomRight = TopRight.ShiftBy(Vector2D{ 0.0f, -Extents.Y });

  // Recurse into this function for each quadrant.
  bool SubdividedBottomLeft =
    SubdivideBox(BottomLeft, Circle, BoxList);
```

```
bool SubdividedTopRight = SubdivideBox(TopRight, Circle, BoxList);
bool SubdividedTopLeft = SubdivideBox(TopLeft, Circle, BoxList);
bool SubdividedBottomRight =
  SubdivideBox(BottomRight, Circle, BoxList);

// If all four subdivisions have resulted in getting added, then
// undo the additions and add this box to the output.
if (SubdividedBottomLeft && SubdividedTopRight &&
    SubdividedTopLeft && SubdividedBottomRight)
{
  BoxList.erase(BoxList.end() - 4, BoxList.end());
  BoxList.push_back(Box);
  return true;
}

return false;
}
```

Rather than erasing all four entries and then immediately adding one back, we can just erase the last three and then overwrite the last one:

```
BoxList.erase(BoxList.end() - 3, BoxList.end());
BoxList.back() = Box;
```

8.4.2 Subdivisions of Two or Three

Now that we have eliminated all of the **A** subdivisions, what remains are the **B** and **C** subdivisions where two or three of the smaller rectangles were added. For the **B** subdivisions where the two quadrants are adjacent, we can merge them into one, and for the **C** subdivisions, we can merge two of the adjacent boxes together. For the **A** boxes, we could just remove all four of the boxes and replace them with the original box, but the **B** and **C** configurations result in a number of different situations that we need to handle. At the end of our output **vector**, there will be either two or three result boxes. We will need to remove two of them and then add the merged box – although, similar to the previous section, we will reuse one of the boxes and replace it instead of removing and then adding.

Let's look at the possible configurations of elements at the end of our output **vector**. We will label the last three elements **X**, **Y**, and **Z**. There

TABLE 8.1 The different possibilities at the end of the output `vector` and the actions that we will take.

Index	Configuration	Action	Merge Offset	Erase Offset
0	$\underbrace{XY}\, Z$	Merge X and Y	3	2
1	$X\, \underbrace{YZ}$	Merge Y and Z	2	1
2	$\underbrace{X\, \overset{\frown}{Y}\, Z}$	Merge X and Z	3	1
3	$\underbrace{XY}$	Merge X and Y	2	1

are four different possibilities, enumerated in Table 8.1. When we determine which index to use, we will take the boxes at the Merge Offset and the Erase Offset entries, merge them together into a bigger box and overwrite the Merge Offset box, and then erase the box at the Erase Offset. The offset values in the table are from the `end()` iterator – in other words, an offset of `1` maps to `end()` − `1`, which is the last entry in the `vector`. If we look at Index 3 in the table, we can see that it is effectively identical to Index 1 except with different labels (**X** and **Y** instead of **Y** and **Z**), so we will use Index 1 to refer to both situations.

Now we know what we will do with the results, but we still need to figure out when to apply these actions by examining the results of the recursion operation. What we will do is assign each smaller box a bit, which lets us assign a numeric value to the resulting configuration. We can then find a mapping from that value to the action to take.

Up until now, it hasn't really mattered what order we subdivided the boxes, but now we will want to subdivide in a particular order so that we can take advantage of the fact that adjacent boxes are also together in value. The code in the previous section subdivided the quadrants in the order Bottom Left (BL), Top Left (TL), Top Right (TR), and Bottom Right (BR). Our new order will be BL, BR, TR, and TL, creating a counterclockwise circle from the bottom left quadrant. Table 8.2 shows the values of the quadrants and their resulting actions. We omit Index 15 in the table because that has all four quadrants included in the output, which we have already handled in Section 8.4.1.

We can put this table into our code without too much trouble, but before we do that, let's see whether we can apply a tool from Boolean logic to simplify the results.

TABLE 8.2   Mapping from Box Layout to Action

Index	Configuration	Output Boxes	Merged Cells	Result	Table 8.1 Index
0		None	None		None
1		BL	None		None
2		BR	None		None
3		BL, BR	BL, BR		1
4		TR	None		None
5		BL, TR	None		None
6		BR, TR	BR, TR		1
7		BL, BR, TR	BL, BR		0
8		TL	None		None

TABLE 8.2 (*Continued*)   Mapping from Box Layout to Action

Index	Configuration	Output Boxes	Merged Cells	Result	Table 8.1 Index
9		BL, TL	BL, TL		1
10		BR, TL	None		None
11		BL, BR, TL	BL, TL		2
12		TR, TL	TR, TL		1
13		BL, TR, TL	TR, TL		1
14		BR, TR, TL	BR, TR		0

8.4.3 Attempting to Simplify the Table

Looking at Table 8.2, we can see that there are some results (1 and None) that show up more often than others. Can we encode the table in code in some way that is simpler? The tool that we will use to investigate this is called a Karnaugh Map, which is a way of organizing a function's output into a grid to make it easier to find patterns. In a Karnaugh Map, the top edge wraps around to the bottom and the left side wraps around to the right, making it a 2D projection of a torus. Although the Karnaugh Map is usually applied to binary operations, it

TABLE 8.3   A Karnaugh Map of the Contents of Table 8.2

TL TR BL BR	00	01	11	10
00	N	N	1	N
01	N	1	0	N
11	1	0	d	2
10	N	N	1	1

can nevertheless be a valuable tool for finding patterns by inspection. Table 8.3 encodes Table 8.2 as a Karnaugh Map. The d in the table represents a "don't care" value where the result can be whatever is most convenient for the functionality – in this case, we've already handled the case, so we can use a "don't care" value.

When analyzing a Karnaugh Map, we look for groups of similar values in rectangular configurations. Unfortunately, what this Karnaugh Map is telling us is that there is not a good way to simplify the table.[1] There are a few patterns that we can find, but there are no surprises hidden in the layout of the table that we can take advantage of to write a simple elegant condition that will encode the table. This result is disappointing, but it is still good confirmation that we are using the correct approach.

8.5 CODE WITH ALL OPTIMIZATIONS APPLIED

In this final version of the code, we make several changes from the previous versions:

- Instead of individual variables for the four quadrants, we store them in an array indexed by an **enum**. This exchanges verbosity for clarity.

- The order of subdivision is now the counterclockwise circle as described in Section 8.4.2.

- Instead of checking the individual results one at a time, we calculate the index value and use that to determine what action to take.

```
static bool SubdivideBox(
  const Box2D& Box, const Circle2D& Circle,
  std::vector<Box2D>& BoxList)
```

```
{
  // If the box is outside of the circle, then we're done.
  if (!DoesBoxIntersectCircle(Box, Circle))
    return false;

  // If the box is at the minimum size or is fully within the circle,
  // then add it to the output.
  if (Box.GetLongestAxis() <= MinAxisLength ||
      IsBoxFullyWithinCircle(Box, Circle))
  {
    BoxList.push_back(Box);
    return true;
  }

  // Split the box into four quadrants.
  auto [Center, Extents] = Box.GetCenterAndExtents();

  enum SubdivisionCorner : uint8_t
  {
    BottomLeft,
    BottomRight,
    TopRight,
    TopLeft,
    Count,
  };

  std::array<Box2D, SubdivisionCorner::Count> Subdivisions;

  Subdivisions[SubdivisionCorner::BottomLeft] =
    { Center - Extents, Center };
  Subdivisions[SubdivisionCorner::TopRight] =
    { Center, Center + Extents };
  Subdivisions[SubdivisionCorner::TopLeft] =
    Subdivisions[SubdivisionCorner::BottomLeft].ShiftBy(
      Vector2D{ 0.0f, Extents.Y });
  Subdivisions[SubdivisionCorner::BottomRight] =
    Subdivisions[SubdivisionCorner::TopRight].ShiftBy(
      Vector2D{ 0.0f, -Extents.Y });

  // Recurse into this function for each quadrant.
  std::array<bool, SubdivisionCorner::Count> SubdivisionResults;
  for (auto i = 0; i < SubdivisionCorner::Count; i++)
```

```
{
  SubdivisionResults[i] =
    SubdivideBox(Subdivisions[i], Circle, BoxList);
}

// Calculate the index value of the subdivision results.
uint8_t SubdivisionSum = std::accumulate(
  SubdivisionResults.begin(), SubdivisionResults.end(),
  static_cast<uint8_t>(0),
  [BitValue = 1](uint8_t Sum, bool SubdivisionResult) mutable
  {
    auto ReturnValue = Sum + SubdivisionResult * BitValue;
    BitValue *= 2;
    return ReturnValue;
  });

// If all four subdivisions have resulted in getting added, then
// undo the additions and add this box to the output.
if (SubdivisionSum == 15)
{
  BoxList.erase(BoxList.end() - 3, BoxList.end());
  BoxList.back() = Box;
  return true;
}
else
{
  // We've subdivided to zero, one, two, or three boxes.

  // Action indexes for merging our subdivisions.
  struct SubdivisionAction
  {
    uint8_t MergedBoxIndexOffset;
    uint8_t EraseIndexOffset;
  };

  // These are the first three entries from Table 8-1, which tell
  // us what to do in each configuration.
  static constexpr
    std::array<SubdivisionAction, 3> SubdivisionActions =
    { {
      { 3, 2 },
      { 2, 1 },
```

```
    { 3, 1 },
  } };

// This is Table 8-2, which tells us what configuration we are in.
static constexpr std::array<int8_t, 15> SubdivisionActionIndexes =
{
  -1, // No subdivisions
  -1, // BL
  -1, // BR
   1, // BL BR
  -1, // TR
  -1, // BL TR
   1, // BR TR
   0, // BL BR TR
  -1, // TL
   1, // BL TL
  -1, // BR TL
   2, // BL BR TL
   1, // TR TL
   1, // BL TR TL
   0, // BR TR TL
};

// Look up which action we should be taking in this configuration.
auto SelectedActionIndex =
  SubdivisionActionIndexes[SubdivisionSum];
if (SelectedActionIndex != -1)
{
  // We have an action that we should be taking, so look that up.
  const auto& SelectedAction =
    SubdivisionActions[SelectedActionIndex];

  // Get the iterators to the boxes that we will be merging and
  // erasing
  auto MergeBoxIt =
    (BoxList.end() - SelectedAction.MergedBoxIndexOffset);
  auto EraseBoxIt =
    (BoxList.end() - SelectedAction.EraseIndexOffset);

  // Merge the boxes and erase
  *MergeBoxIt = MergeBoxIt->MergeWith(*EraseBoxIt);
  BoxList.erase(EraseBoxIt);
}
```

```
    // This function returns true if the input box was added in its
    // entirety, which we never do in this case.
    return false;
  }
}
```

Although this code is much longer than the previous listing in Section 8.4.1, it does not do that much more. The preamble is exactly the same, and the code to subdivide and recurse is morally equivalent – the new code stores the boxes in an array rather than individual named variables. We then use `std::accumulate()` to calculate the table index, which is not the most obvious code. If using the algorithm is confusing, then you can expand it by hand[2]:

```
uint8_t SubdivisionSum =
  SubdivisionResults[SubdivisionCorner::BottomLeft]   * 8 +
  SubdivisionResults[SubdivisionCorner::BottomRight]  * 4 +
  SubdivisionResults[SubdivisionCorner::TopRight]     * 2 +
  SubdivisionResults[SubdivisionCorner::TopLeft]      * 1;
```

With the index calculated, we special-case the value 15 where all four quadrants are included. The remainder of the function encodes the functionality described in Tables 8.1 and 8.2, and much of the code length is taken up with compile-time tables. The actual code looks up the correct action to take from the table, merges the two boxes together, and then erases one of the boxes.

8.6 RESULTS

After applying the code from Section 8.5, we get the results from Figure 8.5, which reduces the total box count from 25 down to 16 - a reduction of roughly 1/3 from the previous step, and less than 1/3 of the original count, which is pretty good! This count is not fully optimal – with some manipulation we can get down to about nine rectangles, but doing that is well into diminishing returns.[3] We'll stop here with a drastic reduction in count that we can now run through our volumetric sound code.

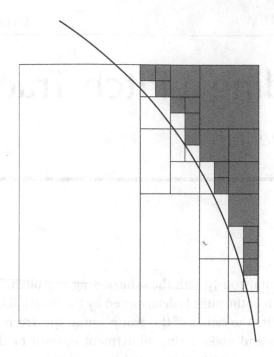

FIGURE 8.5   The resulting boxes after running through the code from Section 8.5.

NOTES

1   Applying the results of a Karnaugh Map to a function is an interesting exercise, but attempting to use the grouping rules for this example will result in a solution that is not much simpler than simply writing out the entire table as a sequence of if() statements.

2   I was about to type in "without loss of generality" until I realized that you do lose generality. Expanding the formula by hand will require minor changes if you expand this function to operate on spheres and 3D boxes. Nevertheless, if you do not expect to make this change, then the non-algorithm code may end up being more readable – the generated assembly is nearly identical.

3   Plus, I haven't actually figured out the algorithm to get the optimal count!

CHAPTER 9

Building a Pitch Tracker

Fundamentals

David Su

Begin simultaneously with the others. Sing any pitch. The maximum length of the pitch is determined by the breath. Listen to the group. Locate the center of the group sound spectrum. Sing your pitch again and make a tiny adjustment upward or downward, but tuning toward the center of the sound spectrum. Continue to tune slowly, in tiny increments toward the center of the spectrum ...

PAULINE OLIVEROS, SONIC MEDITATIONS XVI

9.1 INTRODUCTION

How are our ears able to distinguish between two musical notes and can we build a digital audio system that can make that same distinction? More generally, how can we create audio systems that *listen* to sounds and provide us with useful information about their properties? In addition, what can we do to ensure that such systems run reliably in a real-time interactive environment such as a video game? This is the bread and butter of pitch tracking in games, which we'll be exploring in this chapter as well as in Chapter 10.

Both chapters are inspired in large part by the work I did as the audio programmer on Bad Dream Games' *One Hand Clapping*, a game in which

 DOI: 10.1201/9781003330936-11

the player sings into their microphone to solve musical puzzles. The specific approaches and implementation details might differ, but the pitch tracking in that game is built upon many of the same principles that we'll explore in these chapters.

9.1.1 What Is Pitch Tracking?

Frequency and pitch are closely related, although they are not exactly equivalent. Generally, frequency refers to the physical property of the rate at which a sound wave repeats itself, while pitch refers to the perceptual property of how "high" or "low" a sound feels on the frequency spectrum – indeed, different listeners may perceive different pitches upon hearing the same sound. In this chapter, we'll use the two terms somewhat interchangeably – for our purposes, a higher frequency (i.e., a faster rate of repetition) is generally also associated with a higher pitch. Nevertheless, it's important to keep in mind the distinction between the two.[1]

Pitch tracking refers to the real-time estimation of a signal's pitch – this task is also often referred to as pitch detection or F0 estimation (F0 being a signal's fundamental frequency), although those terms don't always distinguish between real-time and non-real-time applications. Because we're working in the real-time setting of game audio, our pitch detection algorithm (or PDA for short) will need to work in real time.

One important thing to note is that we'll be focusing on *monophonic* pitch tracking – that is, tracking only one pitch at a time. In other words, if the input signal involves two or more simultaneous distinct pitches, the tracker is going to have a hard time. There are certainly some timbres that blur the line between monophony and polyphony (again highlighting the perceptual nature of pitch), but generally we'll assume that our input signal has one distinct pitch at any given moment in time.

9.1.2 Motivation

Probably the most common use case for monophonic pitch tracking is in games that involve live musical input, especially karaoke-based games in which players sing along to existing music – examples include the games *SingStar*, *Karaoke Revolution*, and *Rock Band*. In such games, the audio system must estimate the player's input pitch so that the game can then measure that input pitch's distance to a target pitch (i.e., the current note in a melody) and thus judge how accurate the player's singing is.

More broadly, pitch tracking is a great way to see DSP in action as applied to *analyzing* an audio signal, as opposed to *effecting* it. That's not to say we can't make use of pitch tracking in audio effects as well – in fact, effects such as pitch correction rely on pitch tracking as an internal step since you can't transpose an input signal to the correct pitch without having an idea of what pitch it was playing in the first place!

With all that in mind, let's begin building a pitch tracker.

9.2 SETTING THINGS UP

Before we get to actually implementing the pitch detection portion of our tracker, we'll need to do a bit of setup, mostly to get our input audio in a usable format.

9.2.1 Plugin Scaffolding

We'll be implementing our pitch tracker as a Wwise effect plugin, but the principles here apply regardless of the specific audio engine or middleware you use. If you've got access to buffers of samples in real time, you're good!

Plugins in Wwise are composed of an Authoring portion (which deals with general plugin properties, including UI) and a Sound Engine portion (which deals with the plugin's real-time behavior, including DSP). We'll be focusing on the latter since that's where the audio processing occurs.

Effect plugins in Wwise are implemented via the `AK::IAkPlugin` interface and achieve real-time processing by operating on blocks of samples. This processing occurs within the `AK::IAkPlugin::Execute()` method, which is called at a fixed interval according to the audio device's sample rate. Wwise effect plugins also have an `AK::IAkPlugin::Init()` method (which is called during initialization) and an `AK::IAkPlugin::Term()` method (which is called when the plugin is terminated). Our plugin, which we'll call `GapTuner`,[2] will implement the `AK::IAkInPlaceEffectPlugin` interface via a `GapTunerFX` class – we're able to replace each block's input buffer directly with our processed output, which is why we derive from `AK::IAkInPlaceEffectPlugin` (which itself derives from `AK::IAkPlugin`).

Our plugin will also contain a set of parameters (or properties) that allow the user to control various aspects of the analysis process (the user in this case might be an audio programmer, sound designer, or even the player themselves!). As long as we define these parameters in the implementation of the AK::IAkPluginParam interface (which in this case we'll implement via a GapTunerFXParams struct), we'll have access to the parameters via our GapTunerFX class' m_PluginParams member variable, which we set in our Init() method.

This is what our GapTunerFX class might look like to begin with:

```
//--------------------------------------------------------------
// GapTunerFX.h

#include "GapTunerFXParams.h"

class GapTunerFX : public AK::IAkInPlaceEffectPlugin
{

public:

    // Constructor
    GapTunerFX() = default;

    // Initialize plugin
    AKRESULT Init(AK::IAkPluginMemAlloc* InAllocator,
                  AK::IAkEffectPluginContext* InContext,
                  AK::IAkPluginParam* InParams,
                  AkAudioFormat& InFormat) override;

    // Terminate plugin
    AKRESULT Term(AK::IAkPluginMemAlloc* InAllocator) override;

    // Execute DSP for a block of audio
    void Execute(AkAudioBuffer* InOutBuffer) override;

private:

    // Wwise-plugin-specific members, set in Init()
    GapTunerFXParams* m_PluginParams { nullptr };
    AK::IAkPluginMemAlloc* m_PluginMemoryAllocator { nullptr };
```

```
  AK::IAkEffectPluginContext* m_PluginContext { nullptr };

};

//-------------------------------------------------------------------
// GapTunerFX.cpp

#include "GapTunerFX.h"

AKRESULT GapTunerFX::Init(AK::IAkPluginMemAlloc* InAllocator,
                          AK::IAkEffectPluginContext* InContext,
                          AK::IAkPluginParam* InParams,
                          AkAudioFormat& InFormat)
{
  m_PluginParams = static_cast<GapTunerFXParams*>(InParams);
  m_PluginMemoryAllocator = InAllocator;
  m_PluginContext = InContext;

  return AK_Success;
}

AKRESULT GapTunerFX::Term(AK::IAkPluginMemAlloc* InAllocator)
{
  AK_PLUGIN_DELETE(InAllocator, this);
  return AK_Success;
}

void GapTunerFX::Execute(AkAudioBuffer* InOutBuffer)
{
  // ...
}
```

In addition to user-controlled parameters, we can also make use of output parameters that our plugin will set as a part of its processing – these parameters will be defined as real-time parameter controls or RTPCs for short. This allows the results of our analysis to be easily used to control other properties in Wwise by hooking into these RTPCs. These output parameters also provide a convenient way to expose the estimated pitch to the game at large – the game can call AK::SoundEngine::Query::GetRTPCValue().

We won't go into too much more detail about the scaffolding for Wwise plugin parameters, but if you'd like to learn more about creating Wwise effect plugins, the SDK documentation has a lot of useful information as well as a step-by-step guide [1].

Assuming we've defined an `OutputPitchParameterId` in the non-RTPC part of our `GapTunerFXParams` struct, this is what setting an output pitch parameter looks like in the context of our `Execute()` function:

```
void GapTunerFX::Execute(AkAudioBuffer* InOutBuffer)
{
  // ...

  AkRtpcID OutputPitchParamId =
    m_PluginParams->NonRTPC.OutputPitchParameterId;

  AkRtpcValue OutputPitchParamValue = 0.f;

  // ... Set OutputPitchParamValue at some point ...

  AK::IAkGlobalPluginContext* GlobalContext =
    m_PluginContext->GlobalContext();

  AKRESULT Result =
    GlobalContext->SetRTPCValue(OutputPitchParamId,
                                OutputPitchParamValue);
}
```

Figure 9.1 shows what the UI for our plugin looks like with this output pitch parameter ID set to the ID of a **Pitch** RTPC in a Wwise project.

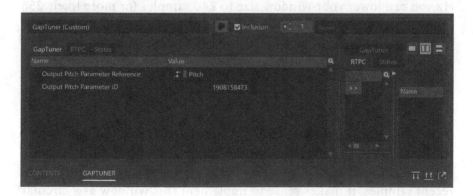

FIGURE 9.1 GapTuner plugin UI, with the output pitch parameter ID hooked up to an RTPC.

9.2.2 Window Size

The buffers that we operate on in our `Execute()` function are generally well-suited for processing audio, but for analysis it can be helpful to operate on larger buffers. One of the first questions we'll need to answer is: what range of pitch do we want to consider? This is the essence of determining an appropriate window size. There's a trade-off between speed and accuracy here – a larger window size allows us to better detect lower frequencies but requires us to wait for more samples, thus incurring latency between the actual audio input and the pitch detection result.

It can be helpful to think of the window size in perceptual terms. Say we have a sample rate of 48,000 Hz and a window size of 512 samples. This means that with this window, we'll be able to represent frequencies as low as $\frac{48,000}{512} = 93.75$ Hz and no lower. If we increase the window size to 1,024 samples, we'll now be able to represent frequencies as low as $\frac{48,000}{1024} = 46.875$ Hz (just above F#1).

Our general pitch tracking approach is going to be based on autocorrelation, which we'll discuss in more detail in Section 9.3.2. For now, one relevant property to note is that the results of the autocorrelation function are only valid for half the window size, which means our window size needs to be twice as large as the lowest pitch we want to estimate. In our case, if we take 46.875 Hz as the lowest considered pitch, then we need a window size of 2,048 samples.

In our plugin, we can parameterize the window size so that the designer can control its behavior – for example, if you know that you only care about pitches above 200 Hz, then at a sample rate of 48,000 Hz you can lower your window size to 240 samples (or more likely 256 samples, to keep the window size a power of 2). In our `GapTuner` plugin, we can get the window size by accessing `m_PluginParams->NonRTPC.WindowSize`.

9.2.3 Analysis Window

In order to perform pitch detection (or any other kind of processing) using our analysis window, we need to actually fill it with samples. Since we'll want to do this in every block, and only care about the most recent samples, it makes sense to implement this window as a circular buffer. In particular, we'll adapt Ethan Geller's `CircularAudioBuffer` class from "Building the Patch Cable," Chapter 7 of *Game Audio*

Programming: Principles and Practices Volume 3 [2], adding a few utility methods for convenience:

```cpp
template <typename SampleType>
class CircularAudioBuffer
{

  // See Section 7.5.1 of Game Audio Programming Vol 3 for full
  // implementation.
  // ...


  // ------------------------------------------------------------
  // Additional convenience methods (not in original implementation)

  // Get the sample at a specific index offset from the read index
  SampleType At(uint32_t InIndex) const
  {
    const uint32_t ReadIndex = ReadCounter.load();
    const uint32_t SampleIndex = (ReadIndex + InIndex) % Capacity;
    const SampleType SampleValue = InternalBuffer[SampleIndex];
    return SampleValue;
  }

  // Push a single sample to the buffer
  uint32_t PushSingle(const SampleType& InSample)
  {
    return Push(&InSample, 1);
  }

  // Set read index to write index
  void AlignReadWriteIndices()
  {
    SetNum(0, false);
  }
};
```

We can set up our analysis window as a private member variable
m_AnalysisWindow and allocate memory for it in our Init() method:

```cpp
//------------------------------------------------------------
// GapTunerFX.h

class GapTunerFX : public AK::IAkInPlaceEffectPlugin
```

```
{
    // ...

private:

    // ...

    CircularAudioBuffer<float> m_AnalysisWindow { };
    uint32_t m_AnalysisWindowSamplesWritten { 0 };

};

// ------------------------------------------------------------------
// GapTunerFX.cpp

AKRESULT GapTunerFX::Init(AK::IAkPluginMemAlloc* InAllocator,
                          AK::IAkEffectPluginContext* InContext,
                          AK::IAkPluginParam* InParams,
                          AkAudioFormat& InFormat)
{
    // Set Wwise-plugin-specific members
    // ...

    // Keep track of sample rate
    m_SampleRate = static_cast<uint32_t>(InFormat.uSampleRate);

    // ----
    // Allocate memory for analysis window
    const uint32_t WindowSize = m_PluginParams->NonRTPC.WindowSize;

    // The circular buffer sets its internal capacity to
    // InCapacity + 1; if we pass in WindowSize - 1, then
    // m_AnalysisWindow.GetCapacity() == WindowSize, which is
    // the result we want
    m_AnalysisWindow.SetCapacity(WindowSize - 1);

    return AK_Success;
}
```

We can then fill the analysis window with samples each time `Execute()` is called (i.e., during each audio block). We'll also start a separate

`GapTunerAnalysis` namespace, which will handle the nitty-gritty of analysis – this is where our `FillAnalysisWindow()` function will live:

```cpp
// -----------------------------------------------------------------
// GapTunerFX.cpp

void GapTunerFX::Execute(AkAudioBuffer* InOutBuffer)
{
  // ----
  // Fill analysis window
  const uint32_t WindowSize = m_PluginParams->NonRTPC.WindowSize;

  const uint32_t NumSamplesPushed =
    GapTunerAnalysis::FillAnalysisWindow(InOutBuffer,
                                         m_AnalysisWindow);

  m_AnalysisWindowSamplesWritten += NumSamplesPushed;

  // Skip analysis if we haven't yet filled a full window
  if (m_AnalysisWindowSamplesWritten < WindowSize)
  {
    return;
  }

  // ...

}

// -----------------------------------------------------------------
// GapTunerAnalysis.h

#include <AK/SoundEngine/Common/IAkPlugin.h>
#include "CircularAudioBuffer/CircularAudioBuffer.h"

namespace GapTunerAnalysis
{
  // Fill an analysis window with samples from an input audio buffer
  uint32_t FillAnalysisWindow(
    AkAudioBuffer* InBuffer,
    CircularAudioBuffer<float>& InOutWindow);
}
```

```cpp
// ---------------------------------------------------------------
// GapTunerAnalysis.cpp

#include "GapTunerAnalysis.h"

namespace GapTunerAnalysis

{
  uint32_t FillAnalysisWindow(AkAudioBuffer* InBuffer,
                              CircularAudioBuffer<float>& InOutWindow)
  {
    const uint32_t NumChannels = InBuffer->NumChannels();
    const uint32_t NumSamples = InBuffer->uValidFrames;
    uint32_t NumSamplesPushed = 0;

    // Set analysis window read index to write index, so that we
    // always write as many samples as we have available
    InOutWindow.AlignReadWriteIndices();

    // Average all input channels so that we only analyze one single
    // buffer
    for (uint32_t SampleIdx = 0; SampleIdx < NumSamples; ++SampleIdx)
    {
      float SampleValue = 0.f;

      // Sum input sample values across channels
      for (uint32_t ChannelIdx = 0;
           ChannelIdx < NumChannels;
           ++ChannelIdx)
      {
        AkSampleType* pChannel = InBuffer->GetChannel(ChannelIdx);
        auto pBuf = static_cast<float*>(pChannel);

        SampleValue += pBuf[SampleIdx];
      }

      // Average summed sample values
      SampleValue /= NumSamples;

      // Add sample to analysis window
      NumSamplesPushed += InOutWindow.PushSingle(SampleValue);
    }
```

```
// Set analysis window read index to new write index (now that
// we've pushed samples), so that we're always reading an entire
// window's worth of samples
InOutWindow.AlignReadWriteIndices();

    return NumSamplesPushed;
  }
}
```

9.3 BASIC PITCH TRACKING

With our plugin scaffolding and analysis window in place, we're finally ready to perform some pitch tracking. One of the most common approaches to monophonic pitch detection is autocorrelation, which essentially involves comparing a waveform with time-displaced, or *lagged*, copies of itself. We can then take the *lag* at which the signal correlates with itself most strongly and use that as our estimated frequency.

9.3.1 Correlation and Lag

Correlation can be computed in many different ways, with one of the most common being to take the dot product. Given input signals x and y, both containing N samples each, their correlation can be defined as follows, outputting a real number[3]:

$$correlation(x, y) = \sum_{n=0}^{N-1} x_n y_n$$

To lag a signal, we time-delay its values by a given amount. To lag an input signal x by time amount t, we can apply the following function, outputting a lagged signal:

$$lag(x, t) = x_{n-t} : n \in \{0, ..., N-1\}$$

Note that for any non-zero lag, we're going to end up with values in the lagged signal that lie outside our original window – in our case, we're going to zero them out, which will let us calculate *linear* autocorrelation. (If we were to wrap the values around instead, we'd be calculating *circular* autocorrelation.) Taking this zeroing out into account, our lag function then looks like this:

$$lag(x, t) = \begin{cases} x_{n-t} : t \in \{0, ..., n-1\} \\ 0 \quad : t \in \{n, ..., N-1\} \end{cases} : n \in \{0, ..., N-1\}$$

9.3.2 Autocorrelation

Putting together our definitions of correlation and lag, the autocorrelation function (often shortened to ACF) for an input signal x containing N samples can be defined as follows, outputting a series of real numbers that each correspond to the autocorrelation for a given lag t:

$$ACF(x)$$
$$= correlation\big(x, lag(x, t)\big) : t \in \{0, \dots, N-1\}$$
$$= \begin{cases} \displaystyle\sum_{n=0}^{N-1} x_n x_{n-t} : t \in \{0, \dots, n-1\} \\ 0 \qquad\qquad : t \in \{n, \dots, N-1\} \end{cases}$$

The last step we'll take is to normalize our ACF output so that all the values end up between –1 and 1. To do this, we divide all our output correlations by the correlation of the first lag:

$$ACF_{normalized}(x)$$
$$= \frac{correlation\big(x, lag(x, t)\big)}{correlation\big(x_0, lag(x, 0)\big)} : t \in \{0, \dots, N-1\}$$
$$= \begin{cases} \displaystyle\sum_{n=0}^{N-1} \frac{x_n x_{n-t}}{(x_0)^2} : t \in \{0, \dots, n-1\} \\ 0 \qquad\qquad : t \in \{n, \dots, N-1\} \end{cases}$$

Let's go ahead and implement this normalized ACF in code[4]:

```cpp
// ----------------------------------------------------------------
// GapTunerAnalysis.h

// ...

#include <vector>

namespace GapTunerAnalysis
{

    // ...
```

```cpp
    // Calculate normalized autocorrelation function for a window
    void CalculateAcf(
      const CircularAudioBuffer<float>& InAnalysisWindow,
      std::vector<float>& OutAutocorrelations);

    // Calculate autocorrelation (using dot product) for a given lag
    float CalculateAcfForLag(
      const CircularAudioBuffer<float>& InSamples,
      const uint32_t InLag);
}

// ------------------------------------------------------------------
// GapTunerAnalysis.cpp

// ...

#include <assert.h>

namespace GapTunerAnalysis
{

  // ...

  void CalculateAcf(
    const CircularAudioBuffer<float>& InAnalysisWindow,
    std::vector<float>& OutAutocorrelations)
  {
    assert(
      InAnalysisWindow.GetCapacity() == OutAutocorrelations.size());

    const size_t WindowSize = InAnalysisWindow.GetCapacity();

    // Calculate ACF for each lag value
    for (uint32_t Lag = 0; Lag < WindowSize; ++Lag)
    {
      OutAutocorrelations[Lag] =
        CalculateAcfForLag(InAnalysisWindow, Lag);
    }

    // Normalize
    const float FirstCorrelation = OutAutocorrelations[0];
    const float NormalizeMultiplier = FirstCorrelation != 0.f
                                      ? 1.f / FirstCorrelation
                                      : 1.f;
```

```
    for (uint32_t Lag = 0; Lag < WindowSize; ++Lag)
    {
      OutAutocorrelations[Lag] *= NormalizeMultiplier;
    }
  }

  float CalculateAcfForLag(
    const CircularAudioBuffer<float>& InSamples,
    const uint32_t InLag)
  {
    const size_t WindowSize = InSamples.GetCapacity();
    float Sum = 0.f;

    for (uint32_t SampleIdx = 0; SampleIdx < WindowSize; ++SampleIdx)
    {
      // All samples before lag amount are zeroed out, so we only
      // need to run calculations for lagged samples
      if (SampleIdx >= InLag)
      {
        const float SampleValue = InSamples.At(SampleIdx);

        const float LaggedSampleValue =
          InSamples.At(SampleIdx - InLag);

        Sum += SampleValue * LaggedSampleValue;
      }
    }

    return Sum;
  }
}
```

Figure 9.2 shows what a plot of the autocorrelation coefficients looks like for a sine wave oscillating at 440 Hz. As you can see, the coefficients themselves comprise a sinusoidal shape, with peaks around 100 samples, 200 samples, and so on. If we zoom in, we can see that the peak occurs at a lag of 109 samples, as shown in Figure 9.3.

Converting this lag value back into Hz, we get $\frac{48,000}{109} \approx 440.367$ Hz, which is pretty darn close! (In fact, note that at our current sample rate of 48,000 Hz, a lag of 108 samples corresponds to 444.444 Hz, and a lag of 110 samples corresponds to 436.364 Hz. This means that our estimate

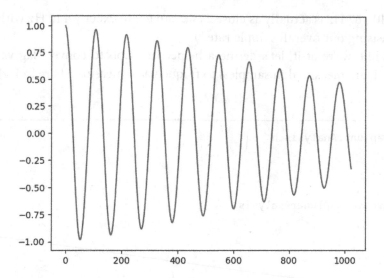

FIGURE 9.2   Plot of autocorrelation coefficients for a sine wave playing at 440 Hz, with a window size of 2,048 samples and sample rate of 48,000 Hz.

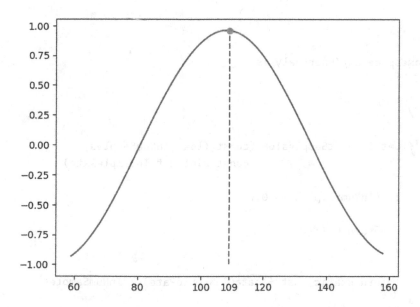

FIGURE 9.3   Zoomed in plot of same autocorrelation coefficients as Figure 9.2, with a point to mark the peak correlation at 109 samples.

of 440.367 Hz is actually as close as we can get to exactly 440 Hz without increasing our overall sample rate.[5])

While we're at it, let's define a helper function to convert lag values (which are measured in samples) to frequencies (measured here in Hz):

```cpp
//-----------------------------------------------------------------
// GapTunerAnalysis.h

// ...

namespace GapTunerAnalysis
{

  // ...

  // Convert from num samples to Hz, based on a given sample rate
  float ConvertSamplesToHz(const float InNumSamples,
                           const uint32_t InSampleRate);
}

//-----------------------------------------------------------------
// GapTunerAnalysis.cpp

// ...

namespace GapTunerAnalysis
{

  // ...

  float ConvertSamplesToHz(const float InNumSamples,
                           const uint32_t InSampleRate)
  {
    if (InNumSamples == 0.f)
    {
      return 0.f;
    }

    return static_cast<float>(InSampleRate) / InNumSamples;
  }

}
```

9.3.3 Peak Picking

Looking back at Figure 9.3, it would be great if we could do the peak-picking process programmatically. A simple approach is to just iterate through all the lag values and pick the highest one. One thing to be careful of is to ignore the very first peak at $t = 0$. The reason for this is that a signal will always have perfect correlation with an un-lagged copy of itself, but this doesn't help us with our goal of pitch detection! A simple way to skip the first peak is to only begin picking peak values after the first zero crossing has been reached. This is what the whole peak-picking process looks like:

```cpp
// ----------------------------------------------------------------
// GapTunerAnalysis.h

// ...

namespace GapTunerAnalysis
{

  // ...

  // Pick the peak lag given the autocorrelation coefficients for a
  // series of time lags
  uint32_t FindAcfPeakLag(
    const std::vector<float>& InAutocorrelations);

}

// ----------------------------------------------------------------
// GapTunerAnalysis.cpp

// ...

namespace GapTunerAnalysis
{

  // ...

  uint32_t FindAcfPeakLag(
    const std::vector<float>& InAutocorrelations)
  {
    const size_t WindowSize = InAutocorrelations.size();
```

```
    uint32_t PeakLag = 0;
    float PeakCorr = 0.f;
    bool bReachedFirstZeroCrossing = false;

    // NOTE: Skip first correlation and only go up to half the window
    //       size, and only start counting after first zero crossing
    for (uint32_t Lag = 1; Lag < WindowSize / 2.f; ++Lag)
    {
      const float Corr = InAutocorrelations[Lag];

      const float PrevCorr = InAutocorrelations[Lag - 1];

      // We've reached first zero crossing when sign changes
      if (Corr * PrevCorr < 0)
      {
        bReachedFirstZeroCrossing = true;
      }

      // Update peak if zero crossing has been reached
      if (bReachedFirstZeroCrossing && Corr > PeakCorr)
      {
        PeakLag = Lag;
        PeakCorr = Corr;
      }
    }

    return PeakLag;
  }
}
```

We can then take that peak lag, convert it to Hz, and set the output pitch parameter. This is what our **GapTunerFX** class looks like with all that in place, with the bulk of the work being done in the **Execute()** method:

```
// ----------------------------------------------------------------
// GapTunerFX.h

#include <AK/SoundEngine/Common/IAkPlugin.h>
#include "CircularAudioBuffer/CircularAudioBuffer.h"
#include "GapTunerFXParams.h"

class GapTunerFX : public AK::IAkInPlaceEffectPlugin
```

```
{

public:

  // Constructor
  GapTunerFX() = default;

  // Initialize plugin
  AKRESULT Init(AK::IAkPluginMemAlloc* InAllocator,
                AK::IAkEffectPluginContext* InContext,
                AK::IAkPluginParam* InParams,
                AkAudioFormat& InFormat) override;

  // Terminate plugin
  AKRESULT Term(AK::IAkPluginMemAlloc* InAllocator) override;

  // Execute DSP for a block of audio
  void Execute(AkAudioBuffer* InOutBuffer) override;

private:

  // Wwise-plugin-specific members, set in Init()
  GapTunerFXParams* m_PluginParams { nullptr };
  AK::IAkPluginMemAlloc* m_PluginMemoryAllocator { nullptr };
  AK::IAkEffectPluginContext* m_PluginContext { nullptr };

  // Sample rate, also set in Init()
  uint32_t m_SampleRate { 48000 };

  // --------
  // Analysis members

  // Analysis window backed by circular buffer class
  CircularAudioBuffer<float> m_AnalysisWindow { };

  // How many samples we've written to the analysis window so far
  uint32_t m_AnalysisWindowSamplesWritten { 0 };

  // Calculated autocorrelation coefficients
  std::vector<float> m_AutocorrelationCoefficients { };

};
```

```cpp
// ---------------------------------------------------------------------
// GapTunerFX.cpp

#include "GapTunerFX.h"

#include <AK/AkWwiseSDKVersion.h>
#include "GapTunerAnalysis.h"
#include "../GapTunerConfig.h"

AKRESULT GapTunerFX::Init(AK::IAkPluginMemAlloc* InAllocator,
                          AK::IAkEffectPluginContext* InContext,
                          AK::IAkPluginParam* InParams,
                          AkAudioFormat& InFormat)
{
  // Set Wwise-plugin-specific members
  m_PluginParams = static_cast<GapTunerFXParams*>(InParams);
  m_PluginMemoryAllocator = InAllocator;
  m_PluginContext = InContext;

  // Keep track of sample rate
  m_SampleRate = static_cast<uint32_t>(InFormat.uSampleRate);

  // ----
  // Allocate memory for analysis window
  const uint32_t WindowSize = m_PluginParams->NonRTPC.WindowSize;

  m_AutocorrelationCoefficients.resize(WindowSize);

  // The circular buffer sets its internal capacity to
  // InCapacity + 1; if we pass in WindowSize - 1, then
  // m_AnalysisWindow.GetCapacity() == WindowSize, which is
  // the result we want
  m_AnalysisWindow.SetCapacity(WindowSize - 1);

  return AK_Success;
}

AKRESULT GapTunerFX::Term(AK::IAkPluginMemAlloc* InAllocator)
{
  AK_PLUGIN_DELETE(InAllocator, this);
  return AK_Success;
}
```

```
void GapTunerFX::Execute(AkAudioBuffer* InOutBuffer)
{
  // ----
  // Fill analysis window
  const uint32_t WindowSize = m_PluginParams->NonRTPC.WindowSize;

  const uint32_t NumSamplesPushed =
    GapTunerAnalysis::FillAnalysisWindow(InOutBuffer,
                                         m_AnalysisWindow);

  m_AnalysisWindowSamplesWritten += NumSamplesPushed;

  // Skip analysis if we haven't yet filled a full window
  if (m_AnalysisWindowSamplesWritten < WindowSize)
  {
    return;
  }

  // ----
  // Perform analysis

  // Autocorrelation
  GapTunerAnalysis::CalculateAcf(m_AnalysisWindow,
                                 m_AutocorrelationCoefficients);

  // ----
  // Peak picking
  const uint32_t PeakLag =
    GapTunerAnalysis::FindAcfPeakLag(m_AutocorrelationCoefficients);

  // ----
  // Conversion
  const float PeakFrequency =
    GapTunerAnalysis::ConvertSamplesToHz(static_cast<float>(PeakLag),
                                         m_SampleRate);

  // ----
  // Set output parameters

  AkRtpcID OutputPitchParamID =
    m_PluginParams->NonRTPC.OutputPitchParameterId;

  AkRtpcValue OutputPitchParamValue = 0.f;
```

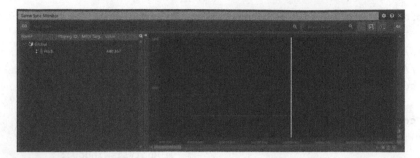

FIGURE 9.4   Wwise Game Sync monitor showing the tracked pitch of the 440 Hz sine wave.

```
// Set to peak frequency
OutputPitchParamValue = PeakFrequency;

// Set RTPC
AK::IAkGlobalPluginContext* GlobalContext =
  m_PluginContext->GlobalContext();

AKRESULT Result =
  GlobalContext->SetRTPCValue(OutputPitchParamID,
                              OutputPitchParamValue);
}
```

Figure 9.4 shows the output pitch in the Wwise Game Sync Monitor (again with a sine wave at 440 Hz). We can see that the chosen peak does indeed correspond to 440.367 Hz.

9.4 CONCLUSION

We've successfully built a pitch tracker! Figure 9.5 shows the UI for our Wwise plugin, with its window size and output pitch parameters. However, our current implementation isn't something that can really be used in a

FIGURE 9.5   UI for our GapTuner Wwise plugin.

real-world setting, as it has performance and accuracy issues. In Chapter 10, we'll discuss some of these issues, along with potential solutions, and adapt the techniques we've explored here into a practical application.

NOTES

1 For more information on this topic, see Christopher Dobrian's "Frequency and Pitch" lesson from his *Physics of Sound* educational materials [3].
2 "Gap," short for "Game Audio Programming" – this book – rather than the word "gap" – Ed.
3 Note that we index starting from 0 instead of 1 in order to maintain consistency with the corresponding implementation in code.
4 Note that the preferred method for storing audio buffers in Wwise plugins is either via the `AkArray` class or via raw arrays in conjunction with `AK_PLUGIN_ALLOC()`. In our case we'll stick with `std::vector`s for the sake of generality and compatibility.
5 Technically, there are ways to get more precision out of our data – for more on that topic, check out Section 10.2.3 of this volume.

REFERENCES

[1] Audio plug-ins. In *Wwise SDK 2022.1.2*. Audiokinetic. https://www. audiokinetic.com/en/library/edge/?source=SDK&id=effectplugin.html
[2] Geller, E. (2020). Building the patch cable. In *Game Audio Programming: Principles and Practices Volume 3* (pp. 93–118). CRC Press. https://www. routledge.com/Game-Audio-Programming-3-Principles-and-Practices/ Somberg/p/book/9780367348045
[3] Dobrian, C. (2019). Frequency and pitch. In *Physics and Sound*. https:// dobrian.github.io/cmp/topics/physics-of-sound/1.frequency-and-pitch. html

CHAPTER 10

Building a Pitch Tracker

Practical Techniques

David Su

> … Each time sing a long tone with a complete breath until the whole group is singing the same pitch. Continue to drone on that center pitch far about the same length of time it took to reach the unison. Then begin adjusting or tuning away from the center pitch as the original beginning was.
>
> PAULINE OLIVEROS, SONIC MEDITATIONS XVI

10.1 INTRODUCTION

In Chapter 9, we wrote a pitch detector that works, but isn't efficient and has accuracy issues. In this chapter, we'll continue that development to make a tool that we can use in a real game.

As a quick refresher, our GapTuner plugin currently computes the autocorrelation function for all lag values in an analysis window, picks the lag value with the highest ("peak") autocorrelation, converts that lag value to frequency, and finally outputs that frequency as the estimated pitch. This all happens in the plugin's Execute() function, which is called every audio frame.

10.2 IMPROVING ACCURACY

Our pitch tracker looks good for a pure sine wave, but if we try it on some more noisy input with varied timbres, we can see that this naive peak-picking method isn't optimal. Figure 10.1a shows the output pitch with

DOI: 10.1201/9781003330936-12

(a)
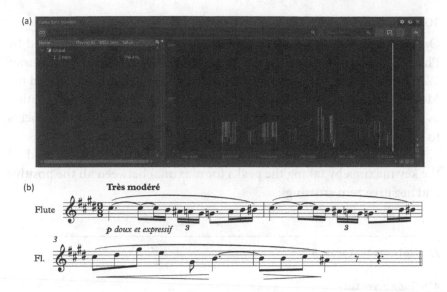

(b)
Flute

Très modéré

p doux et expressif

Fl.

FIGURE 10.1 (a) Tracked pitch for the first four measures of *Prélude à l'après-midi d'un faune*. (b) Musical notation for the first four measures of *Prélude à l'après-midi d'un faune*.

a recording of the first four measures (consisting of solo flute) of Claude Debussy's *Prélude à l'après-midi d'un faune* (*Prelude to the Afternoon of a Faun*), along with its corresponding musical notation in Figure 10.1b.

We can see that the estimate jumps around quite a bit. In particular, if we look closer at the first note, we can see our estimated pitch jumping between 558 and 279 Hz, as shown in Figure 10.2.

Those two frequencies have a ratio of 2:1 – in other words, they're an octave apart! This is what's known as an octave error and is a problem that all pitch detection algorithms have to deal with.

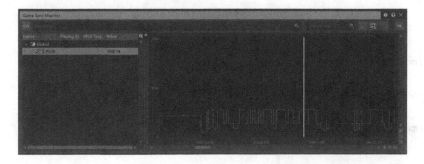

FIGURE 10.2   Zoomed in portion of the tracked pitch from Figure 10.1a, showing octave errors in the first C# note.

10.2.1 Octave Errors

One relatively robust approach for handling octave errors is outlined by Philip McLeod and Geoff Wyvill in their widely cited paper *A Smarter Way to Find Pitch* [1] as part of their pitch detection algorithm dubbed the McLeod Pitch Method (or MPM for short). The MPM uses autocorrelation as its basis[1] and also describes a way to improve the peak-picking process to reduce octave errors.

First, instead of choosing the highest overall peak, we instead find all the key maxima by taking the peaks (or maxima) between all the positive and negative zero crossings:

```
// ----------------------------------------------------------------
// GapTunerAnalysis.h

#include <vector>
#include <AK/SoundEngine/Common/IAkPlugin.h>
#include "CircularAudioBuffer/CircularAudioBuffer.h"

namespace GapTunerAnalysis
{

    // ...

    // Gather a list of key maxima using the MPM's peak-picking process
    uint32_t FindKeyMaxima(std::vector<float>& OutKeyMaximaLags,
                           std::vector<float>& OutKeyMaximaCorrelations,
                           const std::vector<float>& InAutocorrelations,
                           const uint32_t InMaxNumMaxima);
}

// ----------------------------------------------------------------
// GapTunerAnalysis.cpp

#include "GapTunerAnalysis.h"

#include <assert.h>

namespace GapTunerAnalysis
{

    // ...
```

```cpp
uint32_t FindKeyMaxima(std::vector<float>& OutKeyMaximaLags,
                       std::vector<float>& OutKeyMaximaCorrelations,
                       const std::vector<float>& InAutocorrelations,
                       const uint32_t InMaxNumMaxima)
{
  const size_t WindowSize = InAutocorrelations.size();
  uint32_t MaximaIdx = 0;
  float MaximaLag = 0.f;
  float MaximaCorr = 0.f;
  bool bReachedNextPositiveZeroCrossing = false;

  // Again, skip first correlation and go up to half the window size
  for (uint32_t Lag = 1; Lag < WindowSize / 2.f; ++Lag)
  {
    const float PrevCorr = InAutocorrelations[Lag - 1];
    const float Corr = InAutocorrelations[Lag];
    const float NextCorr = InAutocorrelations[Lag + 1];

    // We've reached zero crossing when sign changes
    if (Corr * PrevCorr < 0)
    {
      if (PrevCorr < 0.f && NextCorr > 0.f) // Positive slope
      {
        bReachedNextPositiveZeroCrossing = true;

        // Add peak indices and values
        OutKeyMaximaLags[MaximaIdx] = MaximaLag;
        OutKeyMaximaCorrelations[MaximaIdx] = MaximaCorr;

        // Increment maxima index
        MaximaIdx++;
        if (MaximaIdx >= InMaxNumMaxima)
        {
          break;
        }

        // Reset
        MaximaLag = 0;
        MaximaCorr = 0.f;
      }
      else if (PrevCorr > 0.f && NextCorr < 0.f) // Negative slope
      {
        bReachedNextPositiveZeroCrossing = false;
      }
    }
```

```
  // Update peak if we're between positive and negative zero
  // crossings
  if (bReachedNextPositiveZeroCrossing && Corr > MaximaCorr)
  {
    MaximaLag = static_cast<float>(Lag);
    MaximaCorr = Corr;
  }
}

  // This tells us how many maxima we ultimately found.
  // It will always be <= InMaxNumMaxima
  return MaximaIdx;
}
}
```

Our job is then to pick the most appropriate peak out of those key maxima. To do so, we'll define a threshold multiplier and multiply it by the highest valued maxima – this is our threshold. We can then take the first key maxima whose correlation value is *above* the threshold. This gives us a chance to pick the fundamental frequency even in cases where subharmonics might have a higher correlation. In general, lower harmonics tend to be a bigger issue for pitch detectors than upper harmonics – if you look again at Figure 10.2, you'll notice that all the octave errors result from downward jumps rather than upward ones. Figure 10.3 shows a plot of the

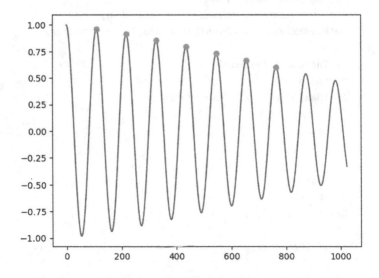

FIGURE 10.3   Plot of key maxima for autocorrelation coefficients of a single analysis window, for a sine wave at 440 Hz.

key maxima for a single analysis window for a sine wave at 440 Hz. Here's what this peak-picking process looks like in code.

```cpp
// ------------------------------------------------------------------
// GapTunerAnalysis.h

// ...

namespace GapTunerAnalysis
{

  // ...

  // Pick the best maxima from a list of key maxima
  uint32_t PickBestMaxima(
    const std::vector<float>& InKeyMaximaLags,
    const std::vector<float>& InKeyMaximaCorrelations,
    const uint32_t InNumKeyMaxima,
    const float InThresholdMultiplier);
}

// ------------------------------------------------------------------
// GapTunerAnalysis.cpp

// ...

namespace GapTunerAnalysis
{

  // ...

  uint32_t PickBestMaxima(
    const std::vector<float>& InKeyMaximaLags,
    const std::vector<float>& InKeyMaximaCorrelations,
    const uint32_t InNumKeyMaxima,
    const float InThresholdMultiplier)
  {
    // This is the index in the array of maxima, not the actual lag
    uint32_t HighestMaximaIdx = 0;
    float HighestMaximaCorr = 0.f;

    // Find highest maxima index and correlation
    for (uint32_t MaximaIdx = 0;
         MaximaIdx < InNumKeyMaxima;
         ++MaximaIdx)
```

```
  {
    const float MaximaCorr = InKeyMaximaCorrelations[MaximaIdx];

    if (MaximaCorr > HighestMaximaCorr)
    {
      HighestMaximaIdx = MaximaIdx;
      HighestMaximaCorr = MaximaCorr;
    }
  }

  // Pick first one that's larger than threshold
  uint32_t BestMaximaIdx = HighestMaximaIdx;
  const float Threshold = HighestMaximaCorr * InThresholdMultiplier;

  for (uint32_t MaximaIdx = 0;
       MaximaIdx < InNumKeyMaxima;
       ++MaximaIdx)
  {
    const float MaximaCorr = InKeyMaximaCorrelations[MaximaIdx];

    if (MaximaCorr >= Threshold)
    {
      BestMaximaIdx = MaximaIdx;
      break;
    }
  }

  return BestMaximaIdx;
  }
}
```

We can now plug this new peak-picking process into our `Execute()` method:

```
// ---------------------------------------------------------------
// GapTunerFX.h

// ...

class GapTunerFX : public AK::IAkInPlaceEffectPlugin
{

// ...
```

```cpp
private:

  // --------
  // Analysis members

  // ...

  // Key maxima lags and correlations, for MPM-based peak-picking
  std::vector<float> m_KeyMaximaLags { };
  std::vector<float> m_KeyMaximaCorrelations { };
};


// --------------------------------------------------------------------
// GapTunerFX.cpp

void GapTunerFX::Execute(AkAudioBuffer* InOutBuffer)
{
  // ----
  // Fill analysis window (same as before)
  // ...


  // ----
  // Perform analysis (same as before)
  // ...

  // ----
  // Peak picking
  const uint32_t MaxNumKeyMaxima =
    m_PluginParams->NonRTPC.MaxNumKeyMaxima;

  const uint32_t NumKeyMaxima =
    GapTunerAnalysis::FindKeyMaxima(m_KeyMaximaLags,
                                    m_KeyMaximaCorrelations,
                                    m_AutocorrelationCoefficients,
                                    MaxNumKeyMaxima);

  const float KeyMaximaThresholdMultiplier =
    m_PluginParams->NonRTPC.KeyMaximaThresholdMultiplier;

  const uint32_t BestMaximaLagIndex =
      GapTunerAnalysis::PickBestMaxima(m_KeyMaximaLags,
                                       m_KeyMaximaCorrelations,
                                       NumKeyMaxima,
                                       KeyMaximaThresholdMultiplier);
```

```
// Best maxima lag and correlation
const float BestMaximaLag = m_KeyMaximaLags[BestMaximaLagIndex];

const float BestMaximaCorrelation =
  m_KeyMaximaCorrelations[BestMaximaLagIndex];

const float BestMaximaFrequency =
    GapTunerAnalysis::ConvertSamplesToHz(BestMaximaLag,
                                         m_SampleRate);

// ----
// Set output parameters

// Set to best maxima frequency
OutputPitchParamValue = BestMaximaFrequency;

// Set RTPC (same as before)
// ...
}
```

Figure 10.4a shows how the tracked pitch looks for those same flute notes, with a threshold multiplier of 0.95. This looks a little better, especially on the static notes, but we can still see some discontinuities. Perhaps we need to decrease our threshold a bit more? Figure 10.4b shows the tracked pitch with a threshold multiplier of 0.8. The static notes are even smoother, which is good, but now we have occasional *upward* octave jumps! This indicates that our thresholding is biasing too strongly against lower frequencies, leading us to pick upper harmonics instead of the fundamental frequency.

It's worth playing around with the threshold value a bit to find what works best for your exact use case – it can be a delicate balancing act. Figure 10.4c shows the tracked pitch with a threshold multiplier of 0.88 (close to midway between 0.8 and 0.95). It's smoother than Figure 10.4a (notice especially the second C#, which has no octave errors at all now) and has many fewer upward octave jumps than Figure 10.4b (only one as opposed to seven) and so feels like a nice compromise between upper and lower octave errors. Still, can we do better?

10.2.2 Noise and Clarity

Going back to the concept of pitch as a perceptual phenomenon, it can be helpful to distinguish between pitched and unpitched sounds. For

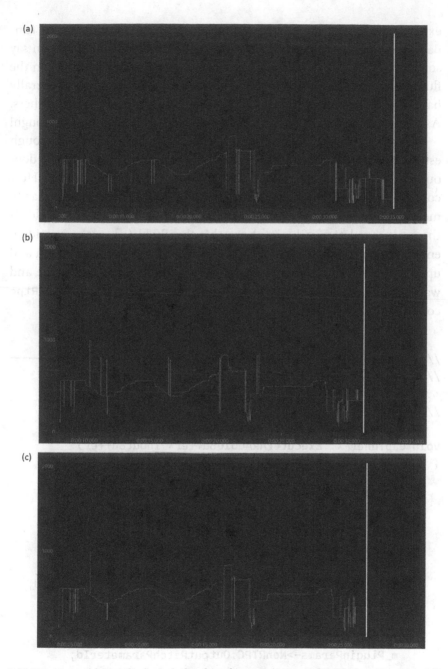

FIGURE 10.4   (a) Tracked pitch for first four measures of *Prélude à l'après-midi d'un faune*, with a key maxima threshold multiplier of 0.95. (b) Tracked pitch for first four measures of *Prélude à l'après-midi d'un faune*, with a key maxima threshold multiplier of 0.8. (c) Tracked pitch for first four measures of *Prélude à l'après-midi d'un faune*, with a key maxima threshold multiplier of 0.88.

example, when we hear a flute playing a note, we can identify a clear fundamental frequency, which is why we think of it as pitched (and can say something like "the flute is playing a C#"). On the other hand, when the flute player takes a breath, the sound is much more noisy, and it's generally hard for us to pinpoint a specific frequency that's stronger than the others. As an exercise, try identifying the pitch of your own breathing – it's tough!

We can use the actual correlation value of our chosen peaks as a rough estimate of how "pitched" a sound is. In other words, how *strongly* does our input signal actually match the peak pitch that we've chosen? How confident are we in our pitch estimate? The MPM calls this the clarity measure, and we can use this measure to define a clarity threshold. If the peak correlation value is above this threshold (i.e., we're confident enough in our pitch estimate), then we'll accept the estimated pitch and update our output parameter – otherwise, we'll discard that value and wait for the next frame. We can accomplish this by defining a **bSetRtpc** condition:

```cpp
//----------------------------------------------------------
// GapTunerFX.cpp

// ...

void GapTunerFX::Execute(AkAudioBuffer* InOutBuffer)
{
  // ...

  // Only set parameter if clarity exceeds threshold
  const float ClarityThreshold =
    m_PluginParams->NonRTPC.ClarityThreshold;

  bool bSetRtpc = BestMaximaCorrelation > ClarityThreshold;
  if (bSetRtpc)
  {
    AkRtpcID OutputPitchParamId =
      m_PluginParams->NonRTPC.OutputPitchParameterId;

    AkRtpcValue OutputPitchParamValue = 0.f;

    // Set to best maxima frequency
    OutputPitchParamValue = BestMaximaFrequency;
```

```
// Set RTPC
AK::IAkGlobalPluginContext* GlobalContext =
  m_PluginContext->GlobalContext();

AKRESULT Result =
  GlobalContext->SetRTPCValue(OutputPitchParamId,
                              OutputPitchParamValue);
  }
}
```

Figure 10.5 shows how the tracked pitch now looks, with a clarity threshold of 0.88 along with a maxima threshold of 0.88 – definitely a lot better than before!

10.2.3 Parabolic Interpolation

In Section 9.3.2 of this volume, I mentioned that we can improve our pitch tracker's precision by increasing the overall sample rate – the higher the sample rate, the less time between samples, and thus the greater the frequency resolution. However, most of the time we don't actually have

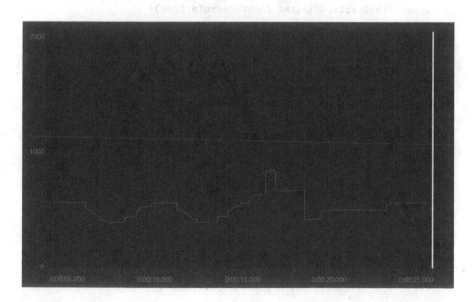

FIGURE 10.5 Tracked pitch for first four measures of *Prélude à l'après-midi d'un faune*, with a key maxima threshold multiplier of 0.88 and clarity threshold of 0.88.

control over the sample rate (and even if we did, we likely wouldn't want to change it just for the sake of pitch detection!).

Luckily, we can use successive parabolic interpolation to arrive at peaks "in between" samples, which allows us to improve precision without messing with the sample rate. For each key maximum, we can also take its left and right neighbors, fit a parabolic curve to those three values, and use the maximum point of that parabola as our estimate. In code, this looks like:

```cpp
// ----------------------------------------------------------------
// GapTunerAnalysis.h

// ...

namespace GapTunerAnalysis
{

    // ...

    // Find the interpolated maxima for a given lag
    float FindInterpolatedMaximaLag(
        const uint32_t InMaximaLag,
        const std::vector<float>& InAutocorrelations);

}


// ----------------------------------------------------------------
// GapTunerAnalysis.cpp

// ...

namespace GapTunerAnalysis
{

    // ...

    float FindInterpolatedMaximaLag(
        const uint32_t InMaximaLag,
        const std::vector<float>& InAutocorrelations)
    {
        const size_t WindowSize = InAutocorrelations.size();
        auto InterpolatedLag = static_cast<float>(InMaximaLag);
```

```
  // Can't interpolate first or last lag value
  if (InMaximaLag < 1 || InMaximaLag >= WindowSize - 1)
  {
    return InterpolatedLag;
  }

  // Get correlations for lags
  const uint32_t LeftNeighborLag = InMaximaLag - 1;
  const uint32_t RightNeighborLag = InMaximaLag + 1;

  const float MaximaCorrelation = InAutocorrelations[InMaximaLag];

  const float LeftNeighborCorrelation =
    InAutocorrelations[LeftNeighborLag];

  const float RightNeighborCorrelation =
    InAutocorrelations[RightNeighborLag];

  // ----
  // Perform interpolation calculation

  const float InterpolationAlpha =
    (MaximaCorrelation - LeftNeighborCorrelation) /
    (InMaximaLag - LeftNeighborLag);

  const float InterpolationBeta =
    (RightNeighborCorrelation - LeftNeighborCorrelation -
      (InterpolationAlpha * (RightNeighborLag - LeftNeighborLag))) /
    ((RightNeighborLag - LeftNeighborLag) *
      (RightNeighborLag - InMaximaLag));

  InterpolatedLag = ((LeftNeighborLag + InMaximaLag) / 2.f) -
                    (InterpolationAlpha / (2 * InterpolationBeta));

  return InterpolatedLag;
}

uint32_t FindKeyMaxima(std::vector<float>& OutKeyMaximaLags,
                       std::vector<float>& OutKeyMaximaCorrelations,
                       const std::vector<float>& InAutocorrelations,
                       const uint32_t InMaxNumMaxima)
{

  // ...
```

```
for (uint32_t Lag = 1; Lag < WindowSize / 2.f; ++Lag)
{
  // ...

  // Update peak if we're between positive and negative zero
  // crossings
  if (bReachedNextPositiveZeroCrossing && Corr > MaximaCorr)
  {
    // With parabolic interpolation
    MaximaLag =
      FindInterpolatedMaximaLag(Lag, InAutocorrelations);

    MaximaCorr = Corr;
  }
}

// ...
}
}
```

Figure 10.6 shows our pitch tracker's output with parabolic interpolation incorporated. At a glance, it doesn't look much different from before. However, if we zoom in a bit, we can see that the tracked pitch is indeed more smooth and continuous than before. Figure 10.7a shows a zoomed in portion of the pitch tracker output without parabolic interpolation – notice

FIGURE 10.6   Tracked pitch for first four measures of *Prélude à l'après-midi d'un faune*, with parabolic interpolation applied to key maxima.

(a)

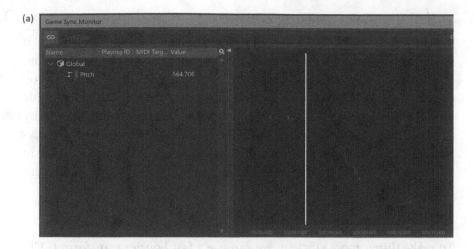

(b)

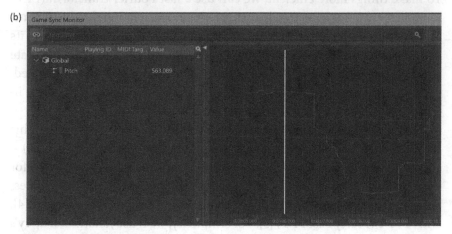

FIGURE 10.7 (a) Tracked pitch for first measure of *Prélude à l'après-midi d'un faune*, without parabolic interpolation. (b) Tracked pitch for first measure of *Prélude à l'après-midi d'un faune*, with parabolic interpolation.

the minor jumps that manifest as sharp corners. Figure 10.7b shows the same portion *with* parabolic interpolation – you can see that the jumps are much more fine-grained owing to the increased precision.

You can also see that the overall tracked pitch values themselves differ slightly – in the frame chosen, the tracked pitch without parabolic interpolation is 564.706 (which corresponds to a lag of 85 samples at 48,000 Hz), whereas the tracked pitch with parabolic interpolation is 563.089 (which corresponds to a lag of 85.244 samples^2 at 48,000 Hz).

10.3 IMPROVING EFFICIENCY

There's one problem with our current implementation that makes it somewhat unsuitable for real-time applications: it is *extremely slow*. If you look back at `CalculateAcf()`, in Chapter 9, Section 9.3.2, you can see that it involves two nested for loops (the second being inside `CalculateAcfForLag()`), which means that its computational complexity is on the order of $O(n^2)$, with n being the number of samples in our analysis window. If you try running this implementation of the pitch tracker in real time, you might start hearing the audio engine stutter, especially with higher window sizes.

10.3.1 Using the FFT

To make things more efficient, we can use a fast Fourier transform (FFT) to implement a mathematically equivalent autocorrelation that has a computational complexity of $O(n \log(n))$. The FFT's efficiency comes from its divide-and-conquer approach, and the reason we can use it to calculate autocorrelation is due to the convolution theorem – if you're interested, you can read more about that in "Filtering and Convolution," Chapter 8 in Allen Downey's excellent *Think DSP* [2].

The exact details of implementing the FFT are beyond the scope of this chapter (one could write a whole separate chapter[3] on the FFT alone!) – suffice to say, there's a wide range of FFT implementations available for you to choose from. Some popular C/C++ libraries include FFTW (Fastest Fourier Transform in the West) [3], Intel MKL (Math Kernel Library) [4], and PFFFT (Pretty Fast FFT) [5]. For simplicity, we'll use Jonathan Dupuy's dj_fft [6] library, which is header-only and public domain. Since our data is one-dimensional, we can adapt the `dj::fft1d()` function, modifying it to operate on `std::vectors` that we pass in by reference (instead of re-allocating and returning new vectors every time we perform an FFT). In our pitch tracker, we'll call that function to compute the FFT:

```
// ----------------------------------------------------------------
// dj_fft.h

// ...

namespace dj {

// ...
```

```
// Overloaded version of fft1d() that takes in both an input vector
// (xi) and an output vector (xo), modifying the output vector
// directly instead of allocating additional memory for a return
// vector.
template <typename T> void fft1d(const fft_arg<T>& xi,
                                 fft_arg<T>& xo,
                                 const fft_dir& dir);

// ...

}

// ------------------------------------------------------------------
// GapTunerAnalysis.h

// ...

#include <complex>
#include "dj_fft/dj_fft.h"

namespace GapTunerAnalysis
{

  // ...

  // Calculate the FFT (forwards or backwards) given an input
  // sequence
  void CalculateFft(
    const std::vector<std::complex<double>>& InFftSequence,
    std::vector<std::complex<double>>& OutFftSequence,
    const dj::fft_dir InFftDirection);

}

// ------------------------------------------------------------------
// GapTunerAnalysis.cpp

// ...

namespace GapTunerAnalysis
{

  // ...
```

```
void CalculateFft(
  const std::vector<std::complex<double>>& InFftSequence,
  std::vector<std::complex<double>>& OutFftSequence,
  const dj::fft_dir InFftDirection)
{
  dj::fft1d(InFftSequence, OutFftSequence, InFftDirection);
}
}
```

To perform autocorrelation using the FFT, we apply the following procedure:

1. Fill the input array with the contents of the analysis window, then zero-pad it so that it's twice the window size.

2. Take the FFT of the zero-padded input.

3. Compute the squared magnitude of each coefficient in the FFT output to get the power spectral density.

4. Take the IFFT (inverse FFT) of the array of squared magnitudes.

5. Take the real part of each value in the IFFT output and divide it by the DC component (first element) – the result gives the correlation coefficient between –1 and 1.

And in code:

```
// ----------------------------------------------------------------
// GapTunerAnalysis.h

// ...

namespace GapTunerAnalysis
{

  // ...

  // Calculate autocorrelation using the FFT
  void CalculateAcf_Fft(
    const CircularAudioBuffer<float>& InAnalysisWindow,
    std::vector<std::complex<double>>& OutFftInput,
    std::vector<std::complex<double>>& OutFftOutput,
    std::vector<float>& OutAutocorrelations);
}
```

```cpp
// --------------------------------------------------------------------
// GapTunerAnalysis.cpp

// ...

namespace GapTunerAnalysis
{

  // ...

  void CalculateAcf_Fft(
    const CircularAudioBuffer<float>& InAnalysisWindow,
    std::vector<std::complex<double>>& OutFftInput,
    std::vector<std::complex<double>>& OutFftOutput,
    std::vector<float>& OutAutocorrelations)
  {
    // 1. Fill the input array with the contents of the analysis
    //    window, then zero-pad it so that it's twice the window size
    assert(
      InAnalysisWindow.GetCapacity() == OutAutocorrelations.size());

    const size_t AnalysisWindowSize = InAnalysisWindow.GetCapacity();

    const size_t FftWindowSize = AnalysisWindowSize * 2;

    for (uint32_t SampleIdx = 0;
         SampleIdx < FftWindowSize;
         ++SampleIdx)
    {
      if (SampleIdx < AnalysisWindowSize)
      {
        float SampleValue = 0;
        SampleValue = InAnalysisWindow.At(SampleIdx);
        OutFftInput[SampleIdx] = std::complex<double>(SampleValue);
      }
      else
      {
        OutFftInput[SampleIdx] = std::complex<double>(0.f);
      }
    }

    // 2. Take the FFT of the zero-padded input
    CalculateFft(OutFftInput,
                 OutFftOutput,
                 dj::fft_dir::DIR_FWD);
```

```
// 3. Compute the squared magnitude of each coefficient in the
//    FFT output, to get the power spectral density
for (uint32_t CoeffIdx = 0; CoeffIdx < FftWindowSize; ++CoeffIdx)
{
  const std::complex<double> Coefficient = OutFftOutput[CoeffIdx];
  const std::complex<double> Conjugate = std::conj(Coefficient);

  const std::complex<double> SquaredMagnitude =
    Coefficient * Conjugate;

  OutFftInput[CoeffIdx] = SquaredMagnitude;
}

// 4. Take the IFFT (inverse FFT) of the array of squared
//    magnitudes
CalculateFft(OutFftInput,
             OutFftOutput,
             dj::fft_dir::DIR_BWD);

// 5. Take the real part of each value in the IFFT output and
//    divide by the DC component (first element) -- the result
//    gives the correlation coefficient between -1 and 1
const auto IfftDcComponent =
  static_cast<float>(OutFftOutput[0].real());

for (uint32_t CoeffIdx = 0;
     CoeffIdx < AnalysisWindowSize;
     ++CoeffIdx)
{
  const auto CoefficientRealComponent =
    static_cast<float>(OutFftOutput[CoeffIdx].real());

  OutAutocorrelations[CoeffIdx] = CoefficientRealComponent /
                                  IfftDcComponent;

  }
 }
}
```

When we run our pitch tracker with this FFT-based approach, the output pitch parameter ends up looking identical to Figure 10.6, at a fraction of the CPU cost – thanks to the FFT, we're able to track pitches more efficiently without sacrificing accuracy at all!

10.3.2 Downsampling

Another way we can make our pitch tracker more efficient is by downsampling our analysis buffer. By decreasing the number of samples we operate on, we can further reduce our pitch tracker's computational load as well as its memory footprint.

To implement downsampling in our pitch tracker, we can add a downsampling factor parameter (accessible via `m_PluginParams->NonRTPC.DownsamplingFactor`) and divide our window size by this factor. Since this will affect the entirety of our analysis process, we'll have to make a few changes:

1. In `GapTunerFX::Init()`, we'll divide by the downsampling factor when setting our analysis window size.

2. In `GapTunerAnalysis::FillAnalysisWindow()`, we'll fill samples in accordance with the downsampling factor (e.g., for a downsampling factor of 4, only fill every 4th sample).

3. In `GapTunerFX::Execute()`, we'll also divide by the downsampling factor when setting `AnalysisSampleRate` (for when we convert the sample index to frequency).

By lowering our analysis sample rate, we also do end up lowering frequency resolution. However, with the addition of the parabolic interpolation we implemented in Section 10.2.3, we're generally able to downsample quite a bit while still retaining accuracy. For example, I tried running the pitch tracker with a downsampling factor of 8 (i.e., with an analysis sample rate of 6,000 Hz instead of 48,000 Hz), and the results look almost identical to Figure 10.6.

10.4 PUTTING IT ALL TOGETHER

For completeness, here are the full implementations of our `GapTuner` plugin's `Init()`, `Term()`, and `Execute()` methods (along with a `GetWindowSize()` helper method), taking into account all of the improvements we've made in this chapter:

```
// ------------------------------------------------------------------
// GapTunerFX.h

#pragma once

#include <complex>
#include <AK/SoundEngine/Common/IAkPlugin.h>
```

```cpp
#include "CircularAudioBuffer/CircularAudioBuffer.h"
#include "GapTunerFXParams.h"

class GapTunerFX : public AK::IAkInPlaceEffectPlugin
{

public:

    // Constructor
    GapTunerFX() = default;

    // Initialize plugin
    AKRESULT Init(AK::IAkPluginMemAlloc* InAllocator,
                  AK::IAkEffectPluginContext* InContext,
                  AK::IAkPluginParam* InParams,
                  AkAudioFormat& InFormat) override;

    // Terminate plugin
    AKRESULT Term(AK::IAkPluginMemAlloc* InAllocator) override;

    // Execute DSP for a block of audio
    void Execute(AkAudioBuffer* InOutBuffer) override;

private:

    // Get our actual window size, taking downsampling into account
    uint32_t GetWindowSize() const;

    // Wwise-plugin-specific members, set in Init()
    GapTunerFXParams* m_PluginParams { nullptr };
    AK::IAkPluginMemAlloc* m_PluginMemoryAllocator { nullptr };
    AK::IAkEffectPluginContext* m_PluginContext { nullptr };

    // Sample rate, also set in Init()
    uint32_t m_SampleRate { 48000 };

    // -------
    // Analysis members

    // Analysis window backed by circular buffer class
    CircularAudioBuffer<float> m_AnalysisWindow { };
```

```cpp
    // How many samples we've written to the analysis window so far
    uint32_t m_AnalysisWindowSamplesWritten { 0 };

    // Calculated autocorrelation coefficients
    std::vector<float> m_AutocorrelationCoefficients { };


    // Key maxima lags and correlations, for MPM-based peak-picking
    std::vector<float> m_KeyMaximaLags { };
    std::vector<float> m_KeyMaximaCorrelations { };

    std::vector<std::complex<double>> m_FftIn { };
    std::vector<std::complex<double>> m_FftOut { };
};


// ------------------------------------------------------------------
// GapTunerFX.cpp

#include "GapTunerFX.h"

#include <AK/AkWwiseSDKVersion.h>
#include "GapTunerAnalysis.h"
#include "../GapTunerConfig.h"

AKRESULT GapTunerFX::Init(AK::IAkPluginMemAlloc* InAllocator,
                          AK::IAkEffectPluginContext* InContext,
                          AK::IAkPluginParam* InParams,
                          AkAudioFormat& InFormat)
{
    // Set Wwise-plugin-specific members
    m_PluginParams = static_cast<GapTunerFXParams*>(InParams);
    m_PluginMemoryAllocator = InAllocator;
    m_PluginContext = InContext;

    // Keep track of sample rate
    m_SampleRate = static_cast<uint32_t>(InFormat.uSampleRate);

    // ----
    // Allocate memory for analysis window
    const uint32_t WindowSize = GetWindowSize();

    m_AutocorrelationCoefficients.resize(WindowSize);
```

```
  // The circular buffer sets its internal capacity to
  // InCapacity + 1; if we pass in WindowSize - 1, then
  // m_AnalysisWindow.GetCapacity() == WindowSize, which is
  // the result we want
  m_AnalysisWindow.SetCapacity(WindowSize - 1);

  // ----
  // Allocate memory for key maxima
  const uint32_t MaxNumKeyMaxima =
    m_PluginParams->NonRTPC.MaxNumKeyMaxima;

  m_KeyMaximaLags.resize(MaxNumKeyMaxima);
  m_KeyMaximaCorrelations.resize(MaxNumKeyMaxima);

  // ----
  // Allocate memory for FFT
  const uint32_t FftWindowSize = WindowSize * 2;

  m_FftIn.resize(FftWindowSize);
  m_FftOut.resize(FftWindowSize);

  return AK_Success;
}

AKRESULT GapTunerFX::Term(AK::IAkPluginMemAlloc* InAllocator)
{
  AK_PLUGIN_DELETE(InAllocator, this);
  return AK_Success;
}

void GapTunerFX::Execute(AkAudioBuffer* InOutBuffer)
{
  // ----
  // Fill analysis window
  const uint32_t WindowSize = GetWindowSize();
  const uint32_t DownsamplingFactor =
    m_PluginParams->NonRTPC.DownsamplingFactor;

  const uint32_t NumSamplesPushed =
    GapTunerAnalysis::FillAnalysisWindow(InOutBuffer,
                                         m_AnalysisWindow,
                                         DownsamplingFactor);

  m_AnalysisWindowSamplesWritten += NumSamplesPushed;
```

```
  // Skip analysis if we haven't yet filled a full window
  if (m_AnalysisWindowSamplesWritten < WindowSize)
  {
    return;
  }

  // ----
  // Perform analysis

GapTunerAnalysis::CalculateAcf_Fft(
    m_AnalysisWindow,
    m_FftIn,
    m_FftOut,
    m_AutocorrelationCoefficients);

  // ----
  // Peak picking
  const uint32_t MaxNumKeyMaxima =
    m_PluginParams->NonRTPC.MaxNumKeyMaxima;

  const uint32_t NumKeyMaxima =
    GapTunerAnalysis::FindKeyMaxima(
      m_KeyMaximaLags,
      m_KeyMaximaCorrelations,
      m_AutocorrelationCoefficients,
      MaxNumKeyMaxima);

  const float KeyMaximaThresholdMultiplier =
    m_PluginParams->NonRTPC.KeyMaximaThresholdMultiplier;

  const uint32_t BestMaximaLagIndex =
      GapTunerAnalysis::PickBestMaxima(
        m_KeyMaximaLags,
        m_KeyMaximaCorrelations,
        NumKeyMaxima,
        KeyMaximaThresholdMultiplier);

  // Best maxima lag and correlation
  const float BestMaximaLag =
    m_KeyMaximaLags[BestMaximaLagIndex];

  const float BestMaximaCorrelation =
    m_KeyMaximaCorrelations[BestMaximaLagIndex];
```

```
// ----
// Conversion
const uint32_t AnalysisSampleRate =
  m_SampleRate / m_PluginParams->NonRTPC.DownsamplingFactor;

const float BestMaximaFrequency =
    GapTunerAnalysis::ConvertSamplesToHz(BestMaximaLag,
                                         AnalysisSampleRate);


// ----
// Set output parameters

// Only set parameter if clarity exceeds threshold
const float ClarityThreshold =
  m_PluginParams->NonRTPC.ClarityThreshold;

bool bSetRtpc = BestMaximaCorrelation > ClarityThreshold;
if (bSetRtpc)
{
  AkRtpcID OutputPitchParamId =
    m_PluginParams->NonRTPC.OutputPitchParameterId;

  AkRtpcValue OutputPitchParamValue = 0.f;

  // Set to best maxima frequency
  OutputPitchParamValue = BestMaximaFrequency;

  // Set RTPC
  AK::IAkGlobalPluginContext* GlobalContext =
    m_PluginContext->GlobalContext();

  AKRESULT Result =
    GlobalContext->SetRTPCValue(OutputPitchParamId,
                                OutputPitchParamValue);
}
}

uint32_t GapTunerFX::GetWindowSize() const
{
  return m_PluginParams->NonRTPC.WindowSize /
         m_PluginParams->NonRTPC.DownsamplingFactor;
}
```

10.5 OTHER METHODS

In this chapter, we've mostly been using direct autocorrelation and the MPM as our base algorithms, but there are plenty of other pitch detection methods worth trying as well. Other autocorrelation-based methods include YIN (named after the concept of yin and yang) [7], subband autocorrelation classification (SacC) [8], and probabilistic YIN (pYIN) [9].

There also exists a wide range of frequency-domain approaches, such as cepstrum pitch determination (CPD) [10], harmonic product spectrum (HPS) [11], maximum likelihood (ML) [12], and FFT phase changes [13]. Indeed, some methods such as YAAPT [14] combine both time-domain and frequency-domain approaches.

Finally, one of the most exciting developments in pitch tracking in recent years has been the onset of deep learning-based approaches such as CREPE [15] and SPICE [16], both of which have achieved state-of-the-art results, with pre-trained models made publicly available.

10.6 INTEGRATION INTO GAMEPLAY

Now that we have a more or less functional pitch tracker, let's zoom out a bit and think about how it might function in a game environment. An important note is that we're doing all this work in the context of an interactive experience – that is, the pitch tracker we've built doesn't exist in a vacuum. As such, we can leverage game-side information to our advantage and also can make some tweaks to accommodate common considerations that arise uniquely in a game setting.

10.6.1 Calibration

One game-side step that can help with the quality of analysis is calibration. This can take many forms, from having the player be silent for a period of time to having them input a specific note (or series of notes).

- Silence-based calibration can be used to establish a noise floor, which we can then filter out in the pitch estimation process – a simple approach is to run that same analysis on the noise floor and then subtract (or otherwise de-bias) our noise floor's correlation coefficients from our analysis results in the actual pitch estimation process. This noise floor can also help us determine a gain threshold below which we can choose not to perform our pitch estimation.

- Note-matching-based calibration can be used to help with octave errors, as we can adjust our key maxima threshold to adapt to the player's input during calibration (assuming the player is providing a pitch-matched signal in good faith). In fact, we could make use of the calibration step to tune other parameters such as the clarity threshold and potentially even choose entirely different pitch detection algorithms based on performance during calibration! That being said, we should take into account the dangers of overfitting when doing this kind of parameter tuning.

10.6.2 Smoothing the Output

One way to make pitch tracking feel smoother to the player is to apply some interpolation to the analysis results. As with many aspects of pitch estimation, there's a trade-off between smoothness and responsiveness at play – indeed, different game mechanics may make use of different interpolation settings. Getting this right is one of those areas where audio programming feels like it's as much of an art as it is a science.

For example, in *One Hand Clapping*, we use a relatively slow interpolation rate for sections where the player generates terrain based on the pitch of their singing, since we want the generated terrain to be smooth and traversable. Then, once the player reaches a call-and-response melody-matching section, we increase the speed of interpolation to allow the note-matching to feel snappy and responsive.

Since our pitch tracker is a Wwise plugin, we can pass in a smoothing rate and interpolation curve to our `SetRTPCValue()` call in `Execute()`. For a pitch tracker that *isn't* a Wwise plugin, any general interpolation implementation should do:

```
void GapTunerFX::Execute(AkAudioBuffer* InOutBuffer)
{
  // ...

  if (bSetRtpc)
  {
    // Set RTPC with interpolation
    AK::IAkGlobalPluginContext* GlobalContext =
      m_PluginContext->GlobalContext();

    const auto SmoothingCurve =
      static_cast<AkCurveInterpolation>(
        m_PluginParams->NonRTPC.SmoothingCurve);
```

```
const uint32_t SmoothingRateMs =
  m_PluginParams->NonRTPC.SmoothingRateMs;

AKRESULT Result =
  GlobalContext->SetRTPCValue(OutputPitchParamId,
                              OutputPitchParamValue,
                              AK_INVALID_GAME_OBJECT,
                              SmoothingRateMs,
                              SmoothingCurve,
                              false);
  }
}
```

10.6.3 Musical Information

Back in Section 10.3.2, we discussed downsampling in order to improve efficiency. We can further reduce our computational load by making use of musical information in a similar way.

For example, if our game is a karaoke game, and we know that the current song only contains notes in the C pentatonic scale, then we only really have to check the player's singing accuracy for the pitch classes $\{C, D, E, G, A\}$. We can then map those pitch classes, across octaves, to their closest corresponding lag values (along with adjacent lag values if we want to continue using parabolic interpolation) and only run our pitch detection algorithm on those lag values.

Similarly, we can use melodic range to determine upper and lower bounds for frequencies we want to consider – we can apply this strategy to a melody to be matched, as in the karaoke game example, or to the player's audio input itself, as part of the calibration process.

In addition to improving efficiency, we can also potentially improve the player experience by biasing our estimation results toward chord tones or target pitches – this can be seen as the pitch-tracking equivalent of "coyote time."[4]

10.6.4 Thread Considerations

In this chapter along with Chapter 9, we've been performing our pitch analysis directly on the audio thread, but it shouldn't be taken for granted that that's what we actually want to do. Where to perform the analysis depends in large part on your game's needs.

On the one hand, performing it on the audio thread gives us the most immediate results, ensuring accuracy on the block level. This also allows us to reliably do further sample-accurate processing based on the analysis results (as in the case of pitch correction) since we're already on the audio thread. Indeed, the current implementation of our pitch tracker as a plugin means that we can place it anywhere in our signal chain – for example, we might want to apply a compressor to the input, perform pitch estimation, and then add some distortion. Similarly, we can easily have multiple instances of the plugin running at once (e.g., if we have a local multiplayer game with several players singing into separate microphones).

On the other hand, performing our analysis on the game thread frees up audio thread resources that can then be devoted to actually generating or processing audio that the player can hear. With that in mind, if you know that you don't need sample-accurate pitch tracking to begin with, and a slower update rate is satisfactory for your use case, then the game thread or a worker thread may be the better place for you to do your analysis.

10.7 CONCLUSION

As with many such chapters, we've only really scratched the surface of pitch tracking – we haven't even touched on topics such as timbral features, noise cancellation, input monitoring, windowing functions, offline analysis, alternate correlation measures, managing audio input devices, multi-microphone setups, or voice-specific considerations.

That being said, it's pretty cool to see that by applying some DSP principles we can actually build a fully functional pitch tracker! Figure 10.8

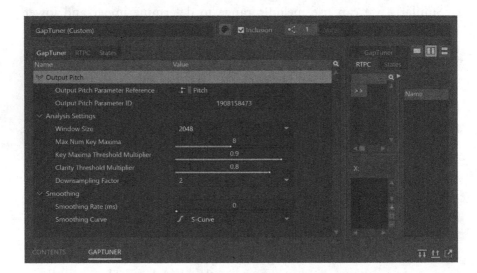

FIGURE 10.8   UI for the final version of our GapTuner Wwise plugin.

shows the final UI of our `GapTuner` plugin, encompassing all the parameters that we've covered. The complete source code for this plugin (which includes `GapTunerFX`, `GapTunerAnalysis`, and our modified implementations of `CircularAudioBuffer` and `dj::fft1d()`) can be found at https://github.com/usdivad/GapTuner.

My hope is that, along with Chapter 9, this chapter serves to whet your appetite for the world of pitch tracking and that it sparks your imagination with ideas for how real-time musical analysis might be applied in a game audio setting.

> Think of the sound of your own voice. What is its fundamental pitch? What is its range? What is its quality? What does it express no matter what you might be verbalizing or singing? What was the original sound of your voice before you learned to sound the way you sound now?
>
> PAULINE OLIVEROS, SONIC MEDITATIONS XX

NOTES

1 More specifically, the MPM uses the normalized square difference function (NSDF) as input to its peak-picking process – the NSDF, in turn, uses autocorrelation as one of its components. For our plugin, we'll stick with direct autocorrelation for simplicity.
2 Incidentally, this is why our definition of `ConvertSamplesToHz()` in Section 9.3.2 of this volume declares `InNumSamples` as a float rather than an int – this way, we can convert the "in-between" interpolated samples as well as the regular integer-indexed samples.
3 Probably even an entire book! – Ed.
4 "Coyote time" is a term that refers to old cartoons – in particular, the roadrunner and coyote cartoons – where a character (usually the coyote) hangs in the air before falling (usually only after looking down.) – Ed.

REFERENCES

[1] McLeod, P., & Wyvill, G. (2005, September). A smarter way to find pitch. In *Proceedings of the 2005 International Computer Music Conference*. https://www.cs.otago.ac.nz/students/postgrads/tartini/papers/A_Smarter_Way_to_Find_Pitch.pdf
[2] Downey, A. (2016). Filtering and convolution. In *Think DSP: Digital Signal Processing in Python* (pp. 89–100). O'Reilly Media. https://greenteapress.com/wp/think-dsp/
[3] Frigo, M., & Johnson, S. G. (2005). FFTW: Fastest Fourier transform in the West [Computer software]. https://www.fftw.org/

[4] FFT functions (2022). In *Developer Reference for Intel® oneAPI Math Kernel Library - C*. Intel. https://www.intel.com/content/www/us/en/develop/documentation/onemkl-developer-reference-c/top/fourier-transform-functions/fft-functions.html

[5] Pommier, J. (2022). PFFFT: Pretty fast FFT [Computer software]. https://bitbucket.org/jpommier/pffft/

[6] Dupuy, J. (2019). dj_fft: Header-only FFT library [Computer software]. https://github.com/jdupuy/dj_fft

[7] De Cheveigné, A., & Kawahara, H. (2002). YIN, a fundamental frequency estimator for speech and music. In *The Journal of the Acoustical Society of America*, *111*(4), 1917–1930. https://asa.scitation.org/doi/abs/10.1121/1.1458024

[8] Lee, B. S. (2012). *Noise robust pitch tracking by subband autocorrelation classification*. Columbia University. https://academiccommons.columbia.edu/doi/10.7916/D8BV7PS0/download

[9] Mauch, M., & Dixon, S. (2014, May). pYIN: A fundamental frequency estimator using probabilistic threshold distributions. In *2014 IEEE International Conference on Acoustics, Speech and Signal Processing (ICASSP)* (pp. 659–663). IEEE. https://ieeexplore.ieee.org/abstract/document/6853678/

[10] Noll, A. M. (1967). Cepstrum pitch determination. In *The Journal of the Acoustical Society of America*, *41*(2), 293–309. https://asa.scitation.org/doi/abs/10.1121/1.1910339

[11] Schroeder, M. R. (1968). Period histogram and product spectrum: New methods for fundamental-frequency measurement. In *The Journal of the Acoustical Society of America*, *43*(4), 829–834. https://asa.scitation.org/doi/abs/10.1121/1.1910902

[12] Wise, J. C. J. D., Caprio, J., & Parks, T. (1976). Maximum likelihood pitch estimation. In *IEEE Transactions on Acoustics, Speech, and Signal Processing*, *24*(5), 418–423. https://ieeexplore.ieee.org/abstract/document/1162852/

[13] Brown, J. C., & Puckette, M. S. (1993). A high resolution fundamental frequency determination based on phase changes of the Fourier transform. In *The Journal of the Acoustical Society of America*, *94*(2), 662–667. https://asa.scitation.org/doi/abs/10.1121/1.406883

[14] Zahorian, S. A., & Hu, H. (2008). A spectral/temporal method for robust fundamental frequency tracking. In *The Journal of the Acoustical Society of America*, *123*(6), 4559–4571. https://asa.scitation.org/doi/abs/10.1121/1.2916590

[15] Kim, J. W., Salamon, J., Li, P., & Bello, J. P. (2018, April). CREPE: A convolutional representation for pitch estimation. In *2018 IEEE International Conference on Acoustics, Speech and Signal Processing (ICASSP)* (pp. 161–165). IEEE. https://ieeexplore.ieee.org/abstract/document/8461329

[16] Gfeller, B., Frank, C., Roblek, D., Sharifi, M., Tagliasacchi, M., & Velimirović, M. (2020). SPICE: Self-supervised pitch estimation. In *IEEE/ACM Transactions on Audio, Speech, and Language Processing*, *28*, 1118–1128. https://ieeexplore.ieee.org/abstract/document/9043478

CHAPTER 11

Flexible Delay Lines

Practical Methods for Varying Sample-Rate Delays During Playback

Robert Bantin

11.1 INTRODUCTION

What is a delay line? Whenever a digital audio system transmits an audio signal from one point in a mix graph to another, irrespective of whether it transmits a single sample frame or a collection of frames in a buffer, that transmission usually represents what is "now" in the timeline. If, for any reason, you require a transmission that represents "the past" in the timeline, whatever signal data that represents "now" for that transmission needs to be stored somewhere so that when it is later retrieved, it is "the past" in relative terms. Since mix graphs are continuous data carrying systems, this store-for-later mechanism also needs to be built as a continuous data carrying system for the sake of compatibility. Put simply, then, a delay line is a store-for-later mechanism that's compatible with digital audio signal data being carried through a mix graph.

What is the use of an audio signal from the past? When we begin to visualize how sound propagates through volumes of air while bouncing off reflective surfaces, it becomes apparent that the direct-line-of-sight signal coming from a sound source to the player's listener position (i.e., "now") would only represent a portion of the total audible sound field of that source in a real-world scenario. The rest is from echoes of "the

DOI: 10.1201/9781003330936-13

past": copies of the same source arriving at us later – albeit colored or even mangled by their journey. When you break down what a reverberation effect is really doing, it's lots of delayed versions of the source colored/mangled and so on as they make their journey through the reverb algorithm.

Even in a simple scenario – let's say an infinitely large wall in a desert – the sound you make as the player would be expected to bounce back at you if you were aiming to simulate some basic acoustic effect. So, the ability to delay copies of a sound source is essential as it can help us create a more "living" acoustic environment. If you already know how memory buffers can be used to delay sample-rate data, you are already in a good position to implement something like the infinitely large wall scenario. There is just one aspect of it that makes things difficult: as soon as the player listener and/or the sound source move to a new position, the required delay time will also change. You will want to be able to handle this without loud artefacts, and so the notion of a flexible delay line that can delay signals transparently is a powerful concept that can be used in lots of different situations.

11.2 THE ANATOMY OF A FLEXIBLE DELAY LINE

A delay line is simply a buffer of sample frames that can be written to and read from with some degree of separation. You could, for instance, alternate the write point between the front and the middle of the buffer while making the simultaneous read point the opposite positions in the buffer. This would make the delay time half the length of the buffer. But this scheme is not flexible enough. What we want is a way to change the degree of separation as we write and read each sample frame.

Consider instead a buffer that can be written to and read from in a circular manner so that the "write" and "read" positions wrap around the buffer's address range and can "chase" each other forever. Figure 11.1 shows an example of this type of circular read/write buffer with 16 sample frames of storage.

An efficient way of implementing this is to allocate a buffer that is 2^N sample frames long. If you do this, determining when the write and read positions need to wrap around can be achieved very cheaply with some non-conditional logic known as a bitmask.

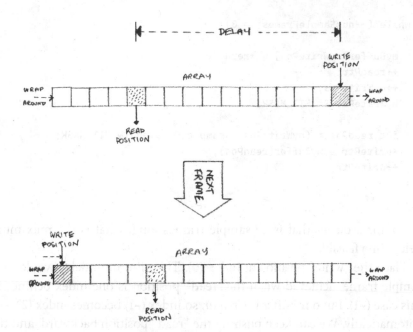

FIGURE 11.1   A circular read/write buffer with 16 sample frames of storage.

```
#define MAX_BUFFER_LEN (131072) // Must be 2^N value for mask to work
#define BIT_MASK (MAX_BUFFER_LEN - 1)

class FlexibleDelayLine
{
public:
  void Process(float* anIObuffer, int numSampleFrames);

private:
  float myCurrentDelayTime;
  int   myWritePos;
  float myBuffer[MAX_BUFFER_LEN];
  float myFloatSamplerate;
};

void FlexibleDelayLine::Process(
  float* anIObuffer, int numSampleFrames)
{
  float* readPtr = anIObuffer;
  float* writePtr = anIObuffer;
  int samplesDelayed =
    static_cast<int>(myCurrentDelayTime * myFloatSamplerate);
```

```
while (--numSampleFrames >= 0)
{
  myBuffer[myWritePos] = *readPtr;
  ++readPtr;
  ++myWritePos;
  myWritePos &= BIT_MASK;

  int readPos = (myWritePos - samplesDelayed) & BIT_MASK;
  *writePtr = myBuffer[readPos];
  ++writePtr;
}
}
```

So, for a buffer that is 2^N sample frames long, what is the maximum delay time feasible?

Place the "write" position at index (0). The minimum delay would be 1 sample frame, achieved when the "read" position is one index behind, in this case (–1). But our buffer is *circular,* so index (–1) becomes index (2^N – 1) automatically. We can keep pushing the "read" position backward, and the delay time gets longer as we do. However, we can't allow the "read" index to collide with the "write" index, so the last feasible index would be index (1). If you count that index and the remaining ones until we get back to the write position, the maximum delay possible is then 2^N – 1 sample frames.

11.3 SOME USEFUL ALLOCATION SIZES

At a sample rate of 48,000 Hz, 1 second of delay = 48,000 sample frames. Since we need to use 2^N for the bitmask, the next position allocation size is 65,536 sample frames, giving us approximately 1.36 seconds of max delay time. In an open world game based on realism, transit distances can be in the range of 900 m (450 m there-and-back). If the speed of sound in air is 343 ms⁻¹, 900/343 = 2.62 seconds. At 48,000 Hz sample rate that is 125,947 sample frames. The next 2^N allocation size is 131,072 sample frames, or 2.73 seconds max delay time. Consider your memory allocation strategy wisely or suffer fragmentation!

11.4 DEALING WITH DISTANCE, MOVEMENT, AND DOPPLER

11.4.1 Distance

A fixed propagation distance $D_{propagation}$ will yield the following delay time in sample frames N_{frames}:

$$N_{frames} = \frac{f_s \cdot D_{propagation}}{c_{air}}$$

where f_s is the sample rate and c_{air} is the speed of sound in air. As an example, a 10 m propagation distance should be about 1,399 sample frames, when f_s is 48,000 Hz and c_{air} is 343 ms⁻¹. Since f_s will be constant, and v_{air} can be assumed constant, this gives us a tidy scale factor of $\frac{f_s}{v_{air}}$ for a samples-per-meter coefficient that we can initialize at a convenient time, leaving us with a simple multiply to scale d with to give us a delay of $T_{seconds}$ (which converts to T_{frames} or "samples delayed" when the moment is right).

```
static const float ourSpeedOfSound = (343.0f);
static const float ourDefaultDelayTime = (0.1f); // E.g. 100ms

class FlexibleDelayLine
{
public:
  void Initialize(int aSamplerate);
  void SetDelayFromDistance(float aDistance);
  void Process(float* anIObuffer, int numSampleFrames);

private:
  float myCurrentDelayTime;
  int   myWritePos;
  float myBuffer[MAX_BUFFER_LEN];
  float myFloatSamplerate;
  float mySamplesPerMetre;
};

void FlexibleDelayLine::Initialize(int aSamplerate)
{
  myCurrentDelayTime = ourDefaultDelayTime;
  myFloatSamplerate = static_cast<float>(aSamplerate);
  mySamplesPerMetre = myFloatSamplerate / ourSpeedOfSound;

  // reset write position
  myWritePos = 0;

  // clear out buffer prior to use
  memset(myBuffer, 0, sizeof(myBuffer[0]) * MAX_BUFFER_LEN);
}

void FlexibleDelayLine::SetDelayFromDistance(const float aDistance)
{
  myCurrentDelayTime = mySamplesPerMetre * aDistance;
}
```

11.4.2 Movement

This is a little trickier, but not by much. Irrespective of how you decide to track movement in your game, you must ultimately determine a current distance and a new distance and then calculate the gradient between the two over the time it takes to make that transition. When you write your DSP code, it should be working in even sized buffers, and so as your flexible delay line is being read out, the read position can be modulated across the length of the buffer using a sample-normalized version of that gradient. Remember, we already know what that sample-normalized formula looks like: it's the same as the one for distance above scaled for the number of sample frames in the buffer.

```cpp
class FlexibleDelayLine
{
public:
  void Initialize(int aSamplerate);
  void SetDelayFromDistance(float aDistance);
  void Process(float* anIObuffer, int numSampleFrames);

private:
  float myCurrentDelayTime;
  float myLastDelayTime;
  int   myWritePos;
  float myBuffer[MAX_BUFFER_LEN];
  float myFloatSamplerate;
  float mySamplesPerMetre;
};

void FlexibleDelayLine::Initialize(int aSamplerate)
{
  myCurrentDelayTime = ourDefaultDelayTime;
  myLastDelayTime    = ourDefaultDelayTime;
  myFloatSamplerate  = static_cast<float>(aSamplerate);
  mySamplesPerMetre  = myFloatSamplerate / ourSpeedOfSound;

  // reset write position
  myWritePos = 0;

  // clear out buffer prior to use
  memset(myBuffer, 0, sizeof(myBuffer[0]) * MAX_BUFFER_LEN);
}
```

```cpp
// Assumed to be called ONLY ONCE between Process() calls
void FlexibleDelayLine::SetDelayFromDistance(const float aDistance)
{
  myLastDelayTime = myCurrentDelayTime;
  myCurrentDelayTime = mySamplesPerMetre * aDistance;
}

void FlexibleDelayLine::Process(
  float* anIObuffer, int numSampleFrames)
{
  float timeGradient =
    (myCurrentDelayTime - myLastDelayTime) /
      static_cast<float>(numSampleFrames);
  float currDelayTime = myLastDelayTime;

  float* readPtr = anIObuffer;
  float* writePtr = anIObuffer;

  while (--numSampleFrames >= 0)
  {
    myBuffer[myWritePos] = *readPtr;
    ++readPtr;
    ++myWritePos;
    myWritePos &= BIT_MASK;

    int samplesDelayed =
      static_cast<int>(currDelayTime * myFloatSamplerate);
    currDelayTime += timeGradient;

    int readPos = (myWritePos - samplesDelayed) & BIT_MASK;
    *writePtr = myBuffer[readPos];
    ++writePtr;
  }
}
```

The key here is to accept that you cannot create delay times of less than one sample frame using this technique, so just quantize the delay times at the start and end of the buffer. The only moment you need to worry about sub-sample delays is when calculating all the other delay times in between, because the sample-normalized gradient will usually produce fractional values. Rounding off every one of those in-between delay times will give you noticeable quantization artefacts. You will need to do some interpolation, and there is a plethora of techniques that could work for you.

11.4.2.1 Linear Interpolation

Perhaps the most obvious approach is to perform a weighted average of the two adjacent sample values in the delay line based on the desired fractional delay point in between.

```
float FlexibleDelayLine::Interpolate(
  const float inputA, const float inputB, const float ratio)
{
  return inputA * (1.0f - ratio) + inputB * ratio;
}

void FlexibleDelayLine::Process(
  float* anIObuffer, int numSampleFrames)
{
  float timeGradient =
    (myCurrentDelayTime - myLastDelayTime) /
      static_cast<float>(numSampleFrames);
  float currDelayTime = myLastDelayTime;

  float* readPtr = anIObuffer;
  float* writePtr = anIObuffer;

  while (--numSampleFrames >= 0)
  {
    myBuffer[myWritePos] = *readPtr;
    ++readPtr;
    ++myWritePos;
    myWritePos &= BIT_MASK;

    float samplesDelayed = currDelayTime * myFloatSamplerate;
    int wholeSampleDelay = static_cast<int>(samplesDelayed);
    float subSampleDelay =
      samplesDelayed - static_cast<float>(wholeSampleDelay);

    currDelayTime += timeGradient;

    int readPosA = (myWritePos - samplesDelayed) & BIT_MASK;
    int readPosB = (myWritePos - samplesDelayed - 1) & BIT_MASK;
```

```
    float valueA = myBuffer[readPosA];
    float valueB = myBuffer[readPosB];

    *writePtr = Interpolate(valueA, valueB, subSampleDelay);
    ++writePtr;
  }
}
```

Linear interpolation is cheap for computations and memory but struggles to get good results when the samples in the delay line are noisy, and pure noise becomes roughly 3 dB quieter than it's supposed to be. The issue is caused by non-deterministic signal values falling in on themselves when they are combined in this way.

11.4.2.2 Power Complimentary Interpolation

Similar to linear interpolation, except that the weights are determined by the Hanning window:

$$w(n) = sin^2\left(\frac{\pi n}{N}\right)\{0 \leq n \leq N\}$$

You can pre-calculate these values in a table, so the execution cost is more or less the same as linear interpolation. Then you implement the same process as linear interpolation but base the weights on the table values rather than overlapping right-hand triangles.

```
// Must be 2^N value
static const int ourStaticInterpolationDepth = 256;
static const float ourPi = 3.141592654f;

class PowercomplimentaryInterpolator
{
public:
  PowercomplimentaryInterpolator()
    : myTableData()
    , myTableLength(ourStaticInterpolationDepth)
    , myTableScale(static_cast<float>(myTableLength - 1))
  {
    float nIdx = 0.0f;

    // modified to give 0..1 range in 2*myTableLength points
    float oneOverTwoNminusOne =
      1.0f / static_cast<float>((myTableLength - 1) << 1);
```

```
    for (int i = 0; i < myTableLength; ++i)
    {
      float val;
      val = std::sin(nIdx * ourPi * oneOverTwoNminusOne);

      ++nIdx;

      myTableData[i] = val * val;
    }
  }

  // Use this method instead of FlexibleDelayLine::Interpolate()
  float Process(
    const float inputA, const float inputB, const float ratio)
  {
    int index =
      (static_cast<int>(ratio * myTableScale)) & (myTableLength - 1);
    float ampA = 1.0f - myTableData[index];
    float ampB = myTableData[index];

    return (inputA * ampA) + (inputB * ampB);
  }

private:
  float myTableData[ourStaticInterpolationDepth];
  int   myTableLength;
  float myTableScale;
};
```

The advantage it has over the linear approach is that it's better at dealing with noisy sample values in the delay line.

11.4.2.3 Polynomial Interpolation

This is a technique that gives slightly better results for deterministic signals such as tones and about the same results as power complimentary interpolation of noisy sample values. The order of the polynomial will determine how good its predictions are and, of course, you'll need to constantly update a collection of values from the delay line to update the prediction. See Ref. [1] for more information.

11.4.2.4 Oversampling

If you up-sample the input signal (e.g., 4×, 8×, 16×) and then store those values in a delay line extended in length by the same scale factor, you can pick the oversampled values in between the base-rate sample values. The higher the oversampling factor, the less quantization artefacts you will introduce.

This oversampling technique does, however, mean that your delay line will allocate much more memory, and it doesn't come cheap either. This technique is usually implemented by inserting the input buffer into a new (larger) buffer at the new sample rate with zeros padded in between the input sample values and then performing a low-pass filter over the new buffer with the cut-off frequency set just below the Nyquist limit of the original sample rate. Sinc function-based interpolation can work well enough for that, but also consider a poly-phase FIR approach that avoids performing multiplies on the zero pad values [2].

11.4.2.5 A Hybrid Solution

You could also create a hybrid solution that interpolates between the oversampled values, possibly making a better trade-off in quality versus performance than by simply doing one or the other.

11.4.3 Doppler

Dealing with movement correctly will force you to build a system that resamples the signal captured in the delay line because the effect of modulating the delay time is to compress and expand time. If things are running well, you should get Doppler for free.

11.5 TYPICAL USE CASES

Let's explore two scenarios that warrant flexible delay lines in order to simulate first-order reflections (i.e., the first bounces of a source).

11.5.1 Scenario A: A Data-Driven Vehicle Game

Consider a map or level where we can place spline curves in order to mark up areas of acoustic reflectivity. This only works in the azimuth plane, and the reflection management system must query the existence of any nearby splines and get the distances to them from a select sound emitter attached to the vehicle that we want the reflection effect to apply to. Let's say it's the engine/motor emitter because it's the loudest on this vehicle. The vehicle can't leave a predefined area (the racetrack), so we don't need to worry about getting behind these splines. Figure 11.2 shows an example plan view of a vehicle between the edges of a racetrack with splines marked out, engine/motor emitter, and reflection points.

Getting the shortest distance to the spline should be computationally cheap, in which case we won't take care of the angle of incidence from the reflective surface. So, this is a quasi-2D reflection system living in the azimuth plane of a 3D world. However, the effect will be absolutely worth the trouble once it's fully implemented, as the player will hear themselves driving through tunnels and under bridges. The delay time from the sides of the car to these reflective surfaces will be based on twice the distance from the sound emitter to the spline (the sound must propagate there-and-back), and the delay effect needs to flip the phase of the delayed signal so that it interferes with the outgoing sound in a similar way to real life. This is a huge simplification, but since we're not going to model acoustic absorption, we may as well assume that all these reflective surfaces are made of flat concrete and then our simplification here holds up.

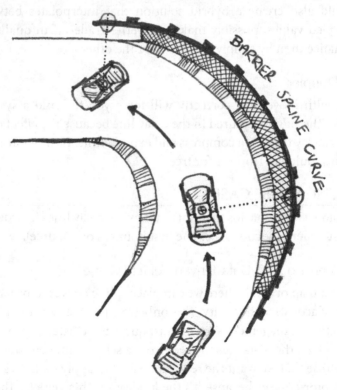

FIGURE 11.2 A vehicle between edges of a racetrack with splines marked out, engine/motor emitter, and reflection points.

Attenuation due to distance also needs to be observed, though, which is why it's convenient to place the reflected sound emitters at that double distance-to-the-spline length away from the engine/motor sound emitter so that your game's spatialization system takes care of the loudness of these reflected sounds automatically. The angle won't be quite correct because we're not observing the angle of incidence, but it won't be far off. In fact, human spatial localization of sound is less accurate at those hard-left and hard-right positions, so let's not worry about it.

11.5.2 Scenario B: A Procedural Walking Simulator

In this scenario, we have no specially prepared data (other than collidable surfaces), so we will use test ray-casts outward from the player's position, derive reflection points from the results, place reflection emitters at those points, and pipe any sound the player makes through those emitters (or as much as we see fit – gunshots, footsteps, VO, etc.). Figure 11.3 shows an example plan view of a human player character walking through a maze.

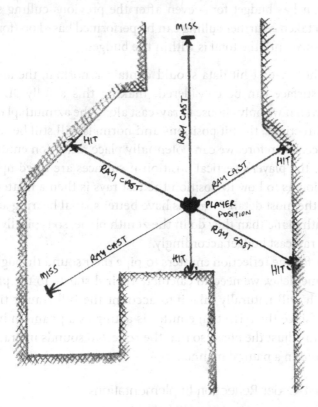

FIGURE 11.3   A player character walking through a maze.

With any procedural system for emitter placement, some criteria need to be met to make sure we don't propagate any weird results. These misreads need to be culled. The typical reasons for culling are:

1. When the system re-raycasts directly to a candidate position as a sanity check, it gets a wildly different result from the original test ray-cast. Clearly, the test ray hit a surface that didn't continue to the spot where the actual reflection would occur from.

2. Some candidate positions are so close that they "flam" or interfere with one another, so we consider them near-duplicates and cull all but one of them.

3. Perhaps we need lots of test ray-casts to get good coverage, but we don't necessarily want all of them to resolve to reflection points as this might sound too chaotic. We could then consider having more test ray-casts than our desired reflection budget would want to handle. If our implementation manages to collect more reflection points than it has budget for – even after the previous culling steps have been taken – further culling can be performed based on (for example) distance until the total is within the budget.

Since the ray-cast hit data should contain a normal, the angle of the reflected surface can be considered, making this a fully 3D system if desired. Even if we only choose to ray-cast along the azimuth plane instead of in all directions, the hit positions and normals will still be represented in 3D space. Therefore, we can potentially place reflection emitters below and above the player's vertical position if surfaces are tilted up or down. The decision as to how to position the test rays is then a matter of where you want the most detail. Humans have better spatial hearing accuracy in the azimuth plane than they do in the zenith plane, so typically we would focus our ray-cast budget accordingly.

Finally, for the reflection emitters to pipe their sound through with the correct time delay, we need to calculate their distance to the player position, which will naturally take into account the full transit time there-and-back (since the reflection emitter is acting as a phantom image). We just need to adjust the phase so that the reflected sounds interact with the direct sound in a natural manner.

11.5.3 First-Order Reflection Implementations

In either scenario, each reflection point found in your ray-casting system will require its own delay line, so they really need to be budget-controlled in some kind of pool. Pooling the delay lines will limit the total memory usage and allocations, and allow the delay lines to be reused frequently without any setup cost.

11.5.3.1 Budgets

In the examples from the previous sections, Scenario A will require two delay lines, and Scenario B will require six delay lines. For each delay line, the total memory they will need to allocate must be greater than or equal to the maximum transit time possible.

Since we know:

$$T_{max} = \frac{D_{max}}{c_{air}}$$

and, typically, f_s = 48,000, if D_{max} = 50 m, multiplying by f_s gives us N_{frames} = 5,418.

Single precision floating point samples will be 4 bytes per sample, and N_{frames} will be 21,670.4 bytes large. Since we need a 2^N length for the bitmask, we need to round up to the next 2^N size, which is 65,536 bytes (or 64 kB). Working that back to a new transit distance gives us d_{max} = 151.2 m. This is the worst-case scenario for a ray-cast hit on an orthogonal surface, so the max ray-casting distance from the origin should be $\frac{D_{max}}{2}$ = 75.6 m.

11.5.3.2 Tips for Scenario A

The spline system should give us the nearest 3D position to it from our point of origin (if there is one in range), but usually without any solid information from which to infer an angle. Instead, we might consider creating a reflection point by doubling the distance along the direction from the origin position to the spline position. This direction vector is obtained by subtracting the spline vector from the origin vector.

$$d = p_{spline} - p_{source}$$

If we add this direction vector to the source vector twice (i.e., doubling the distance), we get a reflection point that is as close to a mirrored phantom position as we can get with the information we have.

$$p_{reflection} = p_{source} + 2d$$

The actual distance is also critical as we will use this with the flexible delay line to create the propagation delay. We can obtain that from either square rooting the sum of squares of the direction vector d we initially got and then multiplying the value by two:

$$D_{propagation} = 2\left(\sqrt[2]{d_x^2 + d_y^2 + d_z^2}\right)$$

or creating a new direction vector by subtracting the candidate reflection vector from the origin vector and then square rooting the sum of squares of that.

$$d' = p_{reflection} - p_{source}$$

$$D_{propagation} = \sqrt[2]{d_x'^2 + d_y'^2 + d_z'^2}$$

We are now ready to place a 3D sound emitter at the reflection point, pipe any sound playing at the origin through that emitter with the prescribed delay taken from the distance, and attenuate it according to that distance. Upon successive game frame updates, we will want to re-query the spline curve, and if we get a new spline point, we can move the reflection point to a new candidate position and recalculate the distance to the origin. The prescribed delay time and attenuation to the distance at that reflection point emitter can then be updated. If the origin position goes out of range to get a new spline position, fade out the sound at the last reflection point quickly and then cull it.

11.5.3.3 Tips for Scenario B

This scenario gets a bit more interesting as you will be able to use mirroring similar to optics. At its core, you get full 3D placement of reflection points from whatever surfaces you ray-cast into, but if you want to clamp them to the azimuth plane, it's a rather small tweak after the fact.

Let's first state some basic ray-cast requirements:

1. A ray-cast must be described as a straight line between two points in 3D cartesian space.

2. It must be configurable what a ray-cast can and can't hit in your game world. For example:

   a. Brick walls – yes.

   b. Hard terrain – yes.

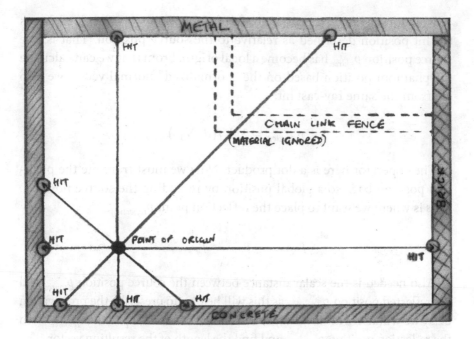

FIGURE 11.4 Rays being cast to hit various surfaces, with a hit mask ignoring certain collisions.

   c. Chain link fences – no.

   d. NPCs and remote players – no.

  3. When a ray-cast gets a hit, the hit information includes a surface normal.

Figure 11.4 shows a plan view of ray-cast with appropriate hit mask. You can also extend this if you want to include physics/collision materials in the hit data or if you want to apply some material-based EQ to the delay lines for added realism. With these three requirements in place, the mathematics for determining the phantom image position from a ray-cast hit is reasonably straightforward.

Let's declare a ray-cast starting a 3D vector p_{source} that extends out to 3D vector $p_{destination}$. If the ray-cast hits a collidable mesh, we will also get p_{hit}. First, take the ray-cast hit position p_{hit} and subtract the source position p_{source}.

$$d = p_{hit} - p_{source}$$

Now we get the direction vector (d) from p_{source} to p_{hit}. Think of this as the hit position described as relative to the source position. That is, the source position p_{source} has become a local origin. From that we can calculate the phantom position based on the "normalized" normal vector we also got from the same ray-cast hit.

$$p_{phantom} = 2N_{hit}\left(d \cdot N_{hit}\right)$$

The $\cdot$ operator here is a dot product. Now we must translate the phantom position back to a global position by re-adding the source position. This is where we want to place the reflection point $p_{reflection}$.

$$p_{reflection} = p_{source} + p_{phantom}$$

Also needed is the scalar distance between the source position p_{source} and the reflected position $p_{reflection}$, as this will help us to prescribe the propagation delay we will use with the delay line. Subtract the source position p_{source} from the reflection position $p_{reflection}$ and find the length of the resulting vector.

$$d' = p_{reflection} - p_{source}$$

$$D_{propagation} = \sqrt[2]{d_x'^2 + d_y'^2 + d_z'^2}$$

The propagation time is therefore the propagation distance divided by the speed of sound in air.

$$T_{propagation} = \frac{D_{propagation}}{c_{air}}$$

And as previously stated in this chapter, multiplying $T_{propagation}$ by f_s gives us the exact number of sample frames to use in the delay line, N_{frames}. Each time the system tests for reflection points, it should ray-cast in enough directions to potentially use all six delay lines stated in the scenario. Figure 11.5 shows the plan view of a human player character walking through a maze with the six ray-casts, normals, and derived reflection points.

Quite often this approach will yield duplicate reflection points, such as when two ray-casts hit the same wall panel. An important step in the

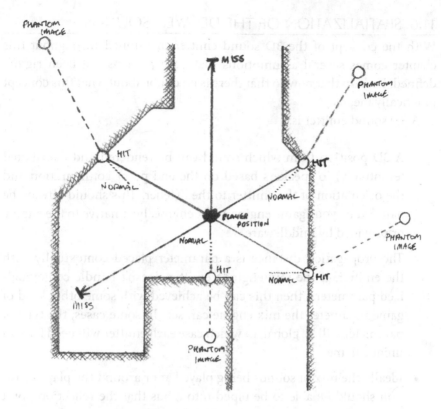

FIGURE 11.5 A player character walking through a maze with six ray-casts, normals, and derived reflection points.

system's processing should be to detect this using proximity testing and cull all but one of the overlapping positions (including those found in previous passes that are still valid).

Another issue is that the system will detect false positives in places where a surface does not continue to the orthogonal position that the phantom position technique assumes, such as when there's an open doorway in the direction that sound is supposed to be reflecting from. In this case, the system can perform a "sanity check" on all the newly found reflection points by directly ray-casting to these new positions and seeing if it gets the same (or similar enough) results. If a proposed new reflection point is wildly different from the position it gets when the ray-cast is applied directly, the sanity check should fail, and this new reflection point culled.

11.6 SPATIALIZATION OF THE DELAYED SOUNDS

With the concept of the 3D sound emitter mentioned throughout this chapter comes several assumptions that have perhaps not been rigidly defined. Let's do that now so that there is no doubt about what this concept practically means.

A 3D sound emitter is:

- A 3D position from which sound can be rendered and distributed (eventually) to speakers based on the end point configuration and the orientation of the emitter to the listener. This should already be handled by your game engine's mix engine, be it native to the engine or provided by middleware.

- The propagation distance is a parameter placed contextually with the emitter. If the mix engine's emitter doesn't handle contextualized parameters, then this can be achieved with some other kind of game parameter the mix engine can see. In some cases, the type of parameter will be global, in which case each emitter will need its own unique name.

- Ideally the mix of sounds being played at or around the player position should be able to be piped into a bus that the reflection point emitters can play out independently with their own delay time applied. If this is not possible, a similar effect can be approximated by playing the same assets through those emitters with their own delay time applied. You can essentially "fake" the propagation of sound at the expense of extra playback voices.

With those technical points met one way or the other, the system should be fairly robust in both channel-based and object-based approaches since the flexible delay lines are doing the bulk of the work. When we talk about the mix engine's ability to surround-pan these 3D emitters as they play out, all they need to do is work out the speaker distribution. In the case of object-panning, the same applies except that the speaker distribution is deferred to later in the pipeline.

However, what you also gain from accurate propagation delays between the emitters is something called interaural time difference or ITD [3]. When spatialization only deals with level difference (as per the norm), the primary spatial hearing mechanism is interaural level difference, or ILD [4]. In humans, this effect can be properly detected only in mid-to-high frequencies [5], meaning the sounds being spatialized by this technique must have mid-to-high frequency content in them for a human to hear the effect. By contrast, humans hear ITD in the low mid frequencies [6] when the sounds arrive at the listener several hundred microseconds (or less) apart. Outside of that they are heard as several distinct sounds – what we normally refer to as "echoes." In the scenarios described in this chapter, it is perfectly possible to support both ITD and normal echoes since it is just a question of delay time. So, by incorporating both level and time difference techniques in spatializing these reflected sounds, you are creating a fuller, more "spatial" image for these reflected sounds than was otherwise possible. This might be something to consider outside of simulating reflections since direct sounds can also benefit from ITD when being spatialized. Figure 11.6 shows just such a time-difference stereo setup. There are a few more parameters to consider in the player's speaker setup [7], but they can be configured by the player during onboarding.

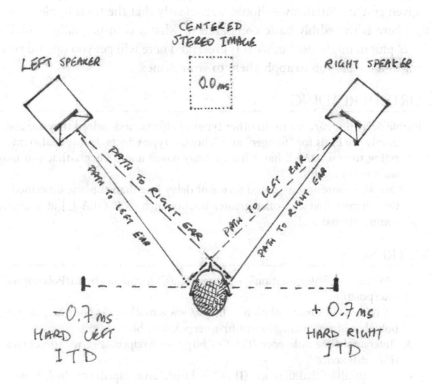

FIGURE 11.6   ITD-based stereo setup.

11.7 CONCLUSIONS

From a very simple concept of delaying sound in a flexible yet reasonably transparent way, we can build some very rich and complex effects. The two scenarios described in this chapter are useful for basic early reflections:

1. A data-driven vehicle game where reflective surfaces are defined by specialized data, such as walls by the side of a road or racetrack.

2. A procedural walking simulator, where any collidable surface such as a wall can be a reflective surface.

Flexible delay lines are broadly useful in plenty of other scenarios, too. For example, they can allow the designer to delve into ITD spatialization, even when just spatializing direct sounds.

Special consideration should be made for memory allocation, since realistic acoustic propagation may require several seconds of delay. Therefore, achievable budgets will inform how many reflections can be supported by a given system. Finally, we should state clearly that the final implementation here is incredibly basic compared to what a commercially available DAW plugin might do, but what is presented here will get you up and running and enable you to apply them to your games.

FURTHER READING

Flexible delay lines are useful in other types of effects, and indeed they are commonly the basis for "flanger" and "chorus" type effects. If this is also interesting to you, DAFX has a list of delay-based audio effects that you may want to try out [8].

There are also more sophisticated forms of delay line than the one described in this chapter that can offer greater fidelity such as PSOLA [9] at a higher computational cost.

REFERENCES

1. "Polynomial interpolation" – https://en.wikipedia.org/wiki/Polynomial_interpolation
2. "Polyphase FIR interpolation" – https://www.mathworks.com/help/dsp/ug/polyphase-implementation-of-fir-interpolation-block.html
3. "Interaural time difference (ITD)" – https://en.wikipedia.org/wiki/Interaural_time_difference
4. "Interaural level difference (ILD)" – https://en.wikipedia.org/wiki/Sound_localization

5. "ILD frequency range" – https://pressbooks.umn.edu/sensationandperception/chapter/interaural-level-difference-draft/
6. "ITD frequency range" – https://www.ncbi.nlm.nih.gov/pmc/articles/PMC6561774/
7. "Time difference stereo" – https://www.dpamicrophones.com/mic-university/stereo-recording-techniques-and-setups
8. "Delay-based audio effects" – p. 75, DAFX (2nd edition), Udo Zölzer, Wiley
9. "Pitch-synchronous overlap and add (PSOLA)" – p. 194, DAFX (2nd edition), Udo Zölzer, Wiley

CHAPTER 12

Thread-Safe Command Buffer

Guy Somberg

12.1 INTRODUCTION

Audio engines are distinctive (although not unique) in their hard real-time requirements. There are parts of our codebases where we cannot perform any operations that can block or perform any sort of kernel system call. Most often, the code that has these requirements lives in the mixer thread – we must perform all of our calculations and completely fill our buffer within a very small number of milliseconds. Failure to do so results in a buffer underrun and an unpleasant pop for the player.

Much of the code that has these strict requirements is already written for us in our audio middleware,[1] so – while we cannot waste cycles willy-nilly – the vast majority of our code is free to follow the normal rules of programming. Every once in a while, though, we are faced with a need to interact directly with the mixer thread. Maybe we're manipulating the DSP graph, or offloading some calculation onto the mixer thread, or we're writing a fancy modern multi-threaded audio engine and the mixer thread is the lowest latency solution for what the "audio thread" should be. In these situations, we are faced with a need to send commands to another thread in a fully lock-free fashion.

Enter a data structure that I call the Thread-Safe Command Buffer or the Atomic-Powered Triple Buffer.[2]

12.2 SENDING DATA TO ANOTHER THREAD

Let's say that I have some data – say, a list of commands – that I would like to send to a worker thread in a lock-free manner. I want to fill the list with

DOI: 10.1201/9781003330936-14

commands, then send them to the worker thread in a batch. The worker thread reads the messages and does its work, then comes back for more. Because we need these operations to be lock-free, we must use operations on `std::atomic` types.

> Atomics are the razor blades of programming: they are the right tool for a certain type of job, but you must handle them with care or you will cut yourself badly. I believe that the code presented in this chapter is correct and bug-free, but you should not just take my word for it.[3] If you use the code here, I encourage you to take time to read it, understand it, and convince yourself of its correctness.[4]

12.2.1 First Attempt: Single Buffer + Atomic Bool

We can use an algorithm like this to make it work:

```
class Buffer
{
public:
  std::vector<Command>* GetSendBuffer()
  {
    if (CommandExchange)
      return nullptr;
    return &Commands;
  }
  const std::vector<Command>* GetReceiveBuffer() const
  {
    if (CommandExchange)
      return &Commands;
    return nullptr;
  }
  void Send()
  {
    CommandExchange = true;
  }
  void CommandsProcessed()
  {
    CommandExchange = false;
  }

private:
  std::vector<Command> Commands;
  std::atomic<bool> CommandExchange = false;
};
```

This data structure will work, and it does solve the problem[5]: lock-free exchange of data. However, it has one fundamental problem that will end up causing all sorts of trouble: the sender cannot write a new buffer of messages while the receiver is still processing messages.

It is highly unlikely that the two threads are operating in lockstep. One or the other will arrive first, and if it is the wrong one, then you can end up in a situation where you're missing updates and adding latency to your messages.

12.2.2 Second Attempt: Double Buffer

Let's try adding another buffer and see how it changes things.

```cpp
class Buffer
{
public:
  std::vector<Command>& GetSendBuffer()
  {
    if (CommandExchange)
      return Commands[0];
    return Commands[1];
  }
  const std::vector<Command>& GetReceiveBuffer() const
  {
    if (CommandExchange)
      return Commands[1];
    return Commands[0];
  }
  bool Send()
  {
    if (ReceiverWorking)
      return false;
    CommandExchange = !CommandExchange;
    ReceiverWorking = true;
  }
  void CommandsProcessed()
  {
    ReceiverWorking = false;
  }

private:
  std::array<std::vector<Command>, 2> Commands;
  std::atomic<bool> CommandExchange = false;
  std::atomic<bool> ReceiverWorking = false;
};
```

This is better! We can now read and write at the same time, at the cost of an extra **bool** and a second **vector** of commands. But we have a problem with threads that are not running in sync, similar to the single-buffer approach: after we have sent the buffer to the other thread, we cannot write again to the send buffer until the worker thread has finished processing its buffer. This will be a problem if the worker thread is taking a long time and the sender thread wants to send more messages.

What we need is a solution that will always allow the sender to write to a buffer and the receiver to read from a buffer.

12.3 THE TRIPLE BUFFER

With one buffer, the sender can't write to the buffer while the worker is processing. With two buffers, the sender can write to a buffer while the receiver is reading, but then has to wait if the receiver is not yet ready. Let's try a triple buffer and see if that gets us what we want.

12.3.1 Buffer Exchange

The buffer management turns out to be more complex with three buffers than with two. In order to make it comprehensible, we'll give the buffers names: *Sender, Receiver*, and *Exchange*, which we will abbreviate as S, R, and X, respectively. In addition, we'll introduce two new variables: the *Expected Exchange Value for Send* and *Expected Exchange Value for Receive*, which will be abbreviated as ES and ER, respectively. ES and ER are the value that X must have in order to be able to send or receive. (We will see how these values are applied later.)

It doesn't matter what default values we select for any of these parameters, so long as they are consistent. We'll pick S = 0, X = 1, and R = 2. But what values do we use for ES and ER? In our default state, we expect to be able to send, but not to receive, and the receiver will get the sender's current value when it does send. This gives us ES = 1 and ER = 0.

12.3.2 Algorithm Walkthrough

Before we start writing a bunch of code, let's go through one send/receive cycle and see what it looks like.[6] We start with the values as described in Section 12.3.1 – our initial state, as shown in Table 12.1.

TABLE 12.1   The Initial State of the Buffer Values

S	X	R	ES	ER
0	1	2	1	0

TABLE 12.2   The State of the Buffer Values
after a Send Operation

S	X	R	ES	ER
1	0	2	2	0

In this initial state, the sending thread can write freely to `Buffers[0]` and the receiving thread can read freely from `Buffers[2]`. `Buffers[1]` is unused in this initial state. In order to be able to send, X (current value: 1) must be equal to ES (current value: 1), which means that we *can* send. And, in order to be able to receive, X (current value: 1) must be equal to ER (current value: 0), which means that we *cannot* receive.

At some point, the sender has filled its buffer and does a send. We perform a send by swapping the values of S and X. We also need to update the value of ES with the current value of R – currently 2. Those operations will leave us with the values given in Table 12.2.

After the send operation, the sending thread can write freely to `Buffers[1]` and the receiving thread can read freely from `Buffers[2]`. `Buffers[0]` contains the messages that the sender wrote and is ready to be read by the receiver. In order to be able to send, X (current value: 0) must be equal to ES (current value: 2), which means that we *cannot* send. And, in order to be able to receive, X (current value: 0) must be equal to ER (current value: 0), which means that we *can* receive.

Finally, the receiver thread has finished its processing and does a receive operation, which is performed similarly to the send. We swap the values of R and X, then update ER to the current value of S. After that, we end up with the values given in Table 12.3.

After the receive operation, the sending thread can write freely to `Buffers[1]` and the receiving thread can read freely from `Buffers[0]`. `Buffers[2]` is unused – after the first send/receive pair, it will contain the messages that the receiver has just finished processing (although in this first send/receive pairing, it will be empty). In order to be able to send, X (current value: 2) must be equal to ES (current value: 2), which means that we *can* send. And, in order to be able to receive, X (current value: 2) must be equal to ER (current value: 1), which means that we *cannot* receive.

TABLE 12.3   The State of the Buffer Values after a Receive

S	X	R	ES	ER
1	2	0	2	1

Having gone through one send/receive cycle, we are now back where we started, except with the values shuffled around from where they were.

12.3.3 The Code (Version 1)

We have our algorithm, but how do we implement the code? Importantly, how do we make sure that this whole operation happens in a lock-free fashion?

Before we get to the atomic core of this structure, let's take a look at the interface first.

```
class Buffer {
public:
  std::vector<Command>& GetSendBuffer() {
    return Buffers[Sender];
  }
  std::vector<Command>& GetReceiveBuffer() {
    return Buffers[Receiver];
  }

  const std::vector<Command>& GetSendBuffer() const {
    return Buffers[Sender];
  }
  const std::vector<Command>& GetReceiveBuffer() const {
    return Buffers[Receiver];
  }

  void Send();
  bool Receive();

private:
  bool DoCompareExchange(uint8_t& Expected, uint8_t& Current);

  std::array<std::vector<Command>, 3> Buffers;
  uint8_t Sender = 0;
  uint8_t Receiver = 2;
  std::atomic<uint8_t> Exchange = 1;
  uint8_t ExpectedExchangeValueForSend = 1;
  uint8_t ExpectedExchangeValueForReceive = 0;
};
```

We've got **const** and mutable accessors for the send and receive buffers, a **Send()** function, and a **Receive()** function. We've also declared a private helper function that will do the heavy lifting. The implementations of `Send()` and `Receive()` are straightforward and relegate the interesting work to the helper function.

```
void Buffer::Send() {
  if (GetSendBuffer().empty())
    return;

  if (DoCompareExchange(ExpectedBufferForSender, Sender)) {
    // We must re-read the send buffer because the exchange
    // operation has switched which buffer is which.
    GetSendBuffer().clear();
  }
}


bool Buffer::Receive() {
  return DoCompareExchange(ExpectedBufferForReceiver, Receiver);
}
```

Both of these operations do the same thing with different parameters, but `Send()` has some convenience functions to skip the send if the buffer is empty and to clear the buffer after a successful send. So far, we haven't done any real work. Let's see how our `DoCompareExchange()` helper function – the workhorse of this implementation – works.

```
bool Buffer::DoCompareExchange(
  uint8_t& ExpectedBuffer, uint8_t& Current) {
  // Take a copy of ExpectedBuffer so that it doesn't get overwritten
  uint8_t ActualBufferValue = ExpectedBuffer;

  // Swap the Current and Exchange values if the Exchange value
  // matches the Expected value.
  if (Exchange.compare_exchange_strong(ActualBufferValue, Current)) {
    // Update the expected buffer
    ExpectedBuffer = 3 - ExpectedBuffer - Current;
    // Update the current value
    Current = ActualBufferValue;
    return true;
  }

  return false;
}
```

The fundamental operation that we are using here is a conditional exchange. That is, *if* the value of X is equal to ES, *then* we exchange the values when sending, and the same when receiving with X and ER. It turns out that this operation is baked into the atomic library as a pair of member functions: `std::atomic<T>::compare_exchange_weak()` and `::compare_exchange_strong()`. The difference between these is that `compare_exchange_weak()` is allowed to have spurious failures (that is, the exchange can fail if the two values are not equal) whereas `compare_exchange_strong()` is not. In general, the guidance is to use `compare_exchange_weak()` if you're retrying in a loop and `compare_exchange_strong()` if you're just doing it once. Regardless, ignoring the spurious failures, the algorithm encoded by these functions is the atomic equivalent of this:

```
// Note: This is pseudocode only!  All of this happens atomically -
// often in a single CPU instruction.
bool atomic<T>::compare_exchange_strong(T& Expected, const T Desired)
{
  if (this->value == Expected) {
    this->value = Desired;
    return true;
  } else {
    Expected = this->value;
    return false;
  }
}
```

This is it! The entire class occupies less than 60 lines of code. In this book, we have the luxury of writing the commentary independently of the code. In shipping code, we really ought to have about a 4 to 1 ratio of comments to actual code, since this is conceptually complex code, even if the implementation is short.

12.4 IMPROVEMENTS

Code similar to Section 12.3 was used to ship Torchlight 3 – it's real stuff! But we can do better. Let's run through our algorithm a few times and examine the values of our buffer indices in Table 12.4.

12.4.1 Removing ES and ER

Our first optimization is to eliminate the values of ES and ER from the table entirely. It turns out that both of these values can be calculated trivially from their respective Send/Receive values.

$$ES = (S+1) \% 3$$
$$ER = (R+1) \% 3$$

TABLE 12.4 Several Iterations of the Send/Receive

Op	S	X	R	ES	ER
Initial	0	1	2	1	0
Send	1	0	2	2	0
Receive	1	2	0	2	1
Send	2	1	0	0	1
Receive	2	0	1	0	2
Send	0	2	1	1	2
Receive	0	1	2	1	0

It's important that ES is calculated only from S and not from R or X (and the same for ER and R). Other than during the moment of exchange, the sender should only be reading the S value and the receiver should only be reading the R value. If we don't obey this rule, then we'll have a data race and undefined behavior. Applying these formulas will simplify the code: we no longer need to store variables for these values or pass them around, and the DoCompareExchange() function will become a bit simpler.

We won't be showing that code because it turns out that we can do much better.

12.4.2 Removing S, X, and R

Let's take another look at our indices from Table 12.4, but with the ES and ER values removed, which we will put into Table 12.5.

The observation that we can make here is that values in the last row of Table 12.5 are exactly the same as the values in the first row, which means that we have a cycle. If we have a cycle, then we can divine the values for

TABLE 12.5 The Same Data from Table 12.4, but with ES and ER Removed

Op	S	X	R
Initial	0	1	2
Send	1	0	2
Receive	1	2	0
Send	2	1	0
Receive	2	0	1
Send	0	2	1
Receive	0	1	2

TABLE 12.6   Row Indices and Send/Receive Added to the Data from Table 12.5

Op	Index	Can Send	Can Receive	S	X	R
Initial	0	☑	✕	0	1	2
Send	1	✕	☑	1	0	2
Receive	2	☑	✕	1	2	0
Send	3	✕	☑	2	1	0
Receive	4	☑	✕	2	0	1
Send	5	✕	☑	0	2	1
Receive	0	☑	✕	0	1	2

the entire table given just the index of the table row, and this is the fundamental premise of our next iteration. Let's add the index and an indicator of whether we can send or receive in Table 12.6.

If we are going to divine the contents of the table from the index, then we need formulas for several things:

- **Can Send** and **Can Receive** – These are easy: we can use the parity of the index.

$$Can\ Send = (Index\ \%\ 2) == 0$$
$$Can\ Receive = (Index\ \%\ 2) == 1$$

- **S, X**, and **R** – These formulas are more complicated, but not too bad.

$$S = \frac{Index + 1}{2}\ \%\ 3$$
$$R = \frac{Index + 4}{2}\ \%\ 3$$
$$X = (7 - Index)\ \%\ 3$$

It turns out that we never actually need the value of X, so while it is interesting that we have a formula to calculate its value, it's not something that we'll be using. With the formulas for S and R, we now have a choice: we can either encode these formulas in our class or just store the values in a lookup table. In practice, this is the difference between an add, a divide, and a modulo[7] versus 12 bytes of static memory. We'll start with the lookup table version for simplicity, but see Section 12.7 for a more in-depth discussion on the subject.

12.4.3 The Code (Version 2)

Let's jump right into the code:

```cpp
class Buffer {
public:
  std::vector<Command>& GetSendBuffer() {
    return CommandBuffers[GetSenderIndex()];
  }
  std::vector<Command>& GetReceiveBuffer() {
    return CommandBuffers[GetReceiverIndex()];
  }

  const std::vector<Command>& GetSendBuffer() const {
    return CommandBuffers[GetSenderIndex()];
  }
  const std::vector<Command>& GetReceiveBuffer() const {
    return CommandBuffers[GetReceiverIndex()];
  }

  bool Send();
  bool Receive();

private:
  enum class Operation : uint8_t {
    Send = 0,
    Receive = 1,
  };
  uint8_t GetSenderIndex() const;
  uint8_t GetReceiverIndex() const;
  static constexpr bool CanDoOperation(
    Operation DesiredOperation, uint8_t CurrentState);
  bool TryIncrementState(Operation DesiredOperation);

  std::array<std::vector<Command>, 3> CommandBuffers;
  std::atomic<uint8_t> State = 0;
  static constexpr inline uint8_t NumStates = 6;
  static constexpr inline
    std::array<uint8_t, NumStates> SendBufferIndexes =
      { 0, 1, 1, 2, 2, 0 };
  static constexpr inline
    std::array<uint8_t, NumStates> ReceiveBufferIndexes =
      { 2, 2, 0, 0, 1, 1 };
};
```

The interface is more or less the same, although the details are quite different. The implementation of the index functions is simply an array lookup:

```cpp
uint8_t Buffer::GetSenderIndex() const {
  return SendBufferIndexes[State];
}

uint8_t Buffer::GetReceiverIndex() const {
  return ReceiveBufferIndexes[State];
}
```

It's worth noting that these functions are our first instance of atomic operations in this implementation. The State variable is of type std::atomic, which provides convenience accessors and conversions. However, if we want to be explicit to the readers of the code that these are atomic operations, then we can replace the references with calls to State.load().

All that's left now is the actual send and receive operations along with their implementation details. Because both send and receive follow exactly the same pattern, we have abstracted it into a single function.

```cpp
bool Buffer::Send() {
  if (GetSendBuffer().empty())
    return false;

  if (TryIncrementState(Operation::Send)) {
    GetSendBuffer().clear();
    return true;
  }
  return false;
}

bool Buffer::Receive() {
  return TryIncrementState(Operation::Receive);
}

bool Buffer::CanDoOperation(
  Operation DesiredOperation, uint8_t CurrentState) {
  return (CurrentState % 2) == static_cast<uint8_t>(DesiredOperation);
}
```

```
bool Buffer::TryIncrementState(Operation DesiredOperation) {
  uint8_t CurrentState = State;
  if (!CanDoOperation(DesiredOperation, CurrentState))
    return false;

  State = (CurrentState + 1) % NumStates;
  return true;
}
```

What I like about this implementation is that it is very straightforward. If we can do the operation, then we increment the index – and the only difference between the send and the receive is the parity that we are checking for. The atomic operations are sufficiently simple that we treat them basically like native integers: no compare-exchange, just loads and stores that are hidden behind operator overloads and implicit conversions. As before, if we want to be explicit, then we can call State.load() and State.store().

That's it! We've rearchitected our class, so we're done, right? Not quite yet.

12.5 FURTHER IMPROVEMENTS

There are three more improvements that we can make to this class: making it a template, splitting out the value implementation from the vector implementation, and applying atomic memory orders.

12.5.1 Making a Template

Rather than passing a single Command structure across, it would be useful to be able to specify the type of data that is being communicated. This change is fairly mechanical: any time that we have a Command, we replace it with T.

```
template<typename T>
class Buffer {
  std::vector<T>& GetSendBuffer() {
    return CommandValues[GetSenderIndex()];
  }
  std::vector<T>& GetReceiveBuffer() {
    return CommandValues[GetReceiverIndex()];
  }

  const std::vector<T>& GetSendBuffer() const {
    return CommandValues[GetSenderIndex()];
  }
```

```cpp
  const std::vector<T>& GetReceiveBuffer() const {
    return CommandValues[GetReceiverIndex()];
  }
  // ...
private:
  // ...
  std::array<std::vector<T>, 3> CommandValues;
  // ...
};
```

12.5.2 Splitting Value from Vector

While the most common use case of this class is a command buffer, there are certain situations where you may want to communicate a single value (or a structure) instead of a buffer of commands. One example would be listener data. While it is possible to encode changes to the listener in commands that are sent as part of the command buffer, it can be more ergonomic to use the structure containing listener data itself as a separate command channel.

The cost in implementation complexity is marginal, so even if there is not an immediate use case for a command value instead of a command buffer, it's an easy thing to add for future use. We will also take this opportunity to rename our class from **Buffer** to something more descriptive of its purpose. Here are the modifications that we will have to make to implement this change:

```cpp
template<typename T>
class ThreadSafeCommandValue
{
public:
  // Renaming these from Buffer to Value
  T& GetSendValue() {
    return CommandValues[GetSenderIndex()];
  }
  T& GetReceiveValue() {
    return CommandValues[GetReceiverIndex()];
  }

  const T& GetSendValue() const {
    return CommandValues[GetSenderIndex()];
  }
  const T& GetReceiveValue() const {
    return CommandValues[GetReceiverIndex()];
  }
```

```cpp
  // ...
  // Implementation of Send() is now simpler and mirrors Receive()
  bool Send() {
    return TryIncrementState(Operation::Send);
  }
  // ...
private:
  // ...
  std::array<T, 3> CommandValues;
  // ...
};

template<typename T>
class ThreadSafeCommandBuffer {
public:
  std::vector<T>& GetSendBuffer() {
    return Value.GetSendValue();
  }
  std::vector<T>& GetReceiveBuffer() {
    return Value.GetReceiveValue();
  }

  const std::vector<T>& GetSendBuffer() const {
    return Value.GetSendValue();
  }
  const std::vector<T>& GetReceiveBuffer() const {
    return Value.GetReceiveValue();
  }

  void Send() {
    if (GetSendBuffer().empty())
      return;

    if (Value.Send())
      GetSendBuffer().clear();
  }

  bool Receive() {
    return Value.Receive();
  }

private:
  ThreadSafeCommandValue<std::vector<T>> Value;
};
```

The only changes we had to make to our original class are renaming a few things, simplifying the implementation of Send(), and changing from an array of vectors to an array of values. The ThreadSafeCommandBuffer<T> class is mostly a wrapper for a ThreadSafeCommandValue<std::vector<T>>, with the vector clearing logic in Send() added back in.

12.5.3 Atomic Memory Orders

So far, the operations that we've been doing with atomics have been fairly straightforward: compare-exchange, which we then removed and replaced with some simple loads and stores. However, with these operations as-is, we are leaving some potential performance improvements on the table, which we can get back if we are willing to take the (metaphorical) safety rails off of our atomics.

> **Warning**: This is an extremely complex topic, and this chapter will only skim the very edges of the surface. I believe that my logic here is sound and that the changes that we will make in this section are valid. Nevertheless, this data structure will work *just fine* with the default sequential consistent memory order. Convince yourself that the changes are valid, but if you don't feel confident in their correctness, then leave them off when you apply this data structure in your own code. For further details, I recommend the talk "atomic<> Weapons: The C++ Memory Model and Modern Hardware" by Herb Sutter from the C++ and Beyond 2012 conference.[8]

By default, C++ atomics use a sequentially consistent memory order called std::memory_order_seq_cst. This means that memory fences are applied that will prevent certain kinds of reordering operations to move after a load or before a store and that all memory accesses will participate in a total order. However, we have more context for how these atomic values are used, so we can do better than the default.

12.5.3.1 Acquire/Release for Incrementing State

The first change is to explicitly request acquire and release semantics for the load and store in TryIncrementState(). Although the sequentially consistent default performs these same acquire/release operations as a part of its semantics, switching to explicit acquire/release means that we are explicitly *opting out* of the total order guarantee. This opt-out has subtle consequences, but ultimately the result is that the compiler has fewer constraints laid upon it and can therefore potentially generate more efficient assembly. Let's first take a look at the code, and then we'll examine the actual instructions to see what the compiler has done with the change.

```
template<typename T>
bool ThreadSafeCommandValue::TryIncrementState(
  Operation DesiredOperation) {
  uint8_t CurrentState = State.load(std::memory_order_acquire);
  if (!CanDoOperation(DesiredOperation, CurrentState))
    return false;

  State.store(
    (CurrentState + 1) % NumStates, std::memory_order_release);
  return true;
}
```

The only changes to this code from the previous version are that we call the load() and store() methods on the atomic state in order to be able to pass in the desired memory orders. This does make the code more complex in some ways, so let's take a look at what the compiler does with this. Of course, every compiler is different and will output different assembly for the same input. The instructions in Table 12.7 and the rest of the assembly code in this chapter were generated using msvc 19.35.32215[9] compiling for x64 in Release mode.[10]

The only difference between the two versions is the last line (marked with a triangle ⚠). The default memory order does an xchg instruction, whereas the acquire/release does a mov. The end result here is the same: memory

TABLE 12.7   Assembly Output of the **Receive()** Function in a Sample Program

Default Memory Order		Acquire/Release	
movzx	ecx,byte ptr [rbx+48h]	movzx	ecx,byte ptr [rbx+48h]
test	cl,1	test	cl,1
je	07FF61AED13A4h	je	07FF6157613A4h
inc	ecx	inc	ecx
mov	eax,0AAAAAAABh	mov	eax,0AAAAAAABh
mul	eax,ecx	mul	eax,ecx
shr	edx,2	shr	edx,2
lea	eax,[rdx+rdx*2]	lea	eax,[rdx+rdx*2]
add	eax,eax	add	eax,eax
sub	ecx,eax	sub	ecx,eax
xchg	cl,byte ptr [rbx+48h] ⚠	mov	byte ptr [rbx+48h],cl ⚠

address [rbx+48h] contains the value of the cl register. The difference is in the locking semantics: with xchg, the processor's locking protocol is automatically implemented for the duration of the exchange operation.[11] The mov instruction, therefore, is slightly cheaper since it does not engage this same lock.

Note that there is no difference between the two for the load operation. This means that we could move that one back to sequentially consistent, at least for this platform/compiler combination. However, it is odd to see a release without a matching acquire, so we will leave it with the acquire in place.

12.5.3.2 Relaxed Semantics for Reads

We've modified the state-increment function and gotten a small improvement. The other atomic operation is the load for the sender/receiver indices when calling GetSenderIndex() or GetReceiverIndex(). How can we reduce the restrictions on this value? It's a bare load, so there's no acquire/release pattern to buy into. We're not going to dive into consume semantics: down that way lies madness. The only other option is relaxed: can we use that?

It turns out that we can: there are no consequences for reordering above or below this function, and nothing that the other thread does could affect the index that we get from this function. We can change our functions thus:

```
template<typename T>
uint8_t ThreadSafeCommandValue::GetSenderIndex() const {
  return SendBufferIndexes[State.load(std::memory_order_relaxed)];
}

template<typename T>
uint8_t ThreadSafeCommandValue::GetReceiverIndex() const {
  return ReceiveBufferIndexes[State.load(std::memory_order_relaxed)];
}
```

This should be safe to do. Let's see if there is any benefit from the compiler. Table 12.8 is the output for one of these functions from the same compiler that was used to generate Table 12.7.

TABLE 12.8 Assembly Output of the GetSendValue() Function in a Sample Program

Default Memory Order		Relaxed	
movzx	eax,byte ptr [rcx+48h]	movzx	eax,byte ptr [rcx+48h]
lea	rdi,[__ImageBase]	lea	rdi,[__ImageBase]
movzx	eax,	movzx	eax,
	byte ptr [rax+rdi+3398h]		byte ptr [rax+rdi+3398h]
lea	rcx,[rax+rax*2]	lea	rcx,[rax+rax*2]

Both listings are identical, at least with this combination of compiler and platform. We saw this same lack of difference earlier with the load operation in the `Receive()` function. Therefore, this optimization is optional – it may generate different (potentially more efficient) code on a different platform, but at least for x64/MSVC, we can take it or leave it.

12.6 A NON-IMPROVEMENT

Let us imagine a situation in which the sender writes some commands to the buffer – say, a collection of "move this event instance to this world location" commands. The receiver thread is still either working or waiting and the sender is running at a particularly high framerate, so the receiver still hasn't gotten around to receiving its last batch of messages when the sender comes back around. Can we add an extra layer of optimization to this system by "un-sending" the last batch of messages and updating the values in place? That way when the receiver does come in, it only has to process each entry once. This will have the benefit of reducing latency as well since only the latest set of commands need to be handled. There are two questions here: *can* we do this operation, and *should* we do it?

The answer to the first question is, yes, we can do it. We can calculate or store what the old value that we sent previously would be and then do a compare-exchange operation to implement the un-sending. We then update the list of commands with updated values and then do a regular `Send()` to give it back to the receiver. Mechanically, it works!

However, we *should not* implement this operation. The reason is that it can result in a denial of service where the receiver thread *never* receives anything at all. Let's take a look at one potential set of timings in Table 12.9 to see why this is.

TABLE 12.9   Potential Timings for the Un-Sending Operation

Sender Thread	Receiver Thread
Send	Other processing/waiting
Un-send	Other processing/waiting
Write to send buffer	Receive (fails due to un-send)
Send	Other processing/waiting
Un-send	Other processing/waiting
Write to send buffer	Receive (fails due to un-send)
Send	Other processing/waiting
Un-send	Other processing/waiting
Write to send buffer	Receive (fails due to un-send)
Send	Other processing/waiting

In Table 12.9, we have a set of timings where the sender has found that the receiver hasn't yet received the last messages it sent, so it un-sends it, writes updated commands, and then re-sends. However, just after the sender thread un-sends, the receiver thread gets scheduled and tries to do a receive. The receive fails because the sender has just un-sent and so there is nothing waiting for it. Table 12.9 shows this continuing three times in a row, but if this timing continues, the receiver thread will *never* get any of the sender's messages!

12.7 ON LOOKUP TABLES VERSUS CALCULATIONS

In Section 12.4.2, we presented the formulas for calculating the sender and receiver indexes, but then opted to use the lookup tables instead. The lookup tables do, in fact, make the code terser, but are they actually better? I cannot answer with certainty, and I will admit to not having done measurements. On the one hand, there is less code with the lookup tables, which means that more fits into the instruction cache. On the other hand, the lookup tables are in static memory that is not likely to be in the data cache, which means a potentially costly data cache miss.

Let's take a look at the actual differences in the code and the generated assembly. First, our C++ version of the `GetSenderIndex()` and `GetReceiverIndex()` changes to look like this:

```
enum class IndexOffsetType : uint8_t {
  Sender = 1,
  Receiver = 4
};
uint8_t GetIndexFromState(IndexOffsetType Offset) const {
  auto CurrentState = State.load(std::memory_order_relaxed);
  return ((CurrentState + static_cast<uint8_t>(Offset)) / 2) % 3;
}


uint8_t GetSenderIndex() const {
  return GetIndexFromState(IndexOffsetType::Sender);
}


uint8_t GetReceiverIndex() const {
  return GetIndexFromState(IndexOffsetType::Receiver);
}
```

TABLE 12.10   Assembly Output of the **GetReceiverIndex()** Function in a Sample Program

Lookup Table		Formula	
movzx	eax,byte ptr [rbx+48h]	mov	eax,0AAAAAAABh
movzx	eax,	movzx	r8d,byte ptr [rbx+48h]
	byte ptr [rax+rdi+3390h]	add	r8d,4
lea	rcx,[rax+rax*2]	shr	r8d,1
		mul	eax,r8d
		shr	edx,1
		lea	eax,[rdx+rdx*2]
		sub	r8d,eax
		movzx	eax,r8b
		lea	rcx,[rax+rax*2]

The generated assembly is listed in Table 12.10 for both the lookup table version and the formula version of **GetReceiverIndex()**.

The lookup table is much shorter since we can just look up the answer directly. Contrariwise, the formula version – despite being six instructions longer – does not do anything more complex than a register-register multiply and may end up being faster due to the aforementioned data cache issue. My gut says that the formula version will be faster,[12] so we will use that one in the code listing in Section 12.8.

12.8 CODE LISTING

We've made a lot of changes to the code in a piecemeal fashion throughout this chapter. Let's get the complete final implementation in one place.

```
template<typename T>
class ThreadSafeCommandValue {
public:
  T& GetSendValue() {
    return CommandValues[GetSenderIndex()];
  }
  T& GetReceiveValue() {
    return CommandValues[GetReceiverIndex()];
  }

  const T& GetSendValue() const {
    return CommandValues[GetSenderIndex()];
  }
  const T& GetReceiveValue() const {
    return CommandValues[GetReceiverIndex()];
  }
```

```cpp
  bool Send() {
    return TryIncrementState(Operation::Send);
  }

  bool Receive() {
    return TryIncrementState(Operation::Receive);
  }

private:
  enum class Operation : uint8_t {
    Send = 0,
    Receive = 1,
  };

  bool TryIncrementState(Operation DesiredOperation) {
    auto CurrentState = State.load(std::memory_order_acquire);
    if (!CanDoOperation(DesiredOperation, CurrentState))
      return false;

    State.store(
      (CurrentState + 1) % NumStates, std::memory_order_release);
    return true;
  }

  enum class IndexOffsetType : uint8_t {
    Sender = 1,
    Receiver = 4
  };

  uint8_t GetIndexFromState(IndexOffsetType Offset) const {
    auto CurrentState = State.load(std::memory_order_relaxed);
    return ((CurrentState + static_cast<uint8_t>(Offset)) / 2) % 3;
  }

  uint8_t GetSenderIndex() const {
    return GetIndexFromState(IndexOffsetType::Sender);
  }

  uint8_t GetReceiverIndex() const {
    return GetIndexFromState(IndexOffsetType::Receiver);
  }

  static constexpr bool CanDoOperation(
    Operation DesiredOperation, uint8_t CurrentState) {
```

```cpp
      return
        (CurrentState % 2) == static_cast<uint8_t>(DesiredOperation);
  }

  std::array<T, 3> CommandValues;
  std::atomic<uint8_t> State = 0;
  static constexpr inline uint8_t NumStates = 6;
};

template<typename T>
class ThreadSafeCommandBuffer {
public:
  std::vector<T>& GetSendBuffer() {
    return Value.GetSendValue();
  }
  std::vector<T>& GetReceiveBuffer() {
    return Value.GetReceiveValue();
  }

  const std::vector<T>& GetSendBuffer() const {
    return Value.GetSendValue();
  }
  const std::vector<T>& GetReceiveBuffer() const {
    return Value.GetReceiveValue();
  }

  void Send() {
    if (GetSendBuffer().empty())
      return;

    if (Value.Send())
      GetSendBuffer().clear();
  }

  bool Receive() {
    return Value.Receive();
  }

private:
  ThreadSafeCommandValue<std::vector<T>> Value;
};
```

12.9 CONCLUSION

One common pattern for audio engines is to put the minimum possible onto the main thread and move much of the management and coordination of the audio engine to a worker thread – often the event thread, but sometimes the mixer thread. In either case, we need an efficient and performant solution, but particularly when interacting with the mixer thread, all communication must be fully lock-free. The Thread Safe Command Buffer implementation presented in this chapter is a great tool for these use cases.

NOTES

1 For those of us who use middleware, that is.
2 Sometimes we can get carried away with naming things. It is, after all, one of the two hardest problems in computer science.
3 I will admit that I have not tested or run the code for the single buffer and the double buffer – the code for those is mostly to demonstrate the short-comings of those strategies, rather than practical code that I'm encouraging people to use. Nevertheless, the code for those sections is as good as I can make it, and I do believe it to be correct. The code for the triple buffer has been thoroughly tested and shipped a real game.
4 This is especially true when it comes to the non-default memory ordering that will come later in the chapter.
5 The code for the single and double buffer solutions is purposefully incomplete – it shows just the exchange mechanism and is missing accessors, convenience functions, and other small details.
6 I hope that you will bear with me as we express very pedantically the operations allowed and repeat very similar patterns three times. It is important to understand these relationships, so a bit of pedantry will hopefully make them all very clear.
7 In practice, compilers are smarter than this and will transform the divide and modulo operations into cheaper instructions.
8 https://herbsutter.com/2013/02/11/atomic-weapons-the-c-memory-model-and-modern-hardware/ (The website contains links to videos of the two-part talk and the talk slides).
9 This corresponds to Visual Studio 2022 v17.5.1, which was the latest stable build as of this writing.
10 Release mode is what it's called in the Visual Studio IDE. The relevant command line options are /O2 /Oi.
11 https://www.felixcloutier.com/x86/xchg
12 If performance matters, of course, then the correct solution is to measure.

III

Tools

CHAPTER 13

Optimizing Audio Designer Workflows

Matias Lizana García

13.1 INTRODUCTION

Audio designers are the creative people behind audio in a game, and it is tempting to think that they spend all their time playing with DAWs, synthesizers, pedals, or doing weird recordings. But the truth is, as they become more technical, they are mostly dragged into the game engine, to set up audio components, systems, and pipelines in addition to bug fixing (maybe they forgot to load a bank or an audio event reference was suspiciously removed). Audio programmers help audio designers by providing them with the best possible pipelines and tools to work with, so here's where we ask ourselves: where do audio designers spend most of their time?

The motivation of this chapter is to take a trip into many aspects of the audio pipeline in a game and examine some of the issues we can face in big productions. We will discuss and define how we should improve all the processes and make them performant and easy to use in order to save as much time as possible for audio designers on their daily workflow.

13.2 ASKING THE RIGHT QUESTIONS

We are often so focused on production times and feature development that it is easy to forget about improving workflows or think of future incoming problems. We must keep a constant attitude of improving things and try to be proactive with the audio designers to see what they need. This is a section that is not strictly unique to audio and can be applied to all

DOI: 10.1201/9781003330936-16

departments in a game, but we will find some examples that make it more specific. Starting with an easy "Is there anything I can help you with?", we can formulate questions that can help improve any project.

13.2.1 Are You Spending a Long Time Setting Something Up?

Usually, a process that takes a long time (such as generating audio assets) is a red flag that something is not implemented properly, and it is also a black hole for productivity. One example can be voice pipelines, where we will be using database queries, downloading assets from a server, integrating them into the middleware, exporting to the engine, etc. Projects are dealing with so many audio assets for the voices that it could potentially take hours to populate new data into the game. Reducing the time or automating the process on how those assets are imported could have a strong impact on our daily workflow. Also, the amount of manual setup or clicking buttons to configure anything in the game is something that needs to be improved.

13.2.2 Are You Doing The Same Process Repeatedly?

There will always be some one-time tasks like setting up a game object or prefab that performs some specific feature, where the asset will probably not be touched again. More commonly, however, audio designers are repeatedly setting up assets using the same processes over and over. One example of this could be setting up interactable objects in a game by tagging the type of object to provide the sound needed when the player interacts with it. Do we really need to manually tag those objects if we have hundreds of them? Would it be better to use a naming convention to automatically tag them, or to create a tool that automatically tags the objects by some heuristic? Any process that repeats more than once needs to be evaluated and improved with a tool or automation.

13.2.3 Is That Issue Happening Again?

Frequently, the root cause of bugs is related to some reference that got lost, or someone changed the structure of a feature and didn't import the audio into the new setup. The most common audio issues involve investigating why sounds are not triggering: things like "footsteps are not playing again" or "this object does not make any sound when colliding." Even if we try to lock those features or make them robust to failure, there is always a chance that they can break due to game object setup and human error. If some feature repeatedly crashes or the same issue appears constantly, it is important to invest time in finding every small thing that can make it break and provide code checks or validation tools to address the issue.

13.3 TOOLS AND MORE TOOLS

If someone tells you in an audio programmer job interview that you are going to spend your time implementing cool DSP effects, they are probably misinformed. In truth, the majority of the work is helping audio designers to do their workflows easier, so it is likely that you are mainly going to spend your time working on tools and more tools.

In the project that I am currently working on, we developed most of the tools by finding a problem with how audio designers used the systems or seeing how much time they spend on a task. From there, we always ask ourselves if there should be a better and faster way for them to work. Here are some examples of tools that we have developed.

13.3.1 Debug Visuals

Visualizations can be as simple as drawing spheres, text, or icons on the screen. Everything that can be printed in the game world has the potential to improve workflow. One of the main visualizations for audio is showing a visualization of audio objects. It can be useful to print a small sphere to show the position of the audio object and change its color depending on if there is any audio playing on the object and showing the event name. We can place text showing the number of voices playing on the object, direction, and distance attenuation. Any object data we can show on the same game object as well, such as velocities, materials, or states, is extremely helpful as we can see the values in the game, and there is no need to manually search or debug.

13.3.2 Validators

We often have features that are applied to thousands of assets, such as collisions with objects or footsteps. Each object needs a proper setup, with some tag that defines the type or some other properties. It is important to have a tool that can validate all those assets and tell if they are set up properly, then generate a warning to spot the error and fix them manually, or even automating the process to fix the issues. These validation tools can run in daily smoke tests so we can get an output list of, for example, how many interactable objects are missing sound in today's build. Validators work particularly well with assets that need a fixed configuration so we can check the desired setup. If we know a character should contain different audio objects to play on each part of the body, we can validate those values with a tool to tell us if some character is missing the proper setup.

13.3.3 Configurations

There are many parameters that the audio designers can use to configure the audio engine. It's important to spend time organizing these settings and making them easy to configure. Even simple things like organizing the settings into categories can make a big difference in usability and discoverability. As new systems get built, expose their configuration parameters so that the audio designers can tweak to get exactly the sound they're looking for. A few examples of the sorts of settings that you might expose to your audio designers are:

- **Audio culling distance** – How far sounds are before they're culled by the game.

- **Debug tool visibility** – Which widgets and gizmos and other debug information are visible by default.

- **Importance setup** – Number of importance levels, effect configuration for each level, max objects at each level, etc.

13.3.4 Audio References

One of the most common issues in audio programming is knowing where a specific audio event is playing from or tracking down why it is not playing correctly. Even though we have profilers in our audio middleware, making tools to search for references inside the engine improves the workflow. A search tool can help find the name of an audio event that has been posted or the audio object it is being played from and make it highlight into the game view so we can easily find it in runtime. We can, for example, find an event called `Firearm_Shoot` when running the game and show in a tool a list of references to the weapons that are playing this event or even use gizmos and filters to highlight those in the same game scene.

13.3.5 Audio Gym

Testing and iterating are important for audio, and gyms are good for that. A gym is basically a game level that contains everything needed to test a feature. A good example is having a gym for footstep materials on player movement. We design a level with all the types of materials on the ground, and we can walk around trying and profiling sound on all different types of terrain. Another example is a gym for having every interactable object, to test grabbing, collisions, and throwing items around. This allows audio designers to go faster on trying every possible sound instead of trying to find them on different levels, with the time consumption attached to it (waiting for the level to load, finding the specific place where the feature needs to be tested, etc.). There can be gyms to test player actions, animations, music states, ambiences, and dialogs – basically any feature you need to test in the game.

13.3.6 Static Ambiences

Many games still rely on manual room setup for creating the ambiences. It can be a tedious job to set up rooms manually with portals attached to them to provide the needed behavior (including occlusion/propagation). There are a bunch of tools that can help, like showing a list of connections between rooms (to identify the sound paths and check if there is any bad setup), being able to search rooms or portals by name on the scene (to easily spot where those are placed as sometimes it can be many layers and many rooms in the same level), or validating if there is some missing portal to attach.

Painting tools can also be helpful to provide a way for designers to tag terrain and populate the level with the audio that will play as an ambience, for instance, having a "pencil" where you can choose the size and material to paint with, and the pencil will always be attached to the terrain surface when painting. Then, our ambience system will read from the terrain and the tagging we made, so it will be able to define the sound in each specific room. A painting tool can also help create rooms automatically using a bounding box of the area we painted. We can also have a tool where we click once inside a room and it reads the meshes around the point using raycasting, so we can check the area size and create a room automatically.

It should be possible to do much of the work of setting up and creating ambiences using room data from level design, with little to no manual setup. That level of automation should be the first goal to achieve on an ambience setup pipeline. Beyond the basics, the focus now is on creating ambience sounds in realtime using raytracing and GPU techniques to read from the actual level geometry and provide the room tones with the real mesh materials and occlusion/propagation setup. These techniques work mostly on games with a realistic aesthetic; games with a more cartoony or 2D vibe will likely need to use different techniques.

13.3.7 Animations

Marking up animations with sounds is one of the most manual parts of the audio designer's job. Frequently, this work ends up being largely placing footstep events on animations when a character's feet hit the ground or placing foley on the clothes when walking. It's all very tedious for the audio designers.

The baseline functionality for this tool is to show a timeline of events, and have the events trigger when the animation is previewed. For common sounds like footsteps, it's a good idea to set up a generic trigger with a data-driven setup. Allow the audio designers to define an event configured by some parameters such as clothes and velocity of the feet. We'll want to put all of this configuration onto the properties on the character itself so that we can read the properties in a systematic way. If there are multiple animations (such as walk, run, and jump) that all want to share the same event (like footsteps), we can create a template tool so that audio designers can just drag an existing template onto the data.

Finally, we can work with the technical artist to find a way to tag the animations in the 3D animation tool, which is then exported to the game. The tech artists and animators can create tools to tag the animations with the information that we need, which the game can import and use with no input from the audio designers.

For more about automated footstep setup, see Chapter 17 of this book – "Automatic Manual Foley and Footsteps" by Pablo Schwilden Diaz.

13.3.8 Cinematics

There is also a lot of work on setting up audio in timelines for cutscenes. Imagine we have a cinematic with multiple characters and they need to trigger foley and voice. We need to manually set up an event for each animation for the cinematic every time the characters trigger a sound or talk. Make sure that the audio designers can play cutscenes in the editor without playing the game, allowing them to scrub forward and backward on the timeline and adjust details as needed to fit the action. Rendering the audio waveform in the audio clips can help the audio designers to find where to place voice lines so that they line up with the action.

Recording and editing the sound foley and voice as an entire cinematic track can help sync the visual content into the whole audio track. If we need to post audio from different emitters, we just need to export any specific audio into a separate track – for instance, any character audio in different tracks each. If we place each audio track at the beginning of the cinematic for each of the characters, they will play together in sync, as if we recorded foley for a film. Sometimes we also rely on cinematic voice tracks coming from a motion capture session, so they will fit perfectly into the action.

Even the simple act of assigning each audio track to each cinematic can be improved and automated by using naming conventions. By naming cinematics and audio tracks with the same prefixes, we can make a tool that automatically populates audio on every cinematic in-game by adding audio tracks matching the name prefix.

13.3.9 Design Graphs

Graph- or node-based programming is a useful tool for game designers and audio designers to create game functionality. By connecting boxes representing logic and other components, they can prototype and iterate on designs without any code support. It is worthwhile to provide entry points to the various audio systems so that audio designers can trigger a sound or voice line, adjust audio parameter values, or manage audio emitters. Make sure to provide context objects as output for the nodes so that the audio events can be stopped or have their parameters adjusted.

One of the problems with graphs is that the game logic and the audio logic are often intertwined: audio is just triggered as part of the graph, making it hard to find and debug. A better way to implement this is to create a graph with triggers for audio events that the game logic can trigger. This will centralize all of the audio behavior into one place and make the audio designers' lives easier as well since they don't need to go find where to post events in different graphs.

13.3.10 Statistics

There is a lot of information to control and monitor how the audio systems are performing. Even with our audio middleware profiler, it is also nice to provide more information inside the engine about gameplay or game states (for example, how many times the player or NPC did a particular action, or how frequently we changed from exploration mode to combat). These stats not only help game designers improve the game but can also help audio designers to make decisions regarding audio triggers. For example, if there is a certain audio stinger that triggers when entering combat, having an understanding of how frequently it plays can inform the audio designers of whether it should play every time or whether it needs more variations.

It can also be valuable to monitor the performance of our systems, beyond what we receive in our middleware. It is interesting to get statistics, for instance, about the number of emitters being handled in our engine, so we can reduce calls to our middleware and virtual voices. We can also glean a lot of statistics from our levels, so we can get location-based statistics instead of relying just on time-based statistics. One useful tool is to implement automation for making the player walk through the level, so we render the audio as if it was normal gameplay, then we can build a heat map of the number of resources used on every part of the map. That will also help audio designers to figure out if there is too much audio in one place, or if our systems collapse in specific situations.

13.3.11 Audio Automation

Any big project needs to deal with a huge amount of audio assets. Audio middleware has a lot of advantages, but generating the assets and importing them into the game engine can be tedious. Every time an audio designer wants to submit a change in the game or even just test locally, there are hoops to jump through. Even with good built-in tooling to update the game's content while it is running, there are still times when they need to generate new assets or new parameters that cannot be updated in realtime.

That is why it is good to author audio automation scripts to handle all of this work. The automation can be as simple as a process that runs during the night so that every day we get fresh assets that were submitted during the previous day. That same script could be hooked up to a build-on-submit trigger, so they can also get the content faster and try it on builds immediately.

Voiceover is one of the features that benefits from these automated builds, as we can end up dealing with hundreds of thousands of assets, and there is no room for manual setup. In addition to generating audio assets, we can also add tools from our engine that need to run to update content, such as reading data from the game engine to populate structures and metadata files, or run audio tests such as the automatic run of the game to visit different parts of the level mentioned in Section 13.3.10. There are a lot of automations we can add to our library, and they are all helpful to improve everyday iteration for audio designers.

13.4 AUDIO EVENTS ARCHITECTURE

A game event is an action happening in the game, like a player jumping, a footstep, opening a door, or hitting an object. An audio event is an audio design element that gets triggered by an action in the game. Those sound similar – are they both the same thing? This question is the starting point for discussion around a lot of issues and decisions. Hooking sounds up is one of the places where, depending on how the architecture is made, audio designers will spend most of their time setting up, so it's worth diving in. Let's start from the beginning and see how far we can improve it.

13.4.1 Triggering an Audio Event

We start coding an audio event trigger from a specific action in the game, so imagine we have a character with a jump action and we go straight to the part in the code where the jump is happening. To post an event at least we need the ID of the event that needs to be triggered and the object where the event will play. Then we will just trigger something like this:

```
void Jump()
{
 ...
  AudioEngine.PostEvent(eventID, gameObjectID)
}
```

It's always a good idea to have a manager/wrapper that handles audio so that we don't couple our engine into the middleware we are using. The transformation is subtle but important:

```
AudioManager.PostEvent(eventID, gameObjectID)
```

Our jumping code, attached to the player, will post the event into an audio object that also lives on the player itself (sometimes the object has its behavior defined in scripts attached to it). Most of the time, however, we will need an external reference to trigger the audio on another object (for example, the script can be in the player top hierarchy as a behavior, but we want to post the jump event on the feet).

Audio objects need to be registered and initialized with the middleware, so game engines provide a component that we can place in a game object to register the audio object automatically to this specific entity. We do the same thing with the eventID, as we create a component to handle the reference of the event (player_jump in this case) and define it manually on the jump script to be triggered in the code. Triggering explicitly this way is useful for fast prototyping and small games, but it scales badly. Imagine we have thousands of assets and each of them contains an object reference and an event to be set up. Sometimes game assets change, or some event gets lost because the audio structure changes as well, or maybe we add more than one audio object component because we forgot there was already one somewhere in the same prefab.

13.4.2 Pooling Audio Objects

To solve the audio object reference issue, we need to think about where they are registered and stored. One good thing about storing audio objects and registering them on the game object is that we just register that object once and it gets created and destroyed with the asset. But that just creates the issue of having references on the game assets that we will need to find later, and we want to avoid that.

One way to solve this problem is to create a pool of audio objects, so every time we need one, we just post the event into one of those, then return it to the pool when the event finishes playing. We first ask the pool to get a new audio object, then we set the position on the post method with the object ID we got from the pool. If we need to update the position over time (the sound is attached to the character as they're moving around), we can store the object and update its position every frame.

One benefit of this approach is performance – registering/unregistering audio objects every time can be expensive. Having a collection of preregistered audio objects that you can reuse by playing/stopping audio and posting new events can be a good solution. Our assets will be free of audio object references, and they will be automatically spawned and managed when needed. For more details on this topic, see Chapter 1 of this book "Audio Object Management Techniques" by Christian Tronhjem.

13.4.3 Centralizing Event References

Finding references to events is another big challenge. When someone implements a feature (whether it is gameplay, UI, AI behavior, or whatever), the logic for triggering the sound events will be customized to that feature. As new features are added, the sound events will be configured along with them, either shown in an inspector or set in a config file for the object. The problem with this approach is that every time we want to find where a particular event is placed, we need to first remember where it was placed and also which game asset contains the reference.

Some cases (such as a player jump animation) are likely easy, but it's not hard to imagine more convoluted cases (where is the shoot event reference for that old weapon version that we did three months ago?). It is often a waste of time for audio designers to spend time finding where event references are, and in big productions, the number of assets in-game can be so big that it becomes unmanageable.

One solution is to create a file that holds all event references in the game (we call it here `AudioEvents`) and we use our `AudioManager` singleton/controller to access this public list:

```
AudioManager.PostEvent(AudioEvents.Jump, gameObjectID)
```

When audio designers ask for audio support on a specific feature, they will not need any specific audio coding support. On our `AudioEvents` list, programmers implementing the feature will just create a new entry and use that event created. For example, if someone implements a weapon shoot, they will add a `weapon_shoot` event entry in our `AudioEvents` list.

Audio designers will see the new field on the `AudioEvents` list every time a new feature is implemented, which will drastically improve the time they invest in finding where to set up the events. That will allow them to spend their energy keeping the list organized, which becomes everyone's responsibility. One good way to maintain this list is using naming conventions and categories, so everything falls into sections like Player, Enemy, Ambience, etc. With the naming convention in place, we can create drop-down lists just to be able to open and close the sections to make this config file more user-friendly.

13.4.4 Avoid Coupling

The last big issue we're going to solve in this chapter is the coupling of audio code with gameplay or game behavior in general. For instance, using the `AudioManager` inside some gameplay code for the jump action. If we want to avoid that as well, it will be better to subscribe to an action instead of triggering the audio code directly from the behavior. We just need to have access to a list of game events published to subscribe to them. This approach will help not only audio but also other reactive components like VFX or UI, and it is important to provide a way in your game code to expose actions to other components.

To implement this system, we create an `EventManager` to handle whatever action comes from the game, and our `AudioManager` will subscribe to the `EventManager`. Events and their associated registrations can be described with an enum and passed through to a single callback so that customers of the `EventManager` don't need to subscribe one by one individually. This is what the code would look like for gameplay:

```
void Jump()
{
    ...
    EventManager.PostEvent(GameEvent.Jump, gameObjectID)
}
```

In our `AudioManager`, we will just receive the event and post what we want. We can also modify our events list to automatically trigger depending on the type we receive from the game event:

```
class AudioManager
{
    OnGameEvent(GameEvent type, int gameObjectID)
    {
        AudioEvents[type].Post(gameObjectID);
    }
}
```

13.4.5 Using Naming Conventions

There is still room for more simplification. Coming from the initial definition of what both game events and audio events are, we should ask ourselves why the audio designers need to manually assign all the references to our audio middleware in the AudioEvents file. Is a jump action event in the game not the same as a jump audio event in the middleware? If they are the same, why can we not just populate them by event type as well? If we define a good naming convention, we can apply it to an event structure that goes into the middleware, automatically correlated with the game events.

Imagine we have some actions for the player and enemies. We can define some categories for both with an underscore connected with the action: `Player_Jump`, `Player_Hit`, `Player_Attack`, `Enemy_Hit`, `Enemy_Die`, etc. We can create a tool that reads all of the game events and parses them with the categories into a structure for our middleware. This tool will detect if there is a new event in the code and add an empty event into our middleware. If the event was already existing, it will keep what was already implemented.

It is difficult to end up with a middleware project that has this perfect setup of events that can be structured automatically, but we can implement tooling that does a best effort. Mainly this is a problem based on how many different events we want to create and for different purposes. In theory, all game events happening should relate to one correlated audio event, so those are the ones that should be created automatically. From there, we can always add more specific events that get triggered from other main events to define a more granular logic.

13.4.6 Events for Actions, Tags for Data

As we have seen, audio events are mostly attached to event actions in the game. Sometimes when we start prototyping a feature, it can be tempting to just start hardcoding the audio events. For instance, in the case of inter-actable objects, we may have two different people start implementing code for a jar and an arrow hitting the floor. They might each code an event called `arrow_hit` and `jar_hit`. Instead, what audio designers should expect is an `object_hit` event with an `object_type` parameter tagged in the object itself. If we do not solve this issue from the beginning, scalability is going to be bad. We always need to think about events addressing actions and tagging all data we can into objects to send to the event.

Let us say that we had the jar and the arrow set up with a parameter to define the type of object, and this is set up on a field in the object itself. We normally define this parameter in our middleware as well when we do the design. We first ask how many objects are going to be in the game, then create a parameter set with all possible object values appearing in the game. Once that is set up, we need to manually select this parameter value on each object to define the type. We would like to avoid all that manual setup.

We discussed already how to get rid of the audio object using the pool and events with our `AudioEvents` list, but how about any data parameter we need to send to the audio object? Every time there is a new object, the audio designers will need to fill in the middleware parameter reference to define which type of object it is (like a jar type for a jar game asset). Instead, we should make use of in-game or model data.

When some artist or game designer creates a jar prop, they will properly tag the object using a good naming convention and tag the object with properties which we can read data from. For instance, we can say a jar contains a tag value of "ceramic" for the material or "big" for the size of the object. We can add more tags and categories as needed. What we need to do from the audio programming side is to make sure all tags are registered into the audio object before posting any event, so we need to make a layer that transforms the tag system into a middleware parameter.

In a perfect scenario, if we do that, audio designers will play the game and profile it with the middleware, and they will start receiving collision events from the objects, with non-defined parameters that they will need to fill. For instance, now there is a small new jar made from wood, so they will just need to fill this instance with a proper sound. There is also room here for more automation since it is possible to read all tags from our engine and populate those values with a tool into our middleware every time we add more values into the tags set, so we always have our parameters updated.

Other examples of this sort of setup are materials for the terrain to provide the correct footstep material, or character clothes where we want to define the type of shoes, pants, or shirt, to change the foley sound in the character. Even if it is a type of chest that we want to open or interact with, it should always be event-based for the action and then send all data possible as parameters. Relying on this architecture, it is mostly automatic for any audio designer to receive data from the engine and just work in the middleware, without having to touch the game engine.

13.5 CONCLUSION

As we can see, there are a lot of ways for a programmer to improve an audio designer's workflow. Creating a good communication culture and trying to find where we all spend most of our time, even if it is a long task or a short one that repeats many times, they all deserve time to investigate how to make them faster. Focusing on tools is also an important part, as we are going to save so much time and make development more user-friendly. And finally, having a solid and data-driven architecture for our game engine will drastically save manual workload time.

Satisfaction with creating all those tools and seeing people happy with their workflows is the best outcome you can get for working on a team with audio designers, and if you invest enough time in all those improvements, you will even manage to get some free time for coding those cool DSP that were promised in the interview.

CHAPTER 14

An Introduction to "An Introduction to Audio Tools Development"

Simon N. Goodwin

14.1 WHAT ARE AUDIO TOOLS AND HOW DO THEY DIFFER FROM GAME PROGRAMMING?

Audio tools are used to author the sound of games. The best tools may be fun to use in their own right, but they are nevertheless a means to an end. That end is making a hit game which will:

- Run well on every platform capable of running it.

- Sound as good as possible in the expectations of the customers.

- Take advantage of unique platform features so that it will be competitive with first-party products.

- Minimize sonic weaknesses compared with rival platforms, some of which might not exist when you set out.

This means that audio tools must be aware of all platforms, even if they only run on a few of the biggest. They must deal with much larger sets of assets than any one release of the game – typically uncompressed audio at the highest sample rate designers can record at, with variants, back-ups, version control, and the other book-keeping necessities of development. All of

DOI: 10.1201/9781003330936-17

this multifarious data is only swept away when the gold master is pressed and the team moves on – hopefully taking some of the tools with them.

If your game is mainly or exclusively played online, there may be no "gold master" milestone, but a drawn-out sequence of betas or soft-launches, content packs and refreshes, crossplay extensions and localizations; these continue until the servers shut down, hopefully a decade or more later. In that case you've traded crunch for a treadmill, so the chance to condense or rationalize audio assets may never come. Readily-available backups and developer-managed version control are especially vital in the toolchains of online titles.

In the simplest, most traditional sense, audio tools *marshal the raw assets* recorded or created by sound designers, then convert them to the formats most suited to the target hardware.[1] They are not part of the game, though they may be incorporated into it in some models of game development. More broadly, audio tools exist to *reconcile static state* – the pre-authored context of the game or a specific level or scenario – with *dynamic state* – the emergent consequences of the players' behavior and their interactions with the entire game world.

Beyond custom-baked audio samples – be those loops, streams, or one-shots; foley, music, speech, or impulse responses – audio tools capture categories and context in the form of metadata which the game audio code, much later, will integrate with gameplay so that the most appropriate sounds play at the right time. Some audio tools also provide means to audition samples in the context of other sounds and predictable states, such as layers of ambience, weather, or crowds.

There is a complex trade-off between doing this auditioning in the game and in the tool.

The audio tools programmer must work closely with the game programmers and designers, not just the audio specialists on either side, to make sure the tool encapsulates the knowledge and intent of the sound designer, to minimize the need for manual markup later, and to thrill the player with sounds which are appropriate to the action in the game and the imagination of the sound designers.

14.2 HOW AUDIO TOOLS MEET THE GAME

There are three broad approaches to audio tool integration, with advantages and disadvantages that vary with the size of the project, the tech used (not just for audio), the target platforms, and the organization of the game team. In practice, you might write tools for a single game that use all three approaches, but it's helpful to compare their constraints and affordances.

14.2.1 Tools in the Game

Unity exemplifies this approach, though it's also common in studios with a mature in-house tech stack.[2] The beauty of placing audio tools directly into the game is that all the game data is available as context for the audio tool. The horror of it – in terms of complexity, fragility, and the need for regular rework – is the same.

Another snag for those targeting a range of platforms (phones, consoles, handheld devices, web, etc.) is that all the constrained platforms become poor relations of the PCs that host the full game and its integrated editors. Designers accustomed to working with mice, MIDI controllers, and multiple screens are not going to find these devices available on all platforms – even if some of them might have enough resources to run the game and the overheads (extra threads, buffers, caches, complications of late binding, etc.) of running tools alongside a game. The more secure (i.e., more monetizable) platforms tend to run apps or games in a sandbox, limited in space and access beyond that, which makes rapid iteration problematic.

14.2.2 Game in the Tool

In this model, parts of the game code and data are shared with the tool; it might use the same audio engine, physics subsystems, or level geometry, but everything else – especially asset streaming and layered post-processed graphics – is left out, to focus on the parts the sound designers most need as context for their work. The key decision governing this approach is where you make the split.

Sharing an audio engine with the game is great, but doesn't give you access to the environmental context. Sharing game geometry is a tougher call. Static objects and lighting and their development affordances help with ambience, reverb, and other environmental aspects of the sound design which may consume far more design time than the compilation and layering of audible assets. But particle systems and game mobiles are generally a step too far, implying a switch from this approach to the first, effectively implementing tools within the game. Look out for the amount of data unrelated to audio that you need to make game code useful in a tool when using this approach. If it dwarfs the audio-specific data, back off.

14.2.3 Standalone Tools

If audio tools are kept strictly apart from game code, they tend to be easier to write and maintain, as they can use whatever tech – scripts, spreadsheets, databases, programming languages – comes readily to hand. Many technologies have a part of the job done for you in terms of user interface, file management, audio output, etc., while eschewing baggage you don't need. A good standalone tool does one thing well and can be used sequentially in conjunction with other tools.[3]

Standalone tools are typically easier to integrate into an automatic test framework; they can still share libraries, or even audio engines or game data, but only to the extent needed for that task. So, for example, a tool for environmental markup might be split into one scripted automatic part and another for interactive tweaking; asset conversion can be separated from rendering, and so on. The lack of coupling allows fast initial progress, but if the results after integration are not as expected, the process to analyze and fix the results can soon get tortuous. This enforced separation is both the strength and the weakness of standalone audio tools.

14.3 DIFFERENCES BETWEEN DEVELOPING AUDIO TOOLS AND AUDIO GAME CODE

The design process and implementation of audio tools is rarely the same as that for code that will ship with the game. This final section highlights seven key differences.

- Audio tools have all the resources of the development computer (RAM, CPU, etc.) to draw upon – not just the fraction allocated to audio runtimes.

- Audio tools do not have the hard real-time constraints of games. Except in relatively rare situations (such as providing audio previews), they don't have to run at a constant high framerate.

- Audio tools typically work with raw rather than baked assets, allowing faster iteration.

- Audio tools can expose information that is valuable to designers – such as which of a set of alternates is the outlier, or the consequences of packaging decisions – which would get in the way of a game. This is because they have access to what might be, as well as what currently is, in the game's repertoire. There can be hundreds of gigabytes of the former, and rarely more than one gigabyte or so of the latter in a finished game, even one stuffed with music and speech.[4]

- The target audiences of audio tools are the sound designers and sometimes game designers – not the game player, producer, or QA department. This affects how the tools communicate with the user. Audio jargon – decibel, filter, codec – is fine and helps with precision, but programmer jargon is no more appropriate here than in the game or installer. That is, it is best avoided, especially if you'd rather be developing than explaining it to your less-technical clients.

- Audio tools do not need to run on low-power target platforms, as long as they're aware of the differences in terms of codecs, file management, and memory management.

- Audio tools and the tech underlying them can be carried from one game to the next more readily than game code, even if the genre or presentation changes.

NOTES

1 Proprietary DSP and codecs invariably outperform "portable" ones and often have access to platform resources denied to cross-platform code and data.

2 We don't often get to see this tech except indirectly in interviews, as it's proprietary and riddled (for better or worse) with trade secrets.

3 This is the Unix philosophy, epitomized in the audio domain by Sound Exchange (AKA SoX), a cross-platform open-source command aptly described as "the Swiss Army knife of sound processing" - Ed.

4 Localization is one area where audio tools generally do a lot more work than other parts of the game toolchain.

CHAPTER 15

An Introduction to Audio Tools Development

Jorge Garcia

15.1 INTRODUCTION

There are already books that will teach you how to build an application or a tool using various technologies, so in this chapter I share part of my journey and discoveries designing and developing tools for sound designers and content creators, explaining what worked and what didn't work. Coming from a background of years writing systems, audio-related code, and frameworks, I started thinking about tools development and asked myself: how hard can it be? Having already written in-game debugging tools and simple user interfaces, at some point I thought that tools and UI development were trivial, a well-solved problem in game audio. I was far from reality.

There are some (non-command line) audio tools where the most complicated and laborious part is the UI and the UX side of things. Think of your favorite DAW or audio middleware authoring app: imagine all the features they deliver and how they are presented. Now think of the years of iteration, maintenance, and fixes it took them to reach a mature state. Designing and developing audio tools is hard in part because they need to serve specialized users, our beloved sound designers and technical sound designers. Sometimes tools are developed for more generalist game developers outside of the audio team, which brings different challenges.

DOI: 10.1201/9781003330936-18

But why do we need to develop audio tools at all? If you are an audio programmer working in a game studio, you probably already have access to the audio middleware tools of choice and the integration with a third-party or proprietary game engine. Most middleware products come with default tools that you can use "out of the box," so you might think that you are good to go for production. But the reality is that there are always ways of improving the process of your designers and helping them be productive. The majority of game projects benefit from having dedicated tools developers because the production needs for a mid- and large-size game can easily fall beyond what your audio middleware provides. As an audio programmer, it's your responsibility to help make the designers and content creators who work on a game more productive and to ensure that the tools they use don't suck. Or, at least, that they don't suck too much [1]!

Designers are very talented individuals who will author incredible content for a game even if the tools aren't very good, but for us tool programmers and designers, that shouldn't be acceptable. Time savings in iteration time will help make a better game and a better experience for the players. Moreover, if the designers enjoy using your tools, the process will be more pleasant for them, which again will lead to having a better game. Great audio tools are the ones designed and developed in close collaboration with the users. These tools understand the user's needs and aims.

This chapter gives an overview of an audio tool development process and some technicalities, in case this is the first time that you are tasked with writing a tool. If you are an experienced tools developer already, you will still find the information presented here useful to improve your tools and development process.

If you read any specialized book on tools development and user experience design ("Designing the User Experience of Game Development Tools" by David Lightbown [2] is a good one), you will see that good tools usually outlive the projects they are built for. A tool that works well may be employed in the development of not just one game, but an entire game franchise, which is economical, as game development timelines are usually tight and need to be optimized as much as possible. This is particularly true in larger projects or in game franchises that release a new title every few years. Tools that are meant to be used by content creators determine the velocity at which a team can create quality content.

Good tools support the adoption of new audio techniques. You may incorporate, for instance, a novel algorithm or an old approach that is now affordable to solve a certain production problem with current hardware or cloud infrastructure. Consider a machine learning model (like a neural network) that will help your sound designers create content. Having a model that is trained to the expected quality with a fast inference time is just part of the battle. A user-friendly interface is key so that users can use the machine learning model efficiently. The model may need to be integrated into your production pipeline and the game engine.

If you are getting into audio tools development, I hope that what I have presented until now in this introduction hasn't bored you. The impact of a tool in the development of a game might sound like a tall order problem, though it should be a shared responsibility across the team, including both designers and programmers. There is also a very nice upside working as an audio tools developer: audio tools offer the opportunity to work on interesting problems and are a great way to leverage your audio skills, knowledge, and interests. So, what problems can audio tools solve?

15.2 DEVELOPING TOOLS FOR HUMANS

An audio tool should solve a problem that your designers and artists have. What is the problem? In general, the goal of an audio tool is to manipulate or transform audio-related data. Some people also present tools as a "game" for content creators, where the goal of this game is to create audio assets for your project. To do that, we need to understand the users' problems and the bottlenecks they face when creating or transforming data. Depending on the size of the studio or company you are working for, this may also involve the audio director, the lead sound designer, the physics programmer, the technical sound designer, or even a level designer who needs to integrate audio content.

An effective audio programmer tries to understand their users' problems. That will help you to speed up development as you can represent your users when they aren't around, allowing you to solve some problems autonomously, or at least know what questions to ask your users. This understanding involves domain knowledge when gathering requirements. If a user asks for the playback preview in the tool mapped to the space bar, you may already know that this is a key binding found in most audio applications and DAWs. You may also find that designers and artists like to count from one and not from zero (as in zero-indexed arrays), so number your UI elements accordingly!

Audio lead Mark Kilborn ran an interesting Twitter poll in March 2022 [3], where he asked what was more important in audio tools: workflow/speed or features/power. After 267 votes, workflow/speed took the majority of the votes with 76.8%. I believe the results of the poll reflect the realities of game development, as having a larger number of features won't make your tool great if the workflow is clunky, or if it takes a long time for users to perform trivial tasks or iterate on their work.

Understanding your users' problems and desires takes time; it's a learning process from both sides – your users also need to understand how the tool could work and get back to you with improvements or preferences in the way they want it to function. This leads to iteration on the original tool idea and workflows – sometimes it won't be possible to know if the solution that the tool provides is a good one until it reaches the hands of your users and they start using it.

15.3 TOOL ARCHITECTURE

To have a tool that can change and evolve over time, we need an architecture that supports this process. This probably doesn't matter much if the tool is just a simple app that can be maintained by a single developer, but having a flexible architecture becomes more relevant once the tool becomes bigger and bigger, and when more than a single pair of hands develops it. David Farley [4] and Titus Winters et al. [5] present this idea of software engineering being "programming over time". If a tool has to adapt to user needs over time, it needs an architecture that can be easily changed, with minimal cost. Object-oriented development principles like SOLID can fit the bill [6]. Here are some typical paradigms in the tools I've worked on, and patterns that you may encounter when contributing to the codebase of an audio tool.

The Model View Controller (MVC) is one of the first architectural patterns you hear about when you start writing applications that have a user interface. It was formulated by Trygve Reenskaug in 1979 while visiting the Xerox Palo Alto Research Center. This pattern is so simple, yet so flexible to various interpretations that it's probably enough for a good amount of audio tools. The three components are:

1. **Model** – Represents user and app data and potentially does some business logic with the data. This could be a database connection, files on disk, or data structures in memory.

2. **Controller** – Accepts input and converts it to commands for the Model or the View.

3. **View** – Carries out the heavy lifting of rendering or representation of information and is responsible for displaying the data.

We can find different flavors or re-imaginations of MVC like Model-View-ViewModel (MVVM) in frameworks such as Microsoft's Windows Presentation Foundation (WPF), which help to separate the development of the GUI via markup language such as XAML or specific GUI code, from the development of the business logic. This way the view isn't dependent on any specific model [7].

Designing and architecting audio applications that aren't native or desktop (such as cloud or server applications) is beyond the scope of this chapter, though some of the aforementioned concepts and ideas still apply. Architecting an application that can run in a browser and do processing in the cloud opens up challenges and operational issues where DevOps and the microservices architecture could help [8]. For the sake of simplicity, we'll stick to desktop applications in this chapter.

One of the particularities of audio tools for game development is the dependencies, the game runtime being one of the most important ones. When I say runtime, I refer to the libraries or parts of the code that are also going to run inside of the game executable that is shipped to players.

It's common for an audio tool or game editor to emulate the audio playback and behaviors of the game, which is useful in a tool where the user creates a sound patch or audio data for the game. Being able to hear a "preview" inside the tool is usually preferable to exporting the data to the game build, which could involve a number of steps,[1] depending on the pipeline design of the project and the target hardware.

Good audio tools are often integrated with the audio engine or the runtimes of the game, and it helps if the playback code used in the audio tool is the same as what is used in the game. This is not just useful to avoid duplicating code or behavior (hence, less code to maintain), but also handy for reproduction of playback issues. Catching issues earlier in the development process and allowing fast iteration times is also one of the most sought features in an audio tool.

15.4 MANAGING TOOL DATA

Earlier I mentioned that transforming and managing data is one of the main goals of a tool. We don't want our users to lose any data or work! This also links to the development process of the team you are part of. Therefore, one of your main tasks as a programmer is to design data structures and data storage formats. This could range from POD types (plain-old-data structures, or passive collections of field values without any object-oriented features) to more sophisticated data structures that may be human-readable (even sound-designer-readable), and which can store a history of changes efficiently or fire events when some data changes.

One of the most requested features for an audio tool is undo and redo. This means that, in some contexts, the users can go to a previous or a later state of their edits or parameter changes. Implementing undo-redo can be quite complex. Two typical approaches are:

- Storing the entire contents of the data after each edit. This takes up more memory while the application is running, but it is a simple approach that may work well with the application framework. It could also potentially be faster as it won't need to recalculate data transformations or use alternative data caches.

- Only store the actions carried out by the user. This way we don't need to store any intermediate data that might be quite big. The downside is that the tool architecture becomes more complex, needing to handle things like the history of changes and the dependencies across them (e.g., the order of transformations in data when, for instance, processing is applied to audio). This is the preferred approach for tools that are expected to grow, as it also helps us to manage complexity.

Data serialization and internal data formats should be considered together. Serialization is one of the pillars of any tool (and one of the "must have" features too), as the users expect to save progress and come back to work on the same project after some time. One part of this is storing the application configuration so that it persists across runs so that it's not lost when the tool is updated or redeployed. The solutions for configuration storage are platform dependent; for example, if your tool runs on Windows, then you may want to save configuration information in the registry. Approaches and frameworks to handle configuration range from just plain JSON or XML serialization to more sophisticated technologies like Google Protocol Buffers [9] or Cereal [10].

We also need to account for versioning of data. Versioning of data containers is important when updating old data with new fields, and especially when making breaking changes that need to be patched and persisted, or to avoid data incompatibilities. Some data from an older version of the tool may become incompatible and it might need additional handling, upgrades, or conversions for the application to continue working with the latest features or fixes. Some scriptable version control systems make these transformations easy to implement as part of the check-in or check-out process – in this case the "tool" may be invisible, like many of the best ones. Additionally, the data exported by your tool may need to have versioning built in, in order to interact with different runtime versions with as few interruptions as possible.

My recommendation is to use existing formats, if available. When saving audio data to a file, for example, the WAV or AIFF formats are simple enough and well-supported by external tools, so that you don't need to reinvent the wheel. However, keep in mind the limitations and issues that these formats could cause (e.g., zero channels in WAVs). In other cases, like bespoke project tool data structures, consider whether XML or JSON is good enough if the designers are familiar with this format. A proprietary exchange format could also become handy if the data needs to interact with a range of applications, be it in-house or third-party. When looking beyond audio-specific data, find out about the containers used by the rest of the game team. Repurposing those with care means non-audio staff will maintain them for you.

15.5 LANGUAGES AND FRAMEWORKS FOR DEVELOPING AUDIO TOOLS

Many frameworks and libraries are created, maintained, or abandoned every year. It's hard to say what will be the best frameworks used for building audio tools even in the near term, but I wanted to list here some of the most popular ones used in game studios and in audio/music companies in the last decade from the time of this writing.

- **WPF** – Introduced by Microsoft in 2006. It's freely available for the development of Windows-based applications and commonly used with the C# programming language. This framework has become very popular for its widespread adoption, flexibility, and customization. There are also various libraries that use WPF as a basis. WPF describes its windows and controls using XAML, an XML-based language that allows defining and linking various interface elements. WPF also allows deploying applications to a website [11].

- **NAudio** – An open-source .NET audio library written by Mark Heath [12]. It contains many abstractions and utilities for building audio applications. Among the features, there are primitives for handling audio playback and reading from various audio formats, format conversion and encoding, mix/manipulation, audio recording, working with soundcards, and even a full implementation of a MIDI event model. If you visit some large and popular game studios, you may still find this library used in various in-house tools.

- **JUCE** – An open-source and cross-platform C++ framework for audio applications development [13]. It is very complete, with abstractions for doing pretty much everything you need in the development of audio tools and plugins. Being available across all major platforms makes it ideal for supporting most users out there, be it on Windows, macOS, or Linux. JUCE contains not only a large number of UI utilities and classes for building audio applications easily but also a DSP library with primitives like filters or effects so that you can put together basic audio apps without much effort. The downside of JUCE being a C++ framework lies, in my view, in the complexity that the programmer needs to handle for creating more elaborate applications.

- **QT** – One of the most popular frameworks for building UI applications in C++ or Python using the **pyQt** bindings [14]. Similar to WPF, if you visit some game studios, you will find QT as a foundation not only for audio tools, but also for helper panels written in Python inside digital content creation 3D-art applications like Maya or Houdini. QT introduces the concepts of signals and slots, which help to implement the observer pattern (more about this later in this chapter). Additionally, the QML declarative language is also part of this framework and allows the scripting of UI interfaces in a simple way.

- **Dear ImGui** – A compact graphical user interface library for C++ with many third-party backends and bindings created by Omar Cornut [15]. This library is also popular in game studios and large publishers. It is a popular option for quickly putting together a tool UI. See Chapter 16 of this book "Audio Debugging Tools and Techniques" by Stéphane Beauchemin for more details on using Dear ImGui.

- **Web-Based Frameworks** – Here we can find a wide range of options like *React, Angular, Vue*, etc. I personally don't have much experience with those but if you have access to web developers or if you have web development skills, they could be a preferred option. There are also web audio apps out there that have a WebAssembly backend, which could ease integration with native audio code.

It's also good practice to find out what tech the game and non-audio tools use and use the same technology if you can. This could simplify the development process later as you can leverage the knowledge and skills of other teams.

15.6 TOOL PROGRAMMING PATTERNS

Once you start looking at the code of an audio app, you will find common patterns that are used to handle state changes, navigation, and data updates. I've listed here some common patterns that I've found when developing tools. These are just "programming tools," so use your discretion with them. Assess what is the problem you need to solve and apply the pattern only if it makes sense to your problem.

- **Observer Pattern** [16] – This pattern is a fundamental one across applications in general. It is used to change the UI or a certain state of the application in response to changes in data. One way to implement the observer pattern yourself is by using lambdas (`std::function` in C++, `lambda` keyword in Python) that are owned by the observer class and passed into the class that acts as observable, which calls the lambda. This pattern is implemented in QT with signals and slots. JUCE implements it as broadcasters and listeners. In C#, this functionality is provided by the templates `IObservable` and `IObserver`.

- **Command and Operations** [17] – A common pattern when building tools that deal with a set of commands and operations done on the data, which helps with abstraction and encapsulation. This pattern can be used when implementing the undo/redo approaches from Section 15.4. Each command has an `execute()` function. The receiver class encapsulates the functionality that comes from each of the commands, effectively decoupling it. The invoker is responsible for registering and invoking each of the commands.

- **Flow Director/Application Navigation** – A pattern that handles the navigation (or flow) of the application. This pattern encapsulates what operations go before or after each of the states (similar to a state machine) in the application, and it can also handle part of the business logic of the tool. This pattern can be implemented in different flavors. For instance, by using lambdas that are called in a certain order depending on the application state. Another typical implementation of application navigation is by using state machines. There are many implementations of FSM (finite state machines) and the state pattern online for all programming languages, so I recommend you find one that fits with the architecture of your tool.

- **Events/Callbacks** – When some user or system event is triggered (e.g., a button has been clicked), a function will be called. For example, in C++ using JUCE, you can use `Button::Listener` to listen for button events within a component.

15.7 BEYOND TOOLS PROGRAMMING

It may sound obvious at this point that programming a tool is just a part of the story. The design of the tool and the user experience are probably even more important than the program itself. There are instances where you might find yourself designing and programming a small tool because the UX designer from your team isn't available, or perhaps there isn't one that has been hired! In this case, I've found it useful to be acquainted with mockup and design tools like Balsamiq [18] or Figma [19]. They are both great tools, handy for quick prototypes and for fleshing out ideas. You can go from just a simple wireframe to a fully fledged design with them if you have the design and artistic skills. These mockups can help you present your ideas to the users of your tool before any implementation takes place, making them powerful communication tools. Having a good-looking and well-designed tool also can help with getting your users engaged and immersed in creating content. As users tell me, having a tool with a nice UI can make it all sound better and more fun.

I don't want to end this chapter without mentioning some of the challenges that might be found in the tool development lifecycle during the production of a game. I believe that good tools are as good as the support and documentation that is provided to your users. Providing this support and documentation can be challenging when having to support various toolsets or projects. Having a testing strategy for your tools becomes important to help with this problem in order to catch any regressions early. Ideally, we want to have low downtime if any problems arise. I've also found that having a continuous integration (CI) environment set up for automatically testing and delivering incremental versions of tools is very handy for providing updates or hotfixes to your users, and it also lowers some risks during the production of a game (like the introduction of breaking changes).

Finally, consider implementing a command-line version of the tool or scriptable alternatives to a UI. These alternatives can be very helpful during game production for batch processing. If you plan for this feature from the start, then your code architecture will lend itself to the implementation, and it will be easier to put together.

ACKNOWLEDGMENTS

I would like to thank Simon N Goodwin for providing feedback, corrections, and comments on the early drafts of this chapter.

NOTE

1 Hopefully automated steps!

REFERENCES

1. https://www.gamedeveloper.com/production/the-6-reasons-your-game-development-tools-suck
2. Designing the user experience of game development tools (David Lightbown, CRC Press)
3. https://twitter.com/markkilborn/status/1499838812477919234
4. Modern software engineering (David Farley, Addison-Wesley Professional)
5. Software Engineering at Google: Lessons learned from programming over time (Titus Winters, Tom Manshreck & Hyrum Wright, O'Reilly)
6. https://en.wikipedia.org/wiki/SOLID
7. https://en.wikipedia.org/wiki/Model-view-viewmodel
8. Fundamentals of Software Architecture (Mark Richards and Neal Ford, O'Reilly Media)
9. https://developers.google.com/protocol-buffers
10. https://uscilab.github.io/cereal/
11. https://en.wikipedia.org/wiki/Windows_Presentation_Foundation
12. https://github.com/naudio/NAudio
13. https://juce.com/
14. https://en.wikipedia.org/wiki/Qt_(software)
15. https://github.com/ocornut/imgui
16. https://en.wikipedia.org/wiki/Observer_pattern
17. https://en.wikipedia.org/wiki/Command_pattern
18. https://balsamiq.com/
19. https://www.figma.com/

CHAPTER 16

Audio Debugging Tools and Techniques

Stéphane Beauchemin

16.1 INTRODUCTION

Can you hear the difference between a sound playing at −4.3 dB and −3.9 dB? Are you able to notice that a sound emitter is panned at 47 degrees from the center, but it should be panned at 54 degrees? Are there three or four instances of the same audio event playing? Let's face it, it is hard to answer those questions relying strictly on our ears. It is much easier to debug audio by augmenting our hearing sense with graphical data. This fact is not new to any audio programmer, but how do we go about implementing these visualizations?

In this chapter, I would like to bring the spotlight on audio debugging tools and techniques. First, I will go over the importance of creating and using debugging tools as early as possible in the development cycle. Then we will look at the different debugging tools that are available in Unreal 5 and the Wwise integration. Using UE5 and Wwise, we will show a few code examples of debug utilities that can be created.

After that, we will jump into using the Dear ImGui library with Unreal 5 and Wwise. In that section, we will go through an overview of ImGui, then we will briefly look at the ecosystem of tools that were built by the community around ImGui. Finally, we will show some fine and concise code examples of ImGui and show why it is such a great library for game audio development. This chapter is not solely intended for people using UE5, Wwise, and ImGUI. The concepts that are presented here can be

DOI: 10.1201/9781003330936-19

easily ported to another game engine or audio engine. If you don't have ImGui, know that it can easily be integrated into any game engine!

16.2 BUILDING DEBUGGING TOOLS FROM THE START

Let's say that you are working on a new audio system in your game project. You already had a few meetings with the audio designers to discuss what the new system should accomplish. You sketched out the architecture of the system and present it to your clients. They are happy with the plan you propose, so you decide to jump on the implementation of the system. You spend two days writing the algorithm for the system you have designed. After the code compiles and looks pretty, you start testing it in the game. Up to now, you are on track with the deadline you have set – you should be able to deliver this by the end of the week.

You start debugging your system. Your code works almost as designed but you know that one behavior is wrong. At this point, you begin with printing console messages to the log. There is not enough information, so you add even more info to the log. After half a day of mad debugging, the log becomes a mess and wrapping your brain around it becomes impossible. Then you realize you spent three days on debugging and that you missed the deadline. Next Monday, you come back to the code, and you eventually find the bug.

How come it took you two days to write the code, but three days to debug? To be honest, I found myself quite often in that kind of situation. We tend to think more about delivering results and not enough on how to get to the finish line in the fastest and safest way possible. Building debug functionalities along with new systems will always save you time down the road. Good debugging APIs will allow you to write debugging code concisely and quickly; it should take very few lines of code to achieve what you need. Not only that, debugging APIs should allow you to display information in a way that is both clear and easy to understand. In the next section, we will begin by looking at a very simple way of adding debug functionality in Unreal: console variables and commands.

16.3 UNREAL CONSOLE COMMANDS AND CONSOLE VARIABLES

Unreal console commands and console variables have been around for a long time, and they are full of features and functionality.[1] It is such a core concept of the engine that it is often overlooked. For example, the current integration of Wwise in Unreal as of this writing has no console variables and no console commands exposed in their integration.

It took me a few years to understand the console command feature set because I never took the time to look at its full functionality. Like many others, I learned about console commands in Unreal by reading the engine code. However, that is a slow process. When reading the code, you often see a console command and realize that this is debugging code. The second after that, your brain just discards it because you are after understanding something else for a game feature.

For many programmers working in Unreal, the console command API is like a Swiss Army knife they have been carrying in their back pocket for many years. They barely know how to use the blade of the Swiss Army knife, and they never took advantage of the various other tools and implements that are part of the knife. In this section, we will shortcut the slow and lengthy learning process by diving into the console command feature set. After reading this section, hopefully you will know how to take advantage of this tool.

16.3.1 Overview of Unreal Console Commands and Console Variables

Conceptually, console commands are quite simple. In some ways, they are similar to DOS or Unix shell commands. The format of the syntax is the name of the command followed by space separated arguments, terminated with a carriage return.

Here are examples of a couple of built-in console commands in Unreal:

- `Gc.CollectGarbageEveryFrame 1` – Tells Unreal to trigger garbage collection every frame, which is useful to find dangling pointers.

- `obj refs name=play_mysound` – Shows references to the `play_mysound` AkAudioEvent.

In the game, you can input console commands from the console input in unreal by typing the backtick (or grave accent) character: `. At the bottom of the Output Log window in the editor, you will find an input box where you can type console commands. They can also be passed as command executable arguments using the following syntax:

```
UE4Editor.exe GAMENAME -ExecCmds="command_0 args,...,command_n args"
```

Finally, on gaming platforms, it is possible to send unreal console commands remotely via the platform development tools.

Up to now, this is far from being rocket science – in fact, it sounds like computer science 101. But the beauty of the way that console commands are implemented in Unreal is that there is a syntax that allows you to a create console variable in just a few lines of C++ code. With very minimal code, you can register your new command, parse arguments, and execute your snippet of debug code.

On top of that, a subset of the console commands, the console variables, are even easier to use. A console variable can store a boolean, an integer, a floating point, or a string value. Using console variables removes the burden of parsing the arguments and storing values. As you might have guessed, the code for creating console variables is more succinct than console commands. Let's look at a few practical examples where the console commands and variables can be very handy in the context of audio debug.

16.3.2 Using a Console Boolean Variable to Conditionally Show 3D Debug Draw

As of this writing, the most recent version of the Wwise Unreal integration (2022.1)[2] does not provide any console commands or variables. However, there are a few in-game 3D debug drawing functions in Wwise. For example, you can choose to see reflection rays from an AkComponent in the world by modifying a member variable. This works, but it is a very cumbersome way of accessing debug draw functionality. Moreover, if your component is created programmatically, it is impossible for a non-programmer to show the debug draw. Let's fix this by using a console variable to provide the same functionality.

First, the console variable can be created like this as a **static** variable:

```
static TAutoConsoleVariable<bool> CVarAudioShowReflectionDebug(
   TEXT("Wwise.AkComponent.ShowReflections"),     // name
   false,                                          // default value
   TEXT("Set to 1 to show reflections"));          // help text
```

Then, the **static** variable can be used in the source code to conditionally show the debug code.

```
if (CVarAudioShowReflectionDebug.GetValueOnGameThread())
{
   // 3d debug draw code here
}
```

By using a console variable instead of member properties, you can now access the debug draw more easily. You or your sound designers can enter `Wwise.AkComponent.ShowReflections` 1 in the console command and your debug draw will appear. With the previous technique of setting a member variable, the debug could only be shown in game (package and standalone) if the asset had been saved with the property set to true.

If you have done the exercise of implementing this console variable, you might have found that there is one drawback compared to the original method. We lost the ability to show the debug view for one component only – we always see the debug draw for all components. This can be fixed by adding a new console command. If we can filter the component by names, then we can filter out uninteresting components. So, let's see how this can be done.

```cpp
static TAutoConsoleVariable<FString> CVarAkCompNameFilter(
  TEXT("Wwise.AkComponent.NameFilter"),     // console command name
  TEXT(""),                                  // default value
  TEXT("Only component with partial name match will be shown"));
```

Now `CVarNameFilter` can be used to filter out components by name if the filter is set.

```cpp
if (CVarAudioShowReflectionDebug.GetValueOnGameThread() &&
    (CVarAkCompNameFilter.GetValueOnGameThread().Len() == 0 ||
      GetName().Contains(CVarAkCompNameFilter.GetValueOnGameThread())))
{
  // 3d debug draw code here
}
```

16.3.3 Creating a Console Command to Trigger Audio Capture

Let's now have a look at our first console command. With a console command, you are responsible for parsing the arguments. Using a lambda function, it is possible to write a console command with very few lines of code. One good use case for a console command is starting and stopping the audio capture in Wwise.

```cpp
static FAutoConsoleCommand CCWwiseAudioCapture(
  TEXT("Wwise.OutputCapture"),
  TEXT("Start capture when filename parameter is passed,")
  TEXT("Stop the capture when no parameter is passed"),
  FConsoleCommandWithArgsDelegate::CreateLambda(
```

```
[](const TArray<FString>& Args)
{
  if (Args.Num() > 0)
  {
    UAkGameplayStatics::StartOutputCapture(Args[0]);
  }
  else
  {
    UAkGameplayStatics::StopOutputCapture();
  }
}));
```

In this example, the audio capture will be started when you pass a parameter. The parameter is the name of the wave file that will be written to disk. When there are no parameters that are passed, the output capture will be stopped. With this little snippet of code, you have a practical debug tool that will create a wave file on disk containing the data that is passed to the soundcard.

16.3.4 Breakpoint on Audio Events

Another cool trick to do with console commands is to add a breakpoint when a particular audio event is being called:

```
static uint32 sBreakEventID = AK_INVALID_UNIQUE_ID;
static FAutoConsoleCommand CCWwiseBreakOnEventName(
  TEXT("Wwise.BreakOnEvent"),
  TEXT("Pass the event name to break on. ")
  TEXT("Pass no parameter to reset"),
  FConsoleCommandWithArgsDelegate::CreateLambda(
    [](const TArray<FString>& Args)
    {
      if (Args.Num() > 0)
      {
        IWwiseSoundEngineAPI* AudioEngine =
          IWwiseSoundEngineAPI::Get();
        check(AudioEngine);
        sBreakEventID = AudioEngine->GetIDFromString(*Args[0]);
      }
      else
      {
        sBreakEventID = AK_INVALID_UNIQUE_ID;
      }
    }
));
```

In order to trigger a breakpoint, insert the following snippet of code in the function UAkAudioEvent::PostEvent():

```
if (sBreakEventID == GetShortID())
{
  UE_DEBUG_BREAK();
}
```

In order for this technique to work, all post-audio event calls must be routed through the same function – UAkAudioEvent::PostEvent() in this example. If this is not the case, it is a good idea to spend some time refactoring the code so that you can use this and similar techniques. Although this example code is specific to Unreal and Wwise, the concept of setting a breakpoint programmatically on an audio event can be implemented on any game engine or sound engine.

This example uses the UE_DEBUG_BREAK() macro, which is available if you are using Unreal. If you are not using Unreal, then you will need to replace that with a different mechanism. Each platform has a different function that needs to be called in order to trigger a breakpoint in the code. For example, on Windows using Microsoft C++, the function to call is __debugbreak().[3]

16.3.5 Going Further with Console Commands

The examples that have been shown in this chapter have been kept simple for readability purposes. In shipping code, we will need to include error checking and compile guards to make sure that debug code is excluded from the release target configuration. There are infinite use cases for console commands, and it only generally takes a few minutes to create a new one. For this reason, it is a powerful development tool that can be used for any purpose. Here are a few ideas for different console commands that you can put together very quickly:

- Disable a prototype system, then give the console command to your QA team so that they can enable it locally to test the prototype code.

- Allow a user to tweak a system value so that they do not need to restart the game in order to change the value they are interested in.

- Trigger a sound a few meters in front of the listener, useful for debugging environmental effects.

- Typing in a console command is much faster than trying to reproduce a gameplay scenario! I sometimes write a custom console command in order to reproduce a bug. In this case, the console command does not end up in source control and is reverted after the bug is fixed. However, given that a console command can take less than a few minutes to write, it is still immensely valuable if you are able to shortcut lengthy bug reproduction steps.

Hopefully, this section has given you ideas on how to take advantage of console commands. They are great for programmers – in just a few lines of code, we create nifty little debug tools. However, as programmers, we're used to interacting with text and commands. For non-programmers, console commands can be inconvenient and intimidating. In the next section, we will look at the friendliest possible debug tool: ImGui.

16.4 I HATE GUI PROGRAMMING, THEREFORE I LOVE IMGUI

One of my first goals when I started programming was to write my own DSP effects. As soon as I became skilled enough to understand the architecture of VST plugins, I started writing my own. I quickly discovered that providing UI to a VST plugin is often more work than writing the actual DSP code behind it. Writing UI code is not a simple task: you need to create UI widgets and handle user input. Often the work is not that complex, but it is very tedious. Because of this tedium, many in-game debug UIs are ugly and painful to use. If you look at Unreal's in-game debug system, you will see that it is quite simple. In fact, it is only a text overlay on the screen.

If you think that such debug system is good enough, it is because you have never seen ImGui in action. ImGui is a game changer in the world of game development. You can write a user interface in few minutes instead of weeks. Adding a button, slider, or text input is just one or two lines of code! For that reason, it has become very popular among game developers. The time that it takes a programmer to implement a UI with ImGui is so short that many things which would have been considered too difficult to implement are now accessible. Moreover, the visual interface that ImGui renders is very user-friendly compared to other debug interfaces.

In this section, we'll take a closer look at ImGui from the lens of audio programming in game development.

16.4.1 ImGui Overview

ImGui is an open-source library written by Omar Cornut, available on GitHub.[4] The author describes ImGui with the following words:

> Dear ImGui is a bloat-free graphical user interface library for C++. It outputs optimized vertex buffers that you can render anytime in your 3D-pipeline-enabled application. It is fast, portable, renderer agnostic, and self-contained (no external dependencies).

ImGui has a wide range of available widgets: text input, button, check box, combo box, slider, list view, plot widget, etc. It is easy to create windows, and it handles mouse input, keyboard input, and even gamepad input. It has enough functionality that it would almost be possible to use ImGui for the UI of an operating system. The library has a tiny footprint: without the examples and documentation, the library is composed of less than a dozen of source files. With the fact that there are no dependencies, the library is very easy to integrate into any game engine.

16.4.1.1 ImGui Integration

I have successfully integrated ImGui into two very different projects up to now: a VST plugin and Unreal Engine 5. For the integration in the VST plugin, I used the provided example from ImGui that shows how to handle input and rendering. For my integration in Unreal Engine 5, I used an open-source integration provided by GitHub user *segross*.[5] The Unreal Engine integration was by far easier than integration in my VST plugin. It took me minutes to get ImGui running in Unreal, while it took me a few hours to get ImGui running in my VST plugin. I'm an audio programmer with very basic knowledge about rendering, and I assume the task would be trivial for a tool programmer with a strong foundation of rendering and input handling. As a matter of fact, if you don't have ImGui in your game, stop thinking about it and just integrate it!

16.4.1.2 ImGui Complementary Tools

The fact that ImGui is an open-source project allows other individuals to provide tools that complement the offerings of ImGui. One extremely useful tool is netImGui.[6] netImGui is composed of a client and a server. The server is an external application that will draw the ImGui interface, and the client runs in the game that implements GUI logic. This separation means that ImGui does not need to be drawn on top of the game, and it can be rendered onto a separate window that is hosted by a different process than the game. The netImGui server can even run on a different machine than the machine that runs the game. This is very useful for platform development since the netImGui server can run on the development PC while the game runs on the console.

16.4.2 ImGui Examples

Now it is time to dive deep into some ImGui audio debug window examples. Let's begin with a practical window for debugging audio.

16.4.2.1 ImGui Audio Component Debug Augmented with 3D Debug Draw

Our first example is an ImGui window that displays the names of all of the `AkComponent`s in the world in a list on the screen. In order to show the position of the audio components, we will use the Unreal functions `DrawDebugCone()` and `DrawDebugString()`. This example also features a text filter that allows the user to filter the components by name. When text is input in the filter, only the items matching the string will be shown in the list and have their position drawn on the screen. Because of the immediate nature of ImGui, the `Draw()` function needs to be called at each frame. An example output of this is shown in Figure 16.1.

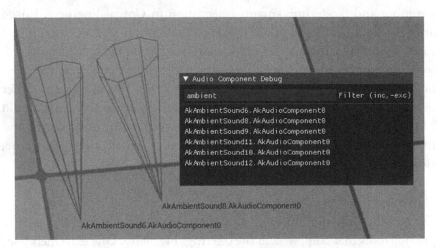

FIGURE 16.1 ImGui audio component debug display, filtering for "ambient" objects and showing 3D positions.

```cpp
#include <imgui.h>
void Draw()
{
  ImGui::Begin("Audio Component Debug");

  static ImGuiTextFilter Filter;
  Filter.Draw();
  ImGui::Separator();
  {
    ImGuiWindowFlags WindowFlags =
      ImGuiWindowFlags_HorizontalScrollbar;

    ImGui::BeginChild(
      "Child AkComponents",
      ImVec2(ImGui::GetContentRegionAvail().x,
      ImGui::GetContentRegionAvail().y - 20.f),
      false, WindowFlags);

    for (TObjectIterator<UAkComponent> It; It; ++It)
    {
      if (!It || It->GetWorld() != GWorld)
      {
        continue;
      }

      FString ComponentName;
      It->GetAkGameObjectName(ComponentName);
      auto Name = StringCast<ANSICHAR>(*ComponentName);
      if (Filter.PassFilter(Name.Get()))
      {
        ImGui::Text("%s", Name.Get());

        const FTransform& ComponentTransform =
          It->GetComponentTransform();
        FVector Origin = ComponentTransform.GetLocation();
        FVector Direction = It->GetComponentRotation().Vector();

        DrawDebugCone(It->GetWorld(), Origin,
                      Direction, 45.0f, 0.20f, 0.3f, 8,
                      FColor::Blue, false, -1.f, 255);
```

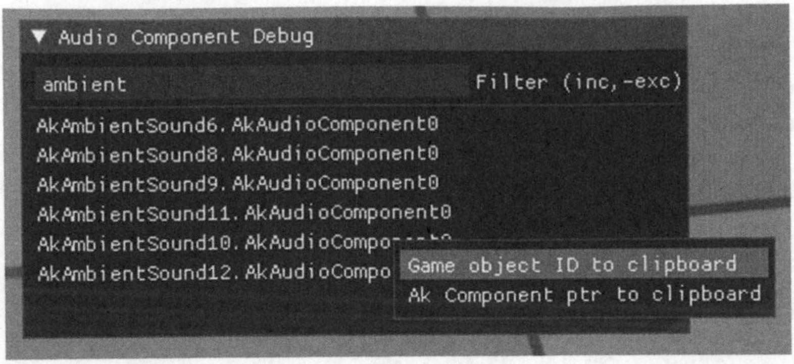

FIGURE 16.2   Contextual menu for the audio component debug window.

```
            DrawDebugString(It->GetWorld(), Origin,
                            ComponentName, nullptr,
                            FColor::Blue, 0.00001f);
        }
    }

    ImGui::EndChild();
}

ImGui::End();
}
```

The code is straightforward and accomplishes the job. This example has some simplifications that real code will have to handle in a more robust fashion. For example, it uses GWorld, which does not support multiplayer configurations. A full-blown audio component debugger would require more code – but not that much!

16.4.2.2 *Extending Audio Component Debug with Contextual Menu*
We will build on the previous example and show how to make it better. Let's add a contextual menu when the user right-clicks on an AkComponent name, shown in Figure 16.2.

```
ImGui::Text("%s", Name.Get());

if (ImGui::BeginPopupContextItem(Name.Get()))
{
    if (ImGui::Selectable("Game object ID to clipboard"))
    {
        FString ClipBoard =
```

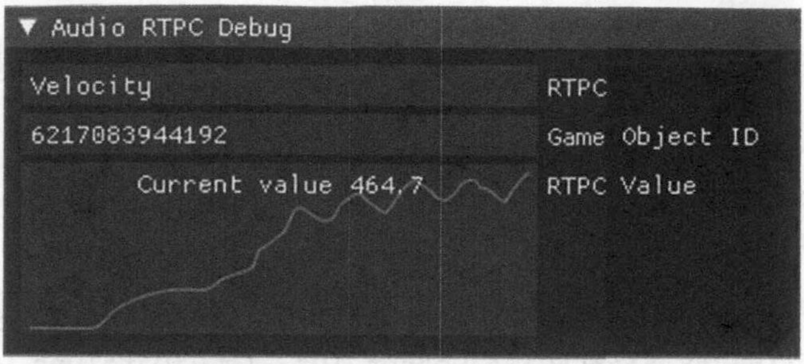

FIGURE 16.3   RTPC plot window.

```
    FString::Printf(TEXT("%llu"), It->GetAkGameObjectID());
  ImGui::SetClipboardText(StringCast<ANSICHAR>(*ClipBoard).Get());
}
if (ImGui::Selectable("Ak Component ptr to clipboard"))
{
  FString ClipBoard = FString::Printf(TEXT("(UObject*)0x%p"), *It);
  ImGui::SetClipboardText(StringCast<ANSICHAR>(*ClipBoard).Get());
}

ImGui::EndPopup();
}
```

When the user right-clicks on a component name, they will see two options: "Game object ID to clipboard" and "Ak Component ptr to clipboard." Copying the game object to the clipboard will be useful in our next example. Copying the game object as a pointer is a great trick for the programmer: pause the execution of the game in your debugger and paste the string in your variable watch window. This is a huge time saver: now you can inspect variables that are not shown by the debug UI.

16.4.2.3 RTPC Plot

In our final example, we will have a look at the plot widget. This widget is useful to show the value of a Wwise RTPC over time. Wwise can already display the information in the authoring tool, but it can still be useful to have the information directly in the game window. An example output is shown in Figure 16.3.

```
#include <imgui.h>
void DrawRTPCWindow()
{
  ImGui::Begin("Audio RTPC Debug");
```

```
static char RtpcName[128] = "";
static ImU64  GameObjID = 0;

// circular buffer of past values
static float RtpcValues[100] = { 0.f };
static int Idx = 0;

ImGui::InputText("RTPC", RtpcName, IM_ARRAYSIZE(RtpcName));
ImGui::InputScalar("Game Object ID", ImGuiDataType_U64,
  &GameObjID, NULL);

AkRtpcValue RtpcValue;
AK::SoundEngine::Query::RTPCValue_type ValueType =
  AK::SoundEngine::Query::RTPCValue_GameObject;
FAkAudioDevice::Get()->GetRTPCValue(
  StringCast<WIDECHAR>(RtpcName).Get(),
  GameObjID,
  AK_INVALID_PLAYING_ID,
  RtpcValue,
  ValueType);

RtpcValues[Idx] = RtpcValue;

char Overlay[32];
sprintf_s(Overlay, "Current value %0.1f", RtpcValue);
Idx++;
Idx %= IM_ARRAYSIZE(RtpcValues);

ImGui::PlotLines("RTPC Value", RtpcValues,
  IM_ARRAYSIZE(RtpcValues),
  Idx,
  Overlay,
  FLT_MAX,
  FLT_MAX,
  ImVec2(0, 80.0f));

  ImGui::End();
}
```

In this window, the RTPC name and the Game Object ID need to be manually entered (or pasted from the clipboard if you have implemented the previous audio component window). The reason behind this choice is to decouple the two IMGui examples. However, in a more full-featured game audio debug tool, the inputs to the RTPC plot widget could be integrated directly with the rest of the debug user interface.

16.4.3 Going Further with ImGui

After using ImGui in the context of game audio development, I find that good debug UI not only helps with debugging but also helps greatly in communication with clients. It becomes easy for an audio programmer to expose the guts of any sound system. When the clients look at those debug systems, they get visibility on things that would otherwise be hidden to them. It leads to a better understanding of the systems from the clients and generally leads to feature requests that are in line with the current implementation.

In this section, we only gave tiny examples of what you can achieve with ImGui. The things you can accomplish with this library are incredible. If you want to get some inspiration, just have a look at this post: https://github.com/ocornut/imgui/issues/123.

16.5 CONCLUSION

When it comes to audio debugging, using the right tools is one of the most important details. With the right tools, you now know that it is easy to add debugging functionality to the systems you create, so you will spend very little time creating debug tools because it is easy and fast. Since it is easy and fast to create debug tools, you do it from the beginning of the development cycle. Consequently, you can build stable audio systems in a way that is very efficient without losing time to debug. Since you are now a very efficient audio programmer, you now have a lot of time to focus on what you really enjoy doing: audio programming!

NOTES

1 https://docs.unrealengine.com/5.2/en-US/console-varaibles-cplusplus-in-unreal-engine/ (Note that the typo "varaibles" is the correct URL. - Ed)
2 As of this writing, the most recent Wwise integration version is 2022.1.7.8290.2779.
3 There is a proposal working its way through the ISO C++ committee to add debugging support functions to the standard library. You can read the latest version of the proposal document (which is currently targeting inclusion in C++26) at https://wg21.link/p2546. If this proposal does make it into the C++ standard, then you will be able to trigger a breakpoint by calling `std::breakpoint()`. – Ed.
4 https://github.com/ocornut/imgui
5 https://github.com/segross/UnrealImGui
6 https://github.com/sammyfreg/netImgui

CHAPTER 17

Automatic Manual Foley and Footsteps

Pablo Schwilden Diaz

17.1 INTRODUCTION

When we think about audio for an animated game, be it 2D or 3D, one of the first things that comes to mind is the movement of characters and their audio representation: foley and footsteps. Unless playing from a very far perspective, these sounds will tend to be ever-present. There are two usual ways of implementing those sound triggers. The first one is to manually place tags, markers, or events on each animation timeline to trigger sounds on certain frames of the animation. The second one is to analyze movement at run-time while the game is playing and detect when a foot hits the ground or a limb moves quickly to trigger a sound at that moment.

17.2 LIMITATIONS OF THE TRADITIONAL SOLUTIONS

These two solutions work perfectly on a lot of different games. You could even say there is no point in bringing this up anymore. However, there is one practical example where both of these solutions have real-life limitations. That example is if we are to have several hours of cutscenes with characters walking, running, and moving around all the time. Think something in the like of *Red Dead Redemption 2* or the recent *God of War* games.

The first solution, manually placing tags on each animation file, could work and would give us satisfying results. However, the amount of manual labor to go across the thousands of unique animation files and place every tag one by one would burn out any audio team before long. Sure, if we can

 DOI: 10.1201/9781003330936-20

burn through an army of juniors and interns, then there is technically "no problem," but this isn't really a satisfying or sustainable approach to the challenge at hand.

The second solution, analyzing movement at run-time and triggering sound on the fly, would solve the issue of manual labor. However, here it implies completely giving artistic control to the analysis and creating a tool that would work in the myriad of different scenarios that are involved. There's always going to be that one scene where the movement is unusual or complex and the analysis will throw sounds at the wrong moment or intensity, breaking the scene. Creating a tool that models real-life movement and impact sounds is theoretically achievable but would again require an enormous amount of effort from the audio programmers to get "just right."

One alternative solution is to go back to the cinema way of doing things: recording all the foley and footsteps in the studio, in sync with the image. However, not only would this require a lot of work, it would also break anytime we bring interactivity back into the game. This isn't a satisfying solution either.

17.3 UNDERSTANDING WHAT WE REALLY WANT

Looking at the limitations, it seems like there's just no way around it. If you want to have a lot of cutscenes in a game with precise control over each individual scene, then you'll need a lot of sound editors mindlessly placing footsteps and foley all over the place for months. That's how we always did it, right? In practice, the fact of having to work long hours to do game audio isn't per se a problem. There are always ways to increase the team, outsource part of the job, or extend the schedule to take more time creating sonic experiences for players.

The issue with the challenge we are facing right now is that the work involved is mindless and most of the time not creative at all. For the one scene where an interesting placement of just the right footstep or movement will bring the drama to the next level, there will be hundreds where the sound editor will have their brain turned off as they go frame by frame looking for the moment where the foot hits the ground. This is neither fun nor creative and isn't what we signed up for when working in a creative industry.

What we really want is to offload the basic work, the boring 80% of the placement, to concentrate on the interesting part, those glorious 20% where we can really make a difference as creatives. The first traditional solution, manually placing tags, entrusts us with the full 100% of the work. The second traditional solution, triggering sounds at run-time, takes away all control and we end up with 0% of the creative work, pouring all our energy into making a system that gets it right 100% of the time. Seeing it laid out with these numbers, what we want becomes clearer: a system that takes care of the boring 80% of the work without taking away the 20% we really like.

This really starts to sound like the work of an intern who makes a first pass on everything before the senior sound designer comes to check and correct mistakes. So, with this in mind let's see if we can create a system that "simulates an intern."

17.4 SIMULATING AN INTERN

Let's have a look at what happens in the brain of an intern were they to manually place footsteps on an animation timeline. On a very broad level, our model intern will first open an animation file inside the game engine. Then they will scroll frame by frame until they find a frame on which the character's foot touches the ground for the first time. On that frame, they will add a marker to the animation timeline to trigger a sound. They will also specify which sound to play based on the info given by their lead about how footstep sounds are named for this character. If our imaginary intern is thorough, they will also choose the sound based on the perceived strength of the footstep detected. Then they will resume scrolling until the end of the animation, marking down every time the feet touch the ground. Finally, they will save and close the animation file, then work on the next one. If our model intern were to work on foley, we can assume that they would follow a similar workflow but based on the movement of the limbs.

Breaking down the steps to their simplest operations, we will have the following sequence:

1. Open the animation file.

2. Find the character's feet.

3. Scroll through every frame.

4. Every frame, check if the feet are touching the ground.

5. If on one frame the foot touches the ground and it didn't before, add a marker.

6. Calculate the strength of the detected footstep.

7. On the created marker, add the correct sound.

8. If not at the end of the animation, loop back to step 3.

9. Save the file and close.

This starts looking like an implementable program, doesn't it?

17.5 THE AUTOMATIC "INTERN" TOOL

Let's start writing our program in pseudo-code. Later, we'll look at an actual implementation of this in Unreal Engine, but the concepts behind can be reused in any kind of game engine.

First off, we know we'll need to pass an animation file as a parameter to our main function.

```
public void AutoGenFootstepEvents (AnimationFile* animationFile) {}
```

After that, we need to do the usual verifications to check if the animation file we were passed exists and we can access it properly.

```
public void AutoGenFootstepEvents (AnimationFile* animationFile)
{
  if (animationFile == nullptr)
  {
    LogError(
      "The animation file passed to the AutoGen doesn't exist");
    return;
  }
}
```

From here, our computerized intern must be able to recognize what are the feet of the character. Whereas a human intern would be able to easily see a foot on their screen, our automatic intern isn't yet capable of such feats, so we will have to find another way to describe what a foot is. Fortunately, most animated characters have skeletons or skeletal meshes which contain all the info about the different mobile parts of that character. Inside these skeletons are bones which are each of the individual moveable parts.

If we know the name of the bone representing the feet, we can tell the computerized intern that it's the object we want to track. For that, we will create an array that holds the names of each bone that the tool needs to follow.

```
public Array<string> feetNames = {"ankle_right", "ankle_left"};
```

This struct will have to be exposed to the engine editor interface or manually edited to match the correct bone names. With this, we can get a reference to the bones we need the tool to track over time.

/.../

```
Skeleton* skeleton = animationFile->GetSkeleton();
Array<Bone*> feetBones = {feetNames.length};
for (int i = 0; i < feetBones.length; i++)
{
    feetBones[i] = skeleton->FindBone(feetNames[i]);
}
```

/.../

That is step 2 completed!

Now we need to go through the animation one frame at a time and check the position of our bones every time. This part is the most dependent on the engine itself. We will write pseudo-code that follows the way to do it in the Unreal Engine – the specific logic might change when using Unity or another engine, but the principle will remain the same.

```
//Our animation files run at 60FPS
const float timeIncrement = 1.0f / 60.0f;
```

/.../

```
for (int footIdx = 0; footIdx < feetBones; footIdx++)
{
    Bone* footBone = feetBones[footIdx];

    for (float time = 0; time < animationFile->AnimationLength;
         time += timeIncrement)
    {
```

```
    Transform footTransform = GetRootToBoneTransform(
      animationFile, footBone, time);
    }
  }
}
```

```
//This method gets the position of a bone relative to the root
//of the animation. It is pseudo-code inspired from an Unreal
//implementation.
Transform GetRootToBoneTransform(
  AnimationFile* anim, Bone* bone, float time)
{
  //This transform is relative to the parent bone
  Transform result = anim->GetBoneTransform(bone, time);
  Bone* currentBone = bone;

  //We crawl bones up the hierarchy until we reach the root which
  //has no parent.
  while(currentBone->parentBone != nullptr)
  {
    currentBone = currentBone->parentBone;

    //The multiplier here offsets a transform by another
    result = result * anim->GetBoneTransform(currentBone, time);
  }

  return result;
}
```

This transform now represents the foot bone in space relative to the root of the animation skeleton at every frame in the animation.

17.6 DEFINING A FOOTSTEP

If you ask any human what a footstep is, they will probably answer that it is the moment a foot touches the ground. How do we translate that in terms of positions? The easy way is to check if the height of the foot is equal or very close to the height of the ground.

We introduce two new variables: groundHeight and deplantHeight. In practice, most of the times groundHeight is the height of the skeleton's root, but if for some reason the skeleton isn't set up that way, we can always change it accordingly. deplantHeight will be the distance under which the foot is "touching" the ground. This value should not be 0 to accommodate for margins of error in the animation or properties of the skeleton (for example, if the character has high heels or big boots). In our example code, we'll set the groundHeight to the root's height and the deplantHeight to three units above the groundHeight.

We also only want to trigger a footstep on the first frame that the foot is in contact with the ground, so we need to have a way to track if the footstep was already touching the ground on the previous frame. The pseudo-code would then look like this:

```
/.../

const float groundHeight = skeleton->rootBone->GetTransform().z;
const float deplantHeight = groundHeight + 3.0f;

for (int footIdx = 0; footIdx < feetBones; footIdx++)
{
  Bone* footBone = feetBones[footIdx];

  //We assume the animation always starts with the feet on the
  //ground.
  bool planted = true;

  for (float time = 0; time < animationFile->AnimationLength;
      time += timeIncrement)
  {
    Transform footTransform = GetRootToBoneTransform(
      animationFile, footBone, time);

    bool isPlanted = footTransform.GetLocation().z <= deplantHeight;

    if(isPlanted && !planted) //New footstep!
    {
      //do stuff
    }

    planted = isPlanted;

  }
}
```

With this code, we should now be able to detect every time the feet touch the ground. Obviously, some footsteps might not be detected correctly depending on the values you use for the ground height and the deplant height, so you might need to tweak those to get good results. However, let's not forget that we are simulating an intern here, which means it's not catastrophic if some very specific or weird footsteps aren't detected. We aren't creating the perfect tool that will detect all footsteps; we are creating a tool that will relieve us from the biggest, most obvious chunk of the work.

Now that we can detect footsteps, we must do something with them. For ease of code, we will just store them in an array for later use. We will use a struct to store the info of each footstep. Our struct includes the footstep strength here, which we do not yet have, but we will get that information shortly.

```
public struct FootstepAudioData
{
    //Name of the bone that did this footstep
    string boneName;

    //Time at which this footstep happened
    float footstepTime;

    //The strength of this footstep
    float footstepStrength;
}
```

How do we get the strength of the footstep? The easiest way is to get the speed at which the foot was traveling just before hitting the ground. The faster it is going, the harder the footstep. As we already have the location of the feet at any given time, deducing its speed is not complex. We could calculate the speed on the last frame before the foot touched the ground, but we found out with practice that it was closer to human perception to take the average speed over a longer time period, so in our example we are going to take the speed over the past 100 milliseconds.

Putting it all together, our first part of the code looks like this:

```
public Array<string> feetNames = {"ankle_right", "ankle_left"};
//Our animation files run at 60FPS
const float timeIncrement = 1.0f / 60.0f;

//Time used to calculate speed of footstep
const float speedCalculationWindow = 0.1f;

public struct FootstepAudioData
```

```
{
  //Name of the bone that did this footstep
  string boneName;

  //Time at which this footstep happened
  float footstepTime;

  //The strength of this footstep
  float footstepStrength;
}

public void AutoGenFootstepEvents (AnimationFile* animationFile)
{
  if (animationFile == nullptr)
  {
    LogError(
      "The animation file passed to the AutoGen doesn't exist");
    return;
  }

  Skeleton* skeleton = animationFile->GetSkeleton();
  Array<Bone*> feetBones = {feetNames.length};

  for (int i = 0; i < feetBones.length; i++)
  {
    feetBones[i] = skeleton->FindBone(feetNames[i]);
  }

  const float groundHeight = skeleton->rootBone->GetTransform().z;
  const float deplantHeight = groundHeight + 3.0f;

  Array<FootstepAudioData> footstepsData = {};
  for (int footIdx = 0; footIdx < feetBones; footIdx++)
  {
    Bone* footBone = feetBones[footIdx];

    //We assume the animation always starts with the feet on the
    //ground.
    bool planted = true;

    for (float time = 0; time < animationFile->AnimationLength;
        time += timeIncrement)
```

```
    {
      Transform footTransform = GetRootToBoneTransform(
        animationFile, footBone, time);

      bool isPlanted = footTransform.GetLocation().z <= deplantHeight;

      if(isPlanted && !planted) //New footstep!
      {
        pastFootTransform = GetRootToBoneTransform(
          animationFile, footBone, time-speedCalculationWindow);

        Vector velocity = footTransform.GetLocation() -
          pastFootTransform.GetLocation() / speedCalculationWindow;

        float speed = velocity.Size();

        FootstepAudioData newFootstep = new FootstepAudioData();

        newFootstep.boneName = footBone.name;
        newFootstep.time = time;
        newFootstep.strength = speed;

        footstepsData.Add(newFootstep);

      }

      planted = isPlanted;

    }
  }

  //Here we can use the footsteps data created
}

//This method gets the position of a bone relative to the root of the
//animation. It is pseudo-code inspired from an Unreal implementation.
Transform GetRootToBoneTransform(
  AnimationFile* anim, Bone* bone, float time)
{
  //This transform is relative to the parent bone
  Transform result = anim->GetBoneTransform(bone, time);
  Bone* currentBone = bone;
```

```
//We crawl bones up the hierarchy until we reach the root which
//has no parent.
while(currentBone->parentBone != nullptr)
{
  currentBone = currentBone->parentBone;

  //The multiplier here offsets a transform by another
  result = result * anim->GetBoneTransform(currentBone, time);
}

  return result;
}
```

17.7 USING THE DATA

Once we have a list of all footsteps detected with their relative speed created by our computerized intern, we can use them to fill out the animation file's timeline. This is very specific to each engine, so we won't go into detail here and we'll just show that part of the code when we show the specific Unreal implementation we did.

The idea here is to use the array of footsteps created to add new markers to the animation timeline one by one and set them up with the correct information. One key suggestion we can make is to try to have that part as accessible as possible to the sound designers using the tool, perhaps by doing it in Blueprints. This means that they can easily change which sound is to be triggered by these markers, how the strength parameter impacts the audio, or even what type of marker they want to use (a marker that also tries to detect the ground type at run-time for example).

17.8 DEFINING FOLEY

Now we have a tool that tries to automatically detect and place footsteps on an animation for us, so we don't have to do it anymore. But we are still missing the foley and we can't directly reuse our footsteps detection algorithm for it. Defining what is foley in computational terms could be the subject of incredible research and debate. We could try and compute every individual bone's movement to have them each contribute to the sound. Or we could try and calculate an "average body movement" and derive a foley sound to accompany it. All of these would be very interesting, but let's remember we are simulating our model intern's editing, not real life. We only have to make it work 80% of the time.

The approach we took when faced with this challenge was a very blunt, simple, and naïve one. As the footsteps were defined by the movement of the lower part of the character, we thought that what needed the most to have foley was the upper part of the character: the arms in particular. The basic movements we wanted to be able to highlight were people waving at each other, shaking hands, or grabbing objects – all of which mostly involve movement of the arms.

To implement this functionality, we analyzed the individual movement of the wrists and triggered foley based on it. More precisely, instead of looking at the location of each wrist on a given frame, we calculated its movement speed at every frame. Whenever this speed would go above a manually set threshold, our "intern" tool would place a marker.

It wasn't perfect, but again we weren't targeting perfection. These markers worked for most of the scenes where the movements weren't specific and for the other scenes, we would just add other markers manually.

17.9 THE END RESULT: AUTOMATIC "MANUAL" MARKER PLACEMENT

What we have now is a tool that will try to replicate human work as closely as possible, but at the speed of light.[1] It will give the same result that a manual marker placement would have done, but in an automatic way. This for us was the best compromise possible between automating and keeping control over the end result.

In practice, we found that we had to intervene in the automatic placement less than 20% of the time. If you were to consider each animation file individually, a lot of imperfections could be heard in the placement and editing of the sounds. However, when checking the result in the context of a game's mix, where there is also music, dialogue, ambiances, and other sound effects, a lot of those imperfections became unnoticeable. We were closer to 95%, where we could really put effort where it mattered the most.

17.10 EXTENDING THE TOOL

While we were happy with the first results of this tool, there are several things we added to extend its functionality over time, saving us more time or giving us better results. A lot of these extensions were quality of life improvements, like analyzing more than one animation file at a time, deleting previously placed markers, or sending the length of a foley movement.

Because we didn't pour our energy into making this tool the best possible realistic footstep generator, but instead into making it the best possible tool for our sound designers to use, we ended up with an incredible tool that saves us a lot of time and is frequently improved with little effort from the audio programmers. Also, we have faced few problems with optimization of the tool, since it runs completely offline in the editor. The only optimization we had to add was a control on the number of events that would be created with a sensitivity filter to avoid spamming sounds too often.

17.11 IMPLEMENTATION EXAMPLE IN UNREAL WITH WWISE

Here is the real tool we created in Unreal 4.27. Some parts of the logic are in Blueprints to manage the Wwise part of things, but the main part of the work is visible here.

```
void UAudioAnimationTools_Widget::AutoGenerateFootstepEvents(
  UAnimSequence* anim,
  TMap<UAnimNotify*, FootstepsData>& createdAnimNotifiesMap)
{
  createdAnimNotifiesMap.Empty()
  if(anim == nullptr)
  {
    UE_LOG(LogTemp, Log, TEXT(
      "The animation file passed to the AutoGen doesn't exist"));
    return;
  }

  const USkeleton* skeleton = animationSequence->GetSkeleton();

  if(skeleton == nullptr)
  {
    UE_LOG(LogTemp, Log, TEXT(
```

```
      "There was an issue getting the skeleton"));
    return;
}

//The foley info data map is defined in the header.
//It's a map editable in blueprint that holds a list of all
//the skeletons in game and the corresponding names of the bones
//of the feet or wrists.
UFoleyBonesInfo* foleyInfo = foleyInfoDataMap.Find(skeleton);

//These variables are defined in the widget blueprint
const float groundHeight = GroundContactThreshold;
const float deplantHeight = groundHeight + GroundDeplantThreshold;

TArray<FootstepsData> footstepsDataArray;
footstepsDataArray.Empty();

for (int footId = 0; footId < foleyInfo->Feet.Num(); footId++)
{
  string footName = foleyInfo->Feet[footId];
  float plantedSinceTime = -1.0f;

  for (float time = timeIncrement; time < anim->SequenceLength;
      time += timeIncrement)
  {
    FTransform rootTransform;
    AnimationUtilities::GetWorldToRootTransform(
      anim, time, rootTransform);
    FTransform footTransform;
    AnimationUtilities::GetRootToBoneTransform(
      anim, footName, time, footTransform);

    FVector footLocation = rootTransform.TransformPosition(
      footTransform.GetLocation());

    bool planted = footHeight <= deplantHeight;

    if (planted && plantedSinceTime < 0.0f)
    {
      plantedSinceTime = time;

      FTransform pastRootTransform;
      AnimationUtilities::GetWorldToRootTransform(
```

```
        anim, time, pastRootTransform);
      FTransform pastFootTransform;
      AnimationUtilities::GetRootToBoneTransform(
        anim, footName, time-speedCalculationWindow,
        pastFootTransform);

      FVector pastFootLocation =
        pastRootTransform.TransformPosition(
        pastFootTransform.GetLocation());

      FVector footVelocity = (footLocation - pastFootLocation) /
        speedCalculationWindow;
      float speed = footVelocity.Size();

      FootstepsData& footstep =
        footstepsDataArray.AddDefaulted_GetRef();

      footstep.boneName = footName;
      footstep.strength = speed;
      footstep.time = time;
    }
    else if (!planted)
    {
      plantedSinceTime = -1.0f;
    }
  }
}


//Anim notifies creation
for (int footId = 0; footId < foleyInfo->Feet.Num(); footId++)
{
  //By default, work on the last track
  int trackIndex = anim->AnimNotifyTracks.Num();

  //Check if there is a track that has the bone name already
  //from a previous generation. Remove all notifies on it.
  for(int trackId = 0; trackId < anim-> trackIndex; trackId++)
  {
    if(anim->AnimNotifyTracks[trackId].TrackName ==
      foleyInfo->Feet[footId])
    {
      anim->Notifies.RemoveAll([trackId](
```

```
        const FAnimNotifyEvent& notify)
        {return notify.TrackIndex == trackId;});
      trackIndex = trackId;
    }
  }


  for (FootstepsData& foostep : footstepsDataArray)
  {
    if(footstep.boneName != foleyInfo->Feet[footId])
      continue;

    FAnimNotifyEvent notifyEvent;
    notifyEvent.NotifyName = "AutoGen_Footstep";

    //We specify the notify class to use in the widget
    //blueprint. This lets us choose the Wwise's
    //AkAnimNotify and cast it in blueprint later.
    UAnimNotify* notify =
      NewObject<UAnimNotify>(anim, animNotifyClass);
    notifyEvent.Notify = notify;
    notifyEvent.SetTime(footstep.time);
    notifyEvent.TrackIndex = trackIndex;

    if(anim->AnimNotifyTracks.Num() <= notify.TrackIndex)
    {
      anim->AnimNotifyTracks.SetNum(notifyEvent.TrackIndex + 1);
      anim->AnimNotifyTracks[notifyEvent.TrackIndex].TrackName =
        footstep.boneName;
    }

    anim->Notifies.Add(notifyEvent);

    createdAnimNotifiesMap.Add(notify, footstep);
  }

}

anim->MarkRawDataAsModified();
anim->Modify(true);
anim->RefreshCacheData();
}
```

The rest is then handled in the Blueprints with the `createdAnim-NotifiesMap` returned filled by the tool's method.

17.12 CONCLUSION

With this tool, we can now handle a lot of animation files without compromising our sound designers' happiness or the quality of the work. Sound designers can now concentrate on what they do best: using their ears to create the best sounding game ever, rather than mindlessly scrolling through long animation files frame by frame.

We have also touched on the idea of creating imperfect but useful tools. By thinking of the tool as an "automatic intern," we lessened the burden of both the audio programmers creating the tool and the sound designers using the tool. We managed to create a tool that does exactly what a sound designer would expect, is easily maintainable, and also has very decent expectations. This is a concept that we now try to apply to all the audio tools development: "How would an intern do it?"

NOTE

1 Well... 99% the speed of light. We can't *actually* reach the speed of light. – Ed.

Index

Printed in the United States
by Baker & Taylor Publisher Services